ISS

Media Audiences

Media Audiences

Edited by Marie Gillespie

Open University Press
in association with The Open University

Open University Press
McGraw-Hill Education
McGraw-Hill House
Shoppenhangers Road
Maidenhead
Berkshire
England
SL6 2QL

email: enquiries@openup.co.uk
world wide web: www.openup.co.uk

and Two Penn Plaza, New York, NY 10121-2289, USA

First published 2005

A catalogue record of this book is available from the British Library

ISBN 0 335 21883 0 (hb) 0 335 21882 2 (pb)

Library of Congress Cataloguing-in-Publication Data

CIP data applied for

Edited and designed by The Open University.

Typeset by The Alden Group, Oxford

Printed and bound in the United Kingdom by The Alden Group, Oxford.

1.1

Contents

The Open University Course Team

Tony Aldgate, Arts Faculty Advisor
Geoff Austin, Leading Technical Developer
Hedley Bashforth, Associate Lecturer and Study Guide Author
Melanie Bayley, Media Project Manager
Tony Bennett, Chapter Author
Chris Bissell, Chapter Author, Faculty of Technology
Kathleen Calder, Editorial Media Developer
Elizabeth Chaplin, Associate Lecturer and Study Guide Author
James Chapman, Reading Member
Giles Clark, Publishing Advisor
Richard Collins, Chapter Author and Book Editor
Lene Connolly, Print Buying Controller
Shanti Dass, Editorial Media Developer
Alison Edwards, Editorial Media Developer
Jessica Evans, Chapter Author and Book Editor
Tot Foster, Consultant Producer, Sound & Vision
Marie Gillespie, Deputy Course Chair, Chapter Author and Book Editor
Richard Golden, Production and Presentation Administrator
R. Harindranath, Critical Reader, 2002–3
Lisa Hale, Media Assistant, Compositor
Alma Hales, Rights Advisor
Celia Hart, Picture Researcher
David Herbert, Chapter Author & Arts Faculty Advisor
David Hesmondhalgh, Course Chair, Chapter Author and Book Editor
Jonathan Hunt, Publishing Advisor
Denise Janes, Course Secretary, 2002–3
Tim Jordan, Critical Reader, 2002–3
Wendy Lampert, Course Manager
Sylvia Lay-Flurrie, Course Secretary
Alex Law, Associate Lecturer and Study Guide Author
Hugh Mackay, Staff Tutor, Teaching Advisor and Critical Reader
Margaret McManus, Media Assistant, Rights
Katie Meade, Contracts Executive
Diane Mole, Graphics Media Developer
Dave Morris, Interactive Media Developer
Martin Moloney, Associate Lecturer and Study Guide Author
Jason Toynbee, Chapter Author and Book Editor

Consultant Authors

Frances Bonner, University of Queensland
Gill Branston, Cardiff University
Nick Couldry, London School of Economics and Political Science
John Downey, Loughborough University
Jostein Gripsrud, University of Bergen
Sonia Livingstone, London School of Economics and Political Science
Nick Stevenson, University of Nottingham
Gillian Ursell, Trinity and All Saints College, University of Leeds

External Assessors

Ann Gray, University of Lincoln
Peter Golding, Loughborough University

Series preface

Understanding Media: Inside Celebrity is the first of four books in a series, also entitled *Understanding Media*. The aim of the series is to provide a cogent and wide-ranging introduction to the study of the media. These four books form the central part of an Open University course with the same title (course code DA204). Each volume is self-contained and can be studied on its own, or as part of a wide range of courses in universities and colleges.

The four books in this series are as follows:

Understanding Media: Inside Celebrity, edited by Jessica Evans and David Hesmondhalgh

Media Audiences, edited by Marie Gillespie

Media Production, edited by David Hesmondhalgh

Analysing Media Texts, edited by Marie Gillespie and Jason Toynbee (with DVD-ROM)

The first book introduces four elements central to any investigation of the media (history, texts, production and audiences) via an analysis of the important media phenomenon of celebrity. The next three books in the series then examine texts, production and audiences in greater detail. Across these different topics, the course addresses three *themes* in media analysis, which the course team believe are fundamental to any appreciation of the importance and complexity of the media. These are

- power
- change and continuity
- knowledge, values and beliefs

These elements and themes can be traced via the index of each book, but the book introductions and conclusions will also help follow how they are pursued across the series.

Understanding Media covers a great deal of media studies curriculum, but of course it still isn't possible for us to cover everything. Nevertheless we have aimed to cover a wide range of media examples, both historically and geographically, and to introduce a number of differing and often competing approaches.

The chapters are designed to be rigorous but student-friendly, and we have sought to achieve this in a number of ways. We have provided clear outlines of the aims of each chapter at its beginning, and summaries at the end, with careful explanations along the way. Activities are built into the chapters, and are designed to help readers understand and retain the key concepts of the course. Just under half of these activities are based around *readings* – extracts drawn from books, academic articles and the media themselves – which are integral to the discussion contained in the chapter. These readings are indicated by a coloured line next to the margin. Each book is thoroughly indexed, so that key concepts can be tracked across the different books in the series. Further reading is indicated at the end of each chapter. Finally, although each book is self-contained, references to other books in the series are indicated by the use of bold type.

A fifth book used on DA204 *Understanding Media* has been published by The Open University alone. This book, entitled *Media Technologies, Markets and Regulation*, is edited by Richard Collins and Jessica Evans and is available from OU Worldwide on +44 (0)1908 858785 (http://www.ouw.co.uk).

Media studies has taken its place as a familiar academic discipline in schools and universities, embraced in large numbers by students, but crassly dismissed by commentators who in most cases seem never to have read a serious analysis of the media. The need to think carefully about the media's role in modern societies is as great as ever. We hope that you find these books a stimulating introduction to this vitally important area of study.

Open University courses are produced by course teams. These teams include academic authors, from The Open University and from other institutions, experienced tutors, External Assessors, editors, designers, audio and video producers, administrators and secretaries. The Open University academics on the *Understanding Media* course team were based mainly in the Sociology discipline, within the Faculty of Social Sciences, but we also drew upon the expertise of colleagues in the Faculty of Arts, in order to construct a course with interdisciplinary foundations and appeal. While book editors have had primary responsibility for each book, the assignment of editors' names to books cannot adequately convey the collective nature of production at The Open University. The names of the *Understanding Media* course team are listed at the front of this book.

I'd like to thank all my colleagues on the course team for their hard work and good humour, especially Wendy Lampert, who has been a really excellent and efficient Course Manager.

David Hesmondhalgh, Course Chair
On behalf of the *Understanding Media* course team

Audiences: living with media

Marie Gillespie

To say that we are all part of a media audience some of the time seems like a simple statement until we start thinking about the details of our own and other people's media experiences. Can you recall your first memories of being part of a media audience? You may not be familiar with the opening lines of *Watch with Mother* (a children's programme broadcast in the UK on the BBC from the 1950s through to 1970) but the phrase 'Are you sitting comfortably?' triggers my earliest memories of childhood pleasures around television. Then there was the weekly trip to the Saturday morning 'flicks' when all the kids in the neighbourhood piled into the local cinema, pushing and shoving in eagerness to get to the best seats. We watched westerns, cartoons and adventure serials, not in silence but shrieking with delight, screaming at the baddies, cheering the goodies, and even dancing in the aisles.

We live with and through media, and our media experiences embed themselves in our biographies, almost imperceptibly. Throughout our lives we create media pathways from the economic and cultural resources available to us. This book is about living with media. It's about how audiences in different parts of the world use and interpret media, and how media affect our lives. It's also about how we think about audiences, what audience research has achieved and how it might be done differently.

Why study media audiences?

In media studies, the term 'audience' usually refers to an assembly of listeners or viewers who come together, if only virtually, through shared consumption of film, television, radio, the internet, music or advertising. The term is also sometimes extended to include readerships of newspapers and magazines. Audiences may appear to be self-selecting, naturally occurring formations, but they are not. They are imagined, targeted and produced by media institutions (**Toynbee, 2006**). They come into being around specific media technologies and texts (or genres) at particular social and historical moments and they need to be understood in relation to these dynamics. Audiences are complex, elusive, shifting social formations but, for all their complexity, they are well worth studying. This book introduces us to the study of audiences through an exploration of these three related questions:

- How do the media exert power over us and what kinds of power do we exercise as audiences?

- How, and to what extent, do the media shape the knowledge, values and beliefs of audiences?

- How do changes in media technologies transform the experiences of audiences and how do audiences change over time?

Studying audiences is important firstly because the media are powerful but the nature and extent of media's power over audiences are not always obvious. Nor, indeed, are the many ways in which we are empowered by the media as individuals and social groups, as citizens and consumers. The media are attributed the power to cause all manner of social ills – from violence and crime to sexism and racism. But media are also regarded as indispensable to living in modern societies. Can you imagine living without media? Try ignoring every billboard or song in public places or not hearing the news in some form even for one day! If we want to understand the power of the media and their paradoxical role in society then we need to study audiences.

This book offers you different theories and examples of empirical research that you can use to situate the often intense and polarised academic and public debates about audiences within broader analytical approaches (such as those discussed by Alasuutari, 1999). You will be able to discern two broad traditions of research: one concentrates on *media effects* and asks 'what do the media do to audiences?' The media are seen as powerful and audiences as passive and vulnerable, prone to manipulation and easily influenced. The other focuses on *media uses* and interpretations and asks 'what do audiences do with media?' 'How do audiences use and make sense of media?' This approach tends to see audiences as more active and selective, creative and powerful.

All theories of audiences have inherent assumptions about power: whether power is concentrated in the hands of many or few, or whether power works on us directly, or whether it works through us in more subtle ways. Different theories of audiences are also based on different models of communication. Some assume communication involves a straightforward transmission of messages between few senders and many passive receivers. Others see media as involving more complex circuits of communication that actively engage us as audiences in the construction of meaningful social worlds.

Studying audiences helps us to become aware of the assumptions we make about the power of the media in society. It shows how the relationship between media and audiences is unpredictable and variable across time and place. We can no more assume that audiences everywhere are the same than we can presume that media have uniform effects. A whole host of contextual and contingent factors intervene in this relationship. But what are they? How do gender, class, ethnicity affect media uses and effects? How do media contribute to our ideas of self and others? Do we have the power to resist media manipulation? Understanding audiences requires more than theoretical speculation about such questions. It needs empirical investigation, and the empirical studies presented here will help you assess the tensions between activity and passivity, choice and control, creativity and constraint.

In studying audiences we must reflect upon our own experiences as audiences and relate them to wider patterns of media consumption, asking what these reveal about the unequal power relations at domestic and local, national and international levels. Our media tastes and choices are not just personal. They are socially stratified and reflect the unequal distribution of economic and cultural resources in society. Our media tastes and choices classify us in important ways. Media consumption patterns reinforce as well as transform social hierarchies, identities and differences (Bourdieu, 1984). Understanding these processes gives us important insights into how media reproduce relations of power and identities.

Given the global scope of media today, we must ask about the impact of powerful, wealthy nations and their media systems (the USA for example) on the audiences of less powerful nations, the poor and disenfranchised. This leads us to the heart of questions about the role of media in reproducing inequalities on an international scale, but also about whether the media are a force for democratisation. When do the media enable audiences to have their voices heard and participate in the political process, and when do they obstruct democratic procedures? What forms of knowledge are required to operate as informed citizens and consumers in today's society? This brings us to the second principal reason why studying audiences is important.

The media are cultural institutions that trade in symbols, stories and meanings. As such they shape the forms of knowledge and ignorance, values and beliefs that circulate in society. If we assume that the media are all powerful and audiences are passive and ignorant (or 'dumbed down') then we might go on to argue that, for example, the pervasiveness and dominance of US media amounts to a form of media imperialism that works to impose 'American' values on audiences on an international or even global scale. Alternatively, we might explore how different audiences around the world respond to US media and, using evidence from empirical research, we might argue that local audiences draw on culturally specific, existing belief and value systems when they use and interpret media, and can be empowered by such experiences.

Thus how we think about power, media and audiences also affects how we understand values and beliefs as fixed or negotiable, contextually shaped or pre-determined, imposed from above or worked through by active audiences.

The third reason for studying media audiences is to understand the dynamics of media change and continuity: how technologies empower or disempower audiences and transform the nature of their media experiences, how audiences themselves change in relation to wider social change. But theories about the putative sweeping changes brought about by media technologies need to be set against the ways in which media reproduce social and power relations: how media contribute to a sense of national or cultural identity, re-invent tradition, crystallise patriarchal values, propagate fundamentalist religious beliefs, reinforce xenophobic political ideologies, obstruct the circulation of new ideas and knowledge, use forms of censorship and self-censorship to keep us ignorant about the workings of government, schedule our lives, and provide the consolations of continuity rather than change.

Despite the conservative tendencies of the media, audiences are changing in response to social and technological change, and our ideas and ways of studying media have to change to reflect this. Consider for a moment the kind of media multi-tasking that is possible today. My 17-year-old nephew appears to be able to watch a DVD film on TV while receiving and sending text messages on his mobile, and e-mails on the computer. He moves fluidly between these activities, interspersing conversations with his friends about who's been thrown out of *Big Brother* (UK, Channel 4, 2000 to present), all the while practising drum beats or guitar riffs. Last summer he used his mobile phone to download and watch movies, took a picture of the planet Venus (when it crossed the face of the sun), superimposed his girlfriend's face on it (a work of art in his view), and received the latest Tottenham Hotspur football scores (a series of disappointing defeats).

Does the fact that this 17-year-old boy is a media-savvy, technically skilled, information-rich kid mean that he has the analytical frameworks required to turn information into knowledge – into intellectual power? Does greater consumer choice or technological skill enrich his media experiences or give him greater power over the media? Is the term 'audience' still appropriate for the kinds of highly individualised pathways that he makes? Do such potential uses of media reflect a shift in the power between producers and audiences? What are the implications of the shift from nationally defined audiences to individualised interactivity on a potentially global scale? What and where is the audience today, as compared with fifty or even a hundred years ago (think of your parents and grandparents and their media use)?

These are just some of the questions that we explore in this book.

The structure of this book

Much of this book is about television audiences, although late nineteenth-century audiences for early cinema also feature. This is because audience research has focused more on television than on other media, largely due to anxieties about its power to influence us, change our behaviour and shape our minds. We offer a series of culturally diverse case studies: from audiences in the UK, USA and Israel to India, Egypt and Trinidad. The case studies highlight the importance of taking an historical and comparative approach to studying audiences. Taking such an approach helps us situate contemporary media experiences and to 'relativise' them (or put them into a comparative perspective). An historical and comparative approach makes myths and crude generalisations about audiences or media power more difficult to defend. Studying media audiences in this way will enable you to see how the media shape lives, and to examine questions of effects and uses, pleasure and power in socially and historically situated ways.

In Chapter 1, 'Media audiences, interpreters and users', Sonia Livingstone introduces us to key debates in media audience research about the power, activity and selectivity of audiences. She shows how the very idea of the audience has been subjected to shifting academic, moral and policy concerns. These concerns determine the questions that get asked about audiences and how they are studied. She introduces one of the dominant paradigms in audience research, the 'media effects' approach, which draws on scientific traditions and uses laboratory and experimental methods. It operates on a cause–effect model of communication, aiming to isolate particular stimuli (say, representations of media violence) and relate it to a specific response (violent behaviour). She contrasts this with 'audience reception' research, which evolved out of literary studies. This conceives of audiences as 'interpreters' and looks at how audiences 'read' and interpret media texts. She leaves us with some valuable suggestions for re-thinking audience research.

In Chapter 2, 'The media sensorium: cultural technologies, the senses and society', Tony Bennett explores how media technologies are mobilised, at key moments, to mould our sensory and social experiences as audiences. He focuses on the transition to sound and the shift from black and white to colour in early cinema. He demonstrates that the way in which these technologies developed was not inevitable but tied to political imperatives – the regulation of spectators and vision. The central argument of the chapter is that how the media act upon and organise relations between the senses plays an important role in understanding how media work, and work upon us, to exercise distinctive forms of power. The 'media sensorium' approach is not concerned so much with the content of the media and its influence on what audiences believe and value, rather it is concerned with the ways in which media organise perception and knowledge.

In Chapter 3, 'Media publics, culture and democracy', David Herbert analyses the concept of audiences in relation to political ideas of 'the public'. Through case studies of media publics set in the Israel and India, he explores the political ramifications of television. He demonstrates how television helped to bring Hindu nationalists to power in India, and contributed to the polarisation of public opinion in Israel. The 'audiences as publics' approach used by Herbert examines how television addresses audiences as citizens, forges media publics and assists or impedes participation in democratic processes.

In Chapter 4, 'Television drama and audience ethnography', I argue that audience ethnography is a particularly valuable approach to studying how audiences live with media. Presenting case studies on television audiences in Trinidad, India and Egypt, I show how different theoretical conceptions of audiences and power have been challenged by ethnographic studies. The 'audience ethnography' approach focuses as much on *how* we come to know audiences as *what* we know. It involves the researcher in participating in the everyday lives of audiences but aims to connect small-scale, local, micro processes of media use, with large-scale, global, macro structures of power.

In Chapter 5, 'The extended audience: scanning the horizon', Nick Couldry argues that, as audiences change and become more diffused across social spaces, we need to take our studies beyond the living room to explore a whole new array of media-related practices. His exploration of 'reality TV' points to new ways of thinking about and researching audiences. He considers the changing boundaries between the real and the virtual, as well as between producers and consumers, texts and contexts, and draws our attention to the limits of interactivity. The 'extended audience' approach focuses on the emergence of new media practices and more individualised media pathways of use but it does so without losing sight of social dynamics or power relations. He ends with some thought provoking questions for us to consider about continuities as well as change. How can we make sense of contemporary media audiences? What are the new challenges facing audience research? How should we understand the changing nature of media power?

We hope that you will enjoy this book and that you will be able to test your own assumptions about audiences and gain insights into how living with media matters. Are you sitting comfortably? Then we'll begin ...

References

Alasuutari, P. (ed.) (1999) *Rethinking the Media Audience*, London, Sage.

Bourdieu, P. (1984/1979) *Distinction: A Social Critique of the Judgement of Taste* (trans. R. Nice), London, Routledge.

Toynbee, J. (2006) 'The media's view of the audience' in Hesmondhalgh, D. (ed.) *Media Production*, Maidenhead, Open University Press/The Open University (Book 3 in this series).

Media audiences, interpreters and users

Chapter 1

Sonia Livingstone

Contents

1 Introduction: what is the audience and why is it important?

Throughout the world, though especially in industrialised countries, people routinely spend a huge amount of time with different forms of media, often more time than they spend at work or school or in face-to-face communication. Within a single generation homes have become media-rich, with multiple televisions, radios, games machines, computers, music systems and telephones – typically shifting from household possessions to personal possessions – accompanying us wherever we go. In our everyday engagement with friends and family, with the community, the political system, the nation and beyond, we draw upon, and increasingly rely upon, a never-ending flood of images, ideas and information about worlds distant in space or time and those close to home.

Imagine our homes without screens, our daily routines without television, our work without the internet, our friendships without shared music interests, and it is obvious how much we are all part of media audiences (see Figure 1.1). Yet the common-sense view of the audience is ambivalent. Most people consider it desirable in practice to be part of the audience – believing that citizens 'should' watch the news, that it is wrong to 'deprive' a child of television, that someone is 'weird' if they do not follow the music scene. But, at the same time, people are reluctant to acknowledge the implications of this 'media dependency' for domestic practices, social relationships, political participation – and for their (our) very identity.

Ever since the media first made 'mass' communication possible, a dominant strand of popular, and academic, thinking about audiences – the very idea of the audience even – has been pejorative. Audiences are seen as mindless, ignorant, defenceless, naïve and as manipulated or exploited by the 'mass media'. We may proclaim ourselves to be discerning, sensible, critical members of the audience – other people, however, and, especially, other people's children in the audience give cause for concern.

This chapter takes this ambivalence about the audience as its starting point. It shows that throughout the history of the media – and the audience – the idea of the audience has been far from taken for granted. Rather, it has been subject to the competing claims of (at least) two dominant discourses, one liberal and the other critical. (A discourse is a way of thinking and talking about a particular subject. It defines what it is possible or permissible to say about a topic.)

The liberal–pluralist discourse locates the audience within the development of western industrialised society, arguing that the media must reach the citizens – in their role as audiences – if they are to gain

Figure 1.1 *A media-rich home*

the information, understanding and shared cultural values required to sustain the informed consent that underpins democratic governance. Yet, within this democratic view of audiences lie also the seeds of doubt – what happens when audiences do not act in a selective or rational manner, or when the media do not provide fair or balanced information?

Such doubts form the starting point for a critical or radical discourse. This positions audiences as consumers rather than citizens, seeing them as the managed subjects of powerful institutional interests, vulnerable to political manipulation and commercial exploitation by the culture industries through subtle and pervasive strategies of mass communication. Yet, here too there are signs of doubt – can the population be castigated so contemptuously for apparently naïve, pleasure-seeking, herd-like behaviour, and is there no defence of the media?

This chapter cannot cover all the research that has sought to understand the multifaceted nature of our relationships with media. Instead, it aims to:

- examine how public concerns about the media drive what gets asked about audiences;
- consider what historical perspective contributes to the debate over active and passive audiences;
- investigate the mixed fortunes of research on media effects;
- look at how audiences make sense of media;
- outline current challenges and future questions for audience research.

2 Moral panics, media effects and the audience research agenda

2.1 Popular anxieties about the media audience

There is a long history of social and political debate underlying ambivalence about the audience. This debate – between the liberal and critical discourses identified in Section 1 – continually resurfaces when we ask, for example, whether children are the technical whizz kids of the cyber-future or whether they are the vulnerable innocents of an increasingly commercialised culture (see Figure 1.2). Is being part of an audience one way of participating as a citizen in a shared community and/or is it just a way of indulging the escapist pleasures of a 'mere consumer'? Does the audience have the collective power to vote with their feet (or fingers on the 'off' button) to ensure that broadcasters give them what they want? Or are we an economic commodity that broadcasters sell (via market researchers' ratings) to the advertising industry?

Not only are the questions about audiences wide-ranging but many policy makers, commercial organisations and academic disciplines have a stake in debating the power and effects of the media. Consider the range of institutions concerned with audiences – from the politician's anxiety about ensuring an informed electorate to the education system's concern with literacy levels, from the advertising industry's relentless competition for market share to the labour market's demand for a hi-tech workforce. Add those who scapegoat the media – for their supposed moral impact on family life, on ethnic stereotyping or on crime statistics – and it should be clear why the notion of audiences is so hotly contested and why the audience research agenda is driven by many conflicting interests.

Activity 1.1

Think about how the media represent audiences. What terms are popularly used to describe audiences? Are they positive or negative? Do they assume the audience to be homogeneous or diverse? Are they describing people like you? What common anxieties are expressed in newspaper headlines, for example? What questions might these perceptions or anxieties lead policy makers to ask researchers? ■ ■ ■

Historians of the media have pointed out that surprisingly similar hopes and fears arise each time a new medium is introduced. At present, these 'moral panics' (spiralling social concerns about moral issues) centre on

Home Office advice over Internet perverts

BAN THE COMPUTER FROM YOUR CHILD'S BEDROOM

PARENTS were warned to move computers out of their children's bedrooms yesterday to protect them from Internet paedophiles.

Youngsters who want to surf the Net should do so where adults can easily check on them.

Otherwise, a Home Office report

By **Michael Clarke**
Home Affairs Correspondent

said, they could be easy prey for perverts who pretend to be children to win their trust and set up a meeting.

The alert comes only days after TV presenter Carol Vorderman published the results of a year-long undercover investigation into the online dangers.

It showed that innocent youngsters may be just three 'clicks' of a com-

puter mouse away from a paedophile.

The Home Office's Internet Crime Forum said chatrooms – websites where children can have typed 'conversations' with strangers – should be monitored by trained moderators who could watch out for perverts.

Sites approved as safe should be granted a kite mark. The unit also wants children to be trained to protect their identities and not to reveal

Turn to Page 6, Col. 4

Figure 1.2 'Ban the computer from your child's room'. Is the front cover of the Daily Mail exaggerating the danger of the internet to children or providing important public information?
Source: The *Daily Mail*, 21 March 2001

the internet, with anxiety expressed about violent, stereotyped, commercially exploitative or pornographic content and about the reinforcement of individualistic, lazy, prejudiced, uncritical or aggressive actions. Yet, these same questions were asked about video games before the internet, about the introduction of television before that, and about radio, cinema and comics back through the decades.

Kirsten Drotner (1992) observed that, as each new medium is introduced, we undergo a kind of 'historical amnesia' about previous panics, as we cheerfully incorporate into our daily lives the medium that preceded it. She argues further that each panic tends to follow a predictable path, starting with a concern among elites that popular media culture will be socially and politically damaging, especially to working class audiences ('pessimistic elitism'). Such a position is associated with calls for technocratic and legalistic measures such as censorship or legal age restrictions to minimise dangers. Moral panics then tend to move to a more positive set of expectations about the social and political effects of popular media culture ('optimistic pluralism'). This is associated with a tolerance of audience diversity along with moral education or media literacy teaching to optimise benefits.

This does not mean, of course, that the concerns expressed in moral panics are necessarily improper, though it does make them less 'new' than their proponents tend to suppose. But often they are misguided, particularly when they seek to blame the media for the wider social ills of society such as social unrest, crime, family breakdown or political apathy, thereby displacing attention from alternative solutions. Moral panics attract an even more critical analysis when they mask intolerant or prejudiced assumptions about audiences other than the 'right-thinking' people making the complaints.

As Stanley Cohen (1972) argued, public anxieties or moral panics about popular pleasures may present themselves as positive and wholesome – what Geoffrey Pearson (1983) termed 'respectable fears' – for example, in the creation of the deviant and stigmatised image of 'youth' (and youth culture) in 1950s Britain or in the rhetoric of a 'golden age' of childhood innocence. When examined closely, these often reveal middle-class concerns about the 'polluting' effect of working-class practices (parents who 'can't control' their children or who do not instil proper 'values', youth 'running amok' in the streets, and children not developing their imagination 'properly'). According to this perspective, moral attacks on the media rest on social inequalities and so should be analysed and resisted rather than taken as the starting point for research investigation.

2.2 Taking the long view: active and passive audiences in historical perspective

Most media research addresses the contemporary scene – today's media, today's audiences, today's concerns. Moreover, considerable research was conducted during the twentieth century (and has continued into the twenty-first), and most has concerned television. But, as historians of the media are keen to point out, the idea of the audience is much older than this (see Figure 1.3). Throughout most of history, the idea of the audience has meant a face-to-face audience in the presence of a communicator or entertainer, whether at a political meeting, the theatre or a concert. Denis McQuail (1997, p.3) suggests that the same features which defined the classical Graeco-Roman audience still define audiences today. He identifies the following six features:

1   planning and *organisation* of viewing and listening, as well as of the performances themselves;

2   events with a *public* and 'popular' character;

3   *secular* content of performance – for entertainment, education and vicarious emotional experiences;

4   *voluntary*, individual acts of choice and attention;

5   *specialisation* of roles of authors, performers and spectators;

6   physical *locatedness* of performance and spectator experience.

The innovation of the 'mass media', after all, was to eliminate the need for physical co-location, for mass communication is communication at a distance, institutionalising a crucial break between performer and spectator or, in today's terms, producer and audience.

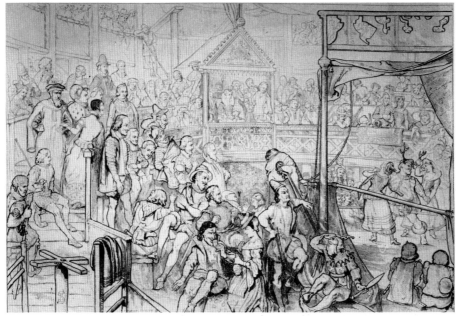

Figure 1.3 *A sixteenth-century drawing of Queen Elizabeth I watching Shakespeare's* The Merry Wives of Windsor *at the Globe Theatre*
Source: Hulton Archive

The history of the audience, therefore, is one of historical continuities as well as discontinuities. Although we tend to find the discontinuities more interesting (or worrying) – how broadcasting breaks with the age of print, how the internet affords unprecedented possibilities for the global dissemination of information, and so on – it is important to bear the continuities in mind also, and to learn the lessons of history when faced with what seems, on first blush, entirely new. This can be seen in Reading 1.1 from Richard Butsch's account of audiences through the centuries.

Reading 1.1 Activity

Now read the following extract from Richard Butsch, 'The making of American audiences: from stage to television 1750–1990' (Reading 1.1), and make notes on these questions:

- What continuities does Butsch see in attitudes towards audiences?
- What is the major contrast between earlier attitudes and those of the twentieth century?

Reading 1.1

Richard Butsch, 'The making of American audiences: from stage to television, 1750–1990'

Popular and scholarly discussions of audiences have long lacked a historical context. Concerns about television viewing, for example, have almost never led to consideration of earlier concerns about radio listening or movie going, let alone popular nineteenth-century entertainments such as melodrama, minstrelsy, and vaudeville. Yet the very issues at the heart of debates today have been played out repeatedly, sometimes in the very same terms, sometimes after inverting these terms.

How *do* nineteenth-century stage entertainments compare to twentieth-century mass media? They differ sharply in institutional form and in technology. Scholars who study one seldom are familiar with the work of those who study the other. And yet there is a continuity of concern about audiences, expressed in the public discourses of the times. Common to all these forms of entertainment is concern about the dangers of and to audiences. Audiences have been worrisome to American elites ever since the Revolution. The written record is a continual flow of worries about social disorder arising from audiences and the consequent need for social control.

While the underlying issues were always power and social order, at different times the causes of the problems of audiences had different sources. In the nineteenth century, the problem lay in the degenerate or unruly people who came to the theater, and what they might do, once gathered. In the twentieth century, worries focused on the dangers of reception, how media messages, might degenerate audiences. In the nineteenth century, critics feared *active* audiences; in the twentieth, their *passivity*.

These changes in the terms of discourse highlight the importance of historicizing the concept of audience. How public discourses construct audiences, how audiences conceive themselves, and what audiences do are historically contingent. Categories like 'the audience' are socially constructed, their attributes typically described in terms of dichotomies. Such dichotomies define the current ideal, what is good, deserves reward, power, privilege.

[...]

In Elizabethan theaters, courtiers and gallants treated theater as their court where they could measure their importance by the attention they received. Fops sat on stage, interrupted performances, and even on occasion grabbed an actress. All of this annoyed the plebeian pit, who shouted, 'Away with them.' But pittites were hardly meek. They too ate, smoked, drank, socialized, and engaged in repartee with actors. Restoration theater was more expensive and exclusive. Still, merchants and professional men, civil servants and their wives, and the critics (poets, writers, and competing playwrights) sat in the pit and squabbled, shouted, teased the women who sold oranges, baited the fops on stage, and wandered from pit to gallery and back. Nobility continued to sit on stage and in boxes, treating the theater as a place to chat, play cards, argue, and even occasionally duel.

By the mid-eighteenth century, London theatergoing was popular among all classes. The privileged continued to give scant attention to the play. Some still sat on stage until David Garrick, director of the Drury Lane Theater, finally succeeded in banning them in 1762. The reputation for rowdiness shifted to the gallery where journeymen, apprentices, servants (footmen) – many of whom could afford theater because they arrived after the featured play and paid only half price – lorded over those below. Instead of the individual display of courtiers of the previous era, this plebeian audience expressed collective opinions, sometimes to the point of riot.

This behavior represents not only an active audience, but a discourse through which audiences insistently constructed themselves as active. Audiences asserted their rights to judge and direct performances. There were two basic traditions of such audience sovereignty which can be characterized as those of the privileged and those of the plebeians – 'the people.' The privileged tradition, rooted in the system of patronage, rested on the status of performers as servants to their aristocratic audience. As with other servants, aristocrats ignored, attended to, or played with actors, as they desired at the moment. It would have violated social order for aristocratic audiences to defer to performers by keeping silent and paying attention. Court theaters were more formal, ritualistic examples of this. More rumbunctious examples were the private theaters frequented by young gentry. Aristocratic audience sovereignty affirmed the social order.

Lower classes too had an honored tradition of rights in the theater that were linked to street traditions of carnival and of crowd actions to enforce a moral economy. Carnival, practiced in parades, hangings, and other public festivities, granted such prerogatives to lower classes on certain occasions when normal social order was turned upside down. The carnival tradition extended to street theater such as *commedia dell'arte* and into popular theaters, which had a rowdier tradition of audience sovereignty. Carnival, like the lesser members of the theater audience, contained lower-class rule within limits and elites to retain control of social order. But carnival also presented the threat of getting out of control.

[...]

Through the nineteenth century, public discussion focused on concerns about *active* audiences. As movies became popular in the early twentieth century, public debate shifted from a focus on audience behavior to worry about the movies' content and its effects *on* audiences, particularly on children. Attention shifted from the place to the play, from effects of dangerous people in those places to effects of dangerous media messages on people. Audiences were being redefined from active to helpless, dependent, and passive, and would remain so through the rest of the twentieth century, as we will see. Concern about what audiences were doing was superseded by what was being done to them, or more precisely what they were learning from the entertainment that they shouldn't. Some of this was evident at the turn of the [nineteenth to the twentieth] century when complaints about small-time vaudeville began to focus on the lewdness of the show. With the movies, however, the attention on the show and its effects clearly became paramount over concerns about activity in theater.

The focus of concern also shifted from women to children as the endangered group. Previously, middle-class women were the ones considered endangered and warned away from theaters and the people who frequented them. Now children were the endangered group, socialized into deviant behavior by movie content. This focus on children was part of many Progressive efforts of the times, and a new middle-class attention to childhood.

Reading source

Butsch, 2000, pp.2–7 ■■■

Butsch makes it clear that modern concerns about audiences go back a long way. But he also suggests that, whereas concerns used to be centred on the activity of audiences and on the possible effects on middle-class women, in the twentieth century, concerns shifted to passivity and the possible effects of such passivity on children. Perhaps most interesting in Butsch's account is the sketch of different kinds of audience from different periods, reminding us of what is too often forgotten when people worry about isolated, vulnerable or passive audiences, namely the liveliness, the whole-hearted engagement and the social complexity of participating in an audience (see Chapter 2).

Butsch is at pains to stress some theoretical points also, particularly the notion that audiences are institutionally planned for and managed (as McQuail, 1997, noted – see the beginning of this section). Audiences themselves know what is expected of them and they develop habits or conventions of behaviour which fit these expectations. Further, notions of the audience are constructed within a moral discourse that posits a break between producers and audiences. And it is this break, this gap, that holds the potential for things going wrong – messages being distorted, audiences not paying proper attention, producers losing touch with their audience – in short, for the unintended consequences of communication. This is less a concern with the media themselves than with the meanings, practices and divisions within a society which depends on the media.

Activity 1.2

Compare the social conventions (the settings, practices and expectations) for audiences at a classical concert and at a cinema. Then compare these social conventions with the conventions surrounding domestic television viewing. What does it mean to 'behave well' in these different circumstances? ■■■

Audiences attending a classical concert will plan their outing, often paying in advance for their tickets. Just before the performance begins, the audience will settle down, sit quietly and await the start of the performance with concentrated attention. During the performance it is important to give applause at the right moment and to avoid disturbing others by coughing excessively or talking. In contrast, the cinema audience is more casual in behaviour but focused on the screen. Advertisements usually precede the film and one can often hear the sound of people eating popcorn and whispering in the dark. As the film begins the audience falls silent, although people often arrive late and so one can expect more disturbances. There are cross-cultural differences in conventions of audience behaviour. In India, for example, cinema spectators often actively perform singing and dancing routines alongside the stars on screen. They might also eat and talk throughout the film. Television audiences are even more casual than cinema audiences. They may or may not choose to watch a programme. The television often provides a background flow of sounds and images and is integrated into the domestic space and its routines. Attention is often distracted and casual, and activities around the television set may have very little to do with viewing. Television audiences may appear to be passive and physically inert but they may be highly active mentally. Let us now turn to the debate about active and passive audiences.

2.3 Twentieth-century debates: oscillating between active and passive audiences

In the second half of the twentieth century, the legacy of ideas and concerns about the mass audience proved decisive in framing the new enterprise of social scientific investigation into the nature and effects of the 'mass media'. Clearly, this is to skip over some crucial stages in a longer historical process, as the media themselves developed through the age of mass printing and what McQuail (1997) terms 'the dispersed reading public', through to the early days of film, with a return to a co-located audience (though not for a live and present communicator, but rather for the vivid 'window on the world' of the cinema screen). Only following this do we get the history of broadcasting – radio as well as television – and this set the stage for the post-Second World War expansion of audience research.

Looking back over the history of media research, it is evident that research is strongly framed by the cultural and historical concerns of its time. The US–Israeli communication researcher Elihu Katz (1980) described an oscillation between the two dominant views of the audience that we identified in Section 1 – the liberal–pluralist view of selective audiences and limited effects, and the critical view of manipulated audiences and strong effects. In accounting for the swings of the pendulum, Katz stressed two mediating factors, which he had discussed in earlier work, that stand between the media and their audience:

1 *Selectivity:* in his development of the 'uses and gratifications' theoretical approach (Blumler and Katz, 1974), Katz asked not what the media do to people but what people do with the media. He did so because, as research readily shows, people are motivated, selective and active in their uses of the media. Others take this further, arguing that people are selective also in their interpretation of the media, guided by their prior knowledge, values and beliefs as well as by the media text.

2 *Interpersonal relations:* In his 'two-step flow' hypothesis (Katz and Lazarsfeld, 1955), Katz argued that because people talk to each other about the media, any media message may be affected, or reshaped, by everyday conversations. Consequently, some people in a community – the 'opinion leaders' – are influential in mediating the effect of the media.

Both 'selectivity' and 'interpersonal relations' led Katz and others to think that the audience is more active than passive, although under certain circumstances – historical, cultural or personal – neither factor is particularly effective. For example, during occasions of national crisis, people share a common anxiety about events and become highly dependent on the media for their information (Ball-Rokeach, 1985).

The influence of the media may also be expected to vary for particular segments of the audience, since people vary in their prior knowledge and interests and in their access to alternative influences, including face-to-face communication. Moreover, as Butsch argued in Reading 1.1, some audiences have always been seen as vulnerable – women, for many centuries, and children, more recently. We will return to the image of women as a 'peculiar' audience in Section 3.3, when we discuss soap operas, but first we pursue the evidence for powerful media effects where it has been most often sought, namely in relation to children.

2.4 Setting the agenda: public concern and research on media effects

Scholars have traced a complex history of relations between public concern about media effects, public funding for research, media effects research itself, and the impact of the research on government policy (Rowland, 1983). Certainly the research agenda is uneven – many studies have examined the potentially harmful effects of the media on children, but few have examined positive effects. Some argue that studies demonstrating harmful effects get published while those that fail to show effects do not. More research is conducted at times of high public concern (see Figure 1.4), often concentrated on the newest medium, while little funding is available for longitudinal studies following children over several years. These biases in the research agenda are rarely discussed. This does not mean that the research which has been conducted is misguided in and of itself, though, as we shall see, researchers have faced other problems.

Figure 1.4 *High profile newspaper stories covering the deleterious effects of the media on our children can cause public concerns. Those concerns can result in more research into the issues. This image appeared in the* Daily Mail *alongside an article that covered the story of a young toddler hooked on video games from a tender age*
Source: courtesy of Solo Syndication, the *Daily Mail*, 28 January 1999

The majority of public interest and public funding, especially in the USA, has been concentrated on experimental research examining the short-term effects of media exposure on behaviours or attitudes – and most of it has focused on the child audience. Other prominent traditions not covered here have investigated the cognitive effects (the effects on the way people think) on adult public opinion of political news, or the reinforcing effect of media coverage on public attitudes and stereotypes of women, ethnic groups, crime and so forth. But although the experiments on children have proved the most controversial, each of these research traditions has produced roughly the same outcome. Whichever way one looks at it, it seems that the media can be shown, under specific circumstances, to have a variety of modest and inconsistent effects on some segments of the population. This tends to disappoint both the liberal–pluralists, who want to know how to use media to appeal to the public, and the critical scholars, who fear that the media have considerable power over their audiences.

As the US communications scholar Wilbur Schramm once elegantly wrote, ironically at the outset rather than at the conclusion of this research programme: 'For some children, under some conditions, some television is harmful. For some children under the same conditions, or for the same children under other conditions, it may be beneficial. For most children, under most conditions, most television is probably neither particularly harmful nor particularly beneficial.' (Schramm et al., 1961, p.11).

On the other hand, another US communications researcher, George Gerbner argued persuasively that, since 'television tells most of the stories to most of the people most of the time', experiments comparing heavy with light users of TV are unlikely to demonstrate significant effects. His point is not that people are unaffected by the media, but rather that everyone is already too much 'under the influence' for a brief experimental intervention to make any difference. As he says: 'If as we argue, the messages are so stable, the medium is so ubiquitous, and accumulated total exposure is what counts, then almost everyone should be affected ... It is clear, then, that the cards are stacked against finding evidence of effects.' (Gerbner et al., 1986, p.21).

Whether the glass is half full or half empty – in other words, whether this is taken as good news or bad news for research, for the media, for children – is a matter of policy and politics. Public policy and public opinion would rather not hear qualifications and excuses. In a parliamentary briefing to the UK government, a committee of psychologists concluded confidently that 'screen violence can desensitise viewers, raise aggression levels, reduce empathy for victims and enhance the role of violence in conflict resolution' (Parliamentary Office of Science and Technology, 1993).

So, what are the conclusions of the studies referred to in the previous section based upon? Let us backtrack and examine the experiments that have been conducted and their findings (see Livingstone, 1996, for an overview).

2.5 What are the effects of the media?

The 'effects tradition' focuses predominantly, but not exclusively, on the effects of television rather than other media – on effects on the child audience especially – on the effects of violent or stereotyped programmes, and on effects on individuals rather than on groups, cultures or institutions. By and large, it tests the idea that exposure to particular media content changes people's behaviour or beliefs (while other research examines whether media reinforce existing beliefs).

Before examining whether media affect behaviour, research must establish a correlation between cause and effect – that is, the more we watch, the greater (or lesser) the behaviour. If there is no correlation, there is no point looking for a causal relation in which watching television actually brings about the change in behaviour. Generally, such correlations are found, though they are usually fairly small (for example, Gerbner et al., 1986). For example, children who watch more 'violent' cartoons (note that there is a debate about what constitutes violence in cartoons) are likely to be more aggressive in the playground.

Causal relations are more difficult to establish, however. Is the correlation really due to an alternative causal factor? Perhaps children who watch a lot of television come from homes both where other activities are lacking and where levels of aggression are higher? This would make the observed correlation between media and behaviour a spurious one, to be explained by social factors rather than by media effects. The direction of causality is also a tricky issue. It could be that playing aggressively in the playground encourages watching violent cartoons on television, so that the behaviour affects media use rather than the other way around. Interestingly, it turns out that research supports all of these hypotheses, including the causal one that media exposure influences behaviour ('media effects' hypothesis). However, clearly social behaviour is multiply determined and no single factor accounts for something as complex as playground behaviour.

Media effects researchers argue that causal connections between media exposure and behaviour can only be inferred through controlled experiments. Controlled experiments seek to vary systematically one causal factor (the 'independent variable'), such as exposure to violent behaviour on film. This enables researchers to observe the effect of that factor on the behaviour of different groups. The experiment relies on two crucial features:

1   People are randomly assigned to experimental and control conditions, so that the social factors which may play a causal role are neutralised, since such factors would apply equally to experimental and control groups.

2   The independent variable (the hypothesised cause – the media exposure) precedes the dependent variable (the hypothesised effect – the measured behaviour), so that the direction of causality within the experimental setting is established.

The classic experiment here is the so-called 'Bobo doll' experiment (see Figure 1.5) – a series of experiments conducted by Albert Bandura, a social learning theorist (see Bandura et al., 1961). Bandura and his colleagues showed children in the experimental condition a film of an adult hitting a large inflatable doll, while the control groups saw a different film or no film at all. He then left the children alone in a playroom for a short time with a variety of toys, including the Bobo doll, and watched how they acted.

Social learning theory proposes that people learn to imitate what they see only if they see the behaviour being rewarded and not if they see it being punished. And this is what happened in Bandura's experiments. Children who saw a film of rewarded aggression were more likely to imitate the aggressive behaviour afterwards in the playroom than were children who saw punished aggression in the film or those who saw no aggression at all. It is argued that part of the significance of the study is that in everyday life, and especially in the media, children witness repeated instances of aggression and also they see aggression being rewarded or approved of rather than punished – hence one should worry much more about Superman or Indiana Jones than about classic 'baddies' in the media.

Figure 1.5 *This young girl was a subject in Albert Bandura's Bobo doll experiment.*
Source: Professor Albert Bandura, Stanford University

This kind of research has been replicated, varied and extended in many different ways. Reviews of the literature agree that viewers learn both pro-social and anti-social attitudes and behaviour from television portrayals – and interestingly, they also agree that pro-social effects (like helping others or being generous) are more pronounced than anti-social effects. Research also shows complex findings – for example, violent images in the news affect older children more than those in younger age groups, while the latter are more affected by cartoons. Younger children, especially boys, are much more likely to be influenced by anti-social contents. However, research is inconsistent over whether the effects last for very long – though some would say that, since children watch similar programmes every day, it hardly matters if the effects are only short-term, since they are never very far from their 'next dose'.

However, none of this need imply, and it certainly does not prove, that beliefs or behaviours learned under experimental conditions can be generalised to viewers' ordinary lives. Results which are relatively consistent under experimental conditions are poorly replicated under naturalistic or everyday conditions. This has led critics to argue that these experiments represent such unusual situations that the results cannot be generalised (indeed, some say that the only thing children learn from experiments is to meet researchers' expectations).

The debate, therefore, concerns not only the nature and consistency of the findings, but also whether the social characteristics of the experimental situation parallel everyday settings in which both viewing and, say, aggression occur. This in turn has led some to conduct field experiments that study the possible changes in children's ordinary behaviour as a result of an experimental intervention into an everyday setting – for example, by positioning researchers as teachers in a nursery where children have time to get used to them and then, over some weeks perhaps, showing children in one nursery one kind of media content and children in a different nursery a different kind. Naturalistic measures of their subsequent behaviour (for example, how often they push or hit other children) can then be taken relatively unobtrusively. Yet, here too there are methodological debates about the design and techniques used in field experiments, with a crucial doubt expressed over whether third causes have been properly dealt with – for random allocation to experimental or control groups may not be possible here. More worryingly, in the best field experiments – that is, those based in the most everyday or ordinary settings – the effects tend to be small to non-existent.

We are faced with a less than ideal situation. Some conclude that the laboratory experiment demonstrates the existence of causal effects, while the weak or absent effects shown in field experiments reflects their poor design and conduct. But others conclude that the laboratory experiment is too artificial to be generalised to everyday life while the lack of effects under naturalistic conditions justifies a 'no effects' conclusion. All agree that more research is needed, but what kind it should be, and how to justify it given the number of studies already conducted, is not easy to resolve.

3 Making sense of television: texts, audiences and meanings

3.1 From media effects to audience reception

Notwithstanding the critique of media effects research, most researchers do in fact believe that the media have effects – why study the media otherwise? Given that the media are thoroughly embedded in our lives, a major source of images and information, especially of social and political phenomena beyond our daily experience, how could we conclude that the media have no effect on how we think or act? Most research therefore draws qualified, modest and contingent or contextualised conclusions regarding media effects, recognising that, as in any other social science field, we will not find the single definitive study which resolves debate. It is to this notion of contingency or context that I now turn.

I will illustrate this with an extract from Ellen Seiter's work, in which she describes a different kind of project on children and media effects.

Reading 1.2 Activity

Now read the following extract from Ellen Seiter, 'Television and new media audiences' (Reading 1.2). In this reading, Seiter adopts a qualitative, ethnographic approach. An ethnographic approach to audience research is based on intensive and extensive participation in and/or observations of a particular group of people in a specific setting (see Chapter 4 on audience ethnography). Seiter, for example, spent lengthy periods of time observing children's play when working in a nursery school. This leads her to critique the experimental approach and to replace it with a culturally grounded analysis of media use. As you read the extract, try to answer the following question: why does Seiter consider the cultural approach to be superior?

Reading 1.2

Ellen Seiter, 'Television and new media audiences'

The scene is a classroom of four-year olds at an upper-middle-class nursery school in a US Midwestern suburb. About twenty children are present, fifteen of them boys. Two teachers are present, one is a woman in her late fifties, the other is a student teacher in her early twenties. It is late morning clean-up time, when the teachers attempt to secure the children's efforts to tidy up the classroom before the children go to the outdoor playground for recess.

Two boys are playing in a corner of the room with tiny toy cars. One is a slender, white, extremely talkative boy named Ian. The other is a small, Chinese-American boy named Wu. Bedlam is all around them.

A third boy, larger and older than Ian and Wu, approaches. His name is Michael. 'Can I play with you?' he asks.

'Sorry, but me and Wu are playing', Ian replies.

A few minutes later, a fourth boy, Casey, who is even larger than Michael and very rambunctious, joins them in play without asking permission.

While Casey plays with the cars and blocks he sings, 'Flintstones, meet the Flintstones have a yabba dabba doo time ...'

Ian and Wu are silent. After a pause in the singing, Ian strikes up some conversation:

Ian: Guess what? You know I heard that the Flintstones are going to see the Jetsons.

Casey: You mean on the cartoons?

Ian: No, the show.

Casey: On the Flintstones show they're going over to see the Jetsons.

The conversation fades out here and the boys continue playing until the student teacher approaches. She asks, 'What are you doing?' in an accusatory way that implies that they should be putting the toys away rather than playing with them.

In high-pitched, joking voices, the boys reply, 'We're trying to sort these [the blocks] out.' Lingering for a moment to check up on them, the teacher observes them hiding the tiny cars behind the blocks as they clean up. Clearly irritated with them for breaking a frequently repeated rule about returning toys to their rightful storage containers, the teacher switches to a commanding tone: 'I want Casey to put the cars away, Wu to put the big blocks away, and Ian to put the small blocks away.'

As she walks away, the boys erupt in laughter, exhilarated by their naughtiness and the discovery of their crime. Casey begins to sing again, and the other boys join in, singing loudly: 'Flintstones, meet the Flintstones.' As they sing, they grow more raucous, boisterous. Wu is laughing hard, intensely enjoying his inclusion in the singing of the song and the rebellion it signifies. The boys repeat the same song lyrics over and over again: 'Flintstones, meet the Flintstones.'

Michael, curious about the good time the three boys are having, wanders over and tries to join them again. Casey immediately grabs a plastic pan and rhythmically hits Michael over the head with it in time to the beat of the music, while singing 'Have a yabba dabba doo time, a dabba doo time ...'

As a qualitative audience researcher observing this scene after some twenty hours of visits to this classroom, and nine months of visits to the school, I see in the boys' classroom interaction the complex ways that popular television is embedded in interpersonal communications, in gendered conflicts, and in the exchange of tokens of cultural capital. To the student teacher walking over to break up the rough-housing between Casey and Michael, the scene might confirm the widely shared conviction among teachers that television produces violent behaviour in children and causes disruptions in the classroom. It must be admitted from the outset that qualitative audience research can do little to confirm or deny such a hypothesis about television's effects. Qualitative research can, however, offer an interpretation of this scene that takes account of the contextual factors at work here, and the various uses of television as a form and topic of communication with others in social settings. The primary contribution of ethnographic audience research since the 1970s has been its demonstration that media consumption is embedded in the routines, rituals, and institutions – both public and domestic – of everyday life. The meanings of the media, whether in the form of print, broadcast, or recorded video, or computer forms, are inseparable from and negotiated within these contexts.

[...]

In this classroom scene, Ian and Casey, two boys who play together infrequently at school, use chat about *The Flintstones* and *The Jetsons* to make conversation. Later, when the boys join together singing the *Flintstones* theme song as a rebel call, Wu is especially exhilarated by it because he is often excluded by Casey from play – as are the other Asian children. On numerous occasions I have observed Wu strategically deploying his knowledge about toys and TV superheroes to gain entry into play situations with some of the dominant (and white) boys in the class.

[...]

It would be erroneous to infer that these three boys are avid fans of *The Flintstones*, for example. Although Michael, who initiates the reference to the cartoon, might recently have seen either the television or the live-action film version, released on video at about the time of this conversation, *The Flintstones* was not a frequent topic of his chat. Something about the blocks and the cars seemed to remind him of the Stone Age cars and garages on the cartoon – or perhaps the song had simply stuck in his mind. Rather than interpreting this scene as an instance of direct effects, it seems typical of the casual references, remembered jingles, and the like that children reuse for their own purposes [...] In this case, the incongruous introduction of TV references into the classroom seems to work for the children and the teacher as a battle cry of rebellion. One of the most salient messages of this use of the *Flintstones* song is: I am doing something naughty, and I refuse to clean up.

[...]

If I had visited this classroom on a single day, I would have had no possibility of understanding the ways in which media references do and also do not serve young children's negotiations and friendships. It is significant, for example, that on many days when I visited the class no references to television were made within my hearing. It is equally significant that fights such as the one between Casey and Michael occurred very frequently, sometimes linked to the media, as in enacting *Power Rangers* karate kicks, and sometimes not. During my first days of classroom observations, the boys were curious, wary, and guarded around me. It was only after several weeks that Casey announced, after starting a fight nearby and looking at me, 'She's not a teacher!' and that the boys engaged in illicit behaviour within my hearing. Thus, doing ethnographic audience research necessitates making contact with informants repeatedly, for as much time as possible, and under as many different circumstances as possible.

Reading source

Seiter, 1999, pp.1–5   ■ ■ ■

Seiter emphasises three points. Firstly, ethnographic research offers a very different methodology from the laboratory experiment. Secondly, only through ethnographic research can key features of the context of media use emerge. Thirdly, interpreting these key contextual features leads to very different research conclusions.

Activity 1.3

Take a moment to elaborate each of these arguments, drawing on Reading 1.2 to illustrate them. Do you find Seiter's case convincing? How does the nursery setting compare with the experimental setting? Can we ask the same types of questions in both settings?   ■ ■ ■

In fact, media researchers have always known that context matters, so that different groups in the audience, for various reasons, interpret media differently, making diverse uses of its content. Consider a famous piece of research conducted even before the days of television.

On 30 October 1938, one million Americans were terrified into believing that Martians were taking over New Jersey during the radio broadcast of H.G. Wells' *The War of the Worlds* (USA, CBS, 1938). This was partly because they did not hear the opening announcement – that it was a drama – and so interpreted the programme as an extended emergency news report (Cantril, 1940). They packed their bags, flooded the churches or ran away. However, the other five million people in the audience were not terrified, for they applied various interpretative checks on what they heard. Some applied 'internal checks', like asking themselves how the Martians could take over so quickly, within the 45-minute time frame of the programme. Others applied 'external checks', looking out of the window to see if the roads were jammed or switching to another channel to see if the same 'news' was to be heard there. Further, some groups – more educated people, for example, or less religious people – were less influenced than others. My point is that an episode commonly cited as evidence for media effects more accurately provided evidence for limited effects, depending on key factors of audience selectivity, interpretation and social context.

Given both the difficulties of establishing direct media effects and the evidence for indirect or contingent effects of the media, a different approach to audiences is warranted. Instead of assuming that all members of the audience are influenced by media messages in the same way, we need an approach which assumes that:

- audiences are plural, diverse and variable;
- the meanings of media texts are a matter of interpretation; and
- the consequences of media 'exposure' or use depend on the social context.

It seems that there is little empirical evidence to suggest that the audience is a homogeneous mass of gullible dopes (though recall Gerbner's caution about the limits of the empirical method here). Do we instead find evidence that audiences are selective and rational in their approach to the media, as the liberal approach would have it? And where does this leave the question of media power?

3.2 Contrasting models of the communication process

To ask about media power, rather than the effects of the media on its audience, we must return to the big picture. Thus, questions about audiences should be connected to questions about media institutions (broadcasters, producers, regulators, advertisers) and about media forms (technologies, channels, genres, contents). The above discussion supports two possible directions, each complicating any simple assumption of a direct relationship between production and audience.

The first approach, associated with the liberal–pluralist tradition, retains the key assumptions of effects research but argues that matters are more complicated. It asserts a linear communication process, following from Harold Lasswell's (1948) influential challenge to early communication research, namely to discover 'who says what in which channel to whom and with what effect'. This model is commonly summarised thus:

Given the lack of empirical evidence for a direct path, many researchers acknowledge the contingent and contextual factors which complicate the process, framing these as intervening variables in the same linear process, albeit now a more indirect one, thus:

Hence the number of stages in the communication process, and the number of factors which must be examined, is increased. For example, in Figure 1.6 (a) – taken from George Comstock's model of learning from television news – a series of intervening factors is included to account for the considerable limits on what people understand of and learn from the news. Still, the model remains linear, following the 'transmission' metaphor of communication in which media messages are treated as packages of meanings which are transported from the sender along a more or less hazardous path towards the receiver (Carey, 1989).

The critiques levelled at this model stimulated the development of an alternative model. One widely influential version of this from the critical tradition is Stuart Hall's Encoding/Decoding model (Hall, 1980). This proposes a cyclic rather than linear view of communication and centres on processes (encoding, decoding) rather than on actors (sender, receiver). Hall adopts a semiotic view of media contents in which 'the range of meaning depends very much on the nature of the language and on the significance attached to the patterned arrangement of given signs and symbols within a culture shared by sender (encoder) and receiver (decoder) alike' (McQuail and Windahl, 1993, p.146). However, he also acknowledges that the cultures of sender and receiver may not be identical – for each is structurally positioned differently in society, most notably in terms of social class. As a result, although Hall emphasises the power of the encoded text, he allows for the possibility that audiences can resist this power. Consider the contrasting models in Figure 1.6 and complete Activity 1.4. (Note that Hall's classic drawing poorly represents the cyclic process he proposed.)

Activity 1.4

Compare and contrast these two models of the communication process. What have they in common and what are the key differences? Does it make a difference to focus on the social actors involved (producers and audiences) or the social processes (encoding and decoding)? Do the different models prioritise different research questions? ■ ■ ■

One difference between these models is that in the linear model the audience is placed at the end-point of the influence process. This makes it easier to ask how the audience is influenced by media than how it participates in the communication process (although some versions of the model have added feedback loops to indicate audience ratings, letters to the editor, and so on). These questions of impact are more naturally asked from the standpoint of the sender, leading one to ask how much

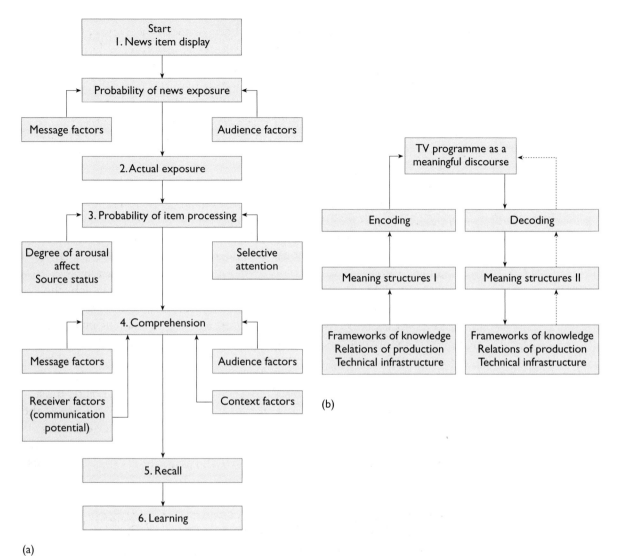

Figure 1.6 *(a) Transmission model of news learning and (b) Hall's Encoding/Decoding model*
Source: adapted from Figures 3.6.1 and 5.3.1 in McQuail and Windahl, 1993

of what the sender intended actually reaches the audience and what gets
lost or altered along the way.

Problematically, this leads to the question of what producers 'intend'
(a difficult question given the complexity of media institutions) and to
judging transformations in messages in terms of degradation, loss or bias
as they pass from sender to receiver. It makes it harder to see that
audiences also have intentions or – better – that they too are socially
located, motivated and selective in their approach to (rather than their
'response' to) the media. It makes it particularly hard to see how

audiences play an interpretative role in co-constructing the meanings of media messages. As McQuail puts it:

> Early audience research had been framed in the shadow of a model of communication as a linear process of transmission of 'messages' that privileged message 'content' and its 'impact' and treated audience 'exposure' as an aggregate of unrelated individual selections. The important thing was for messages to be consciously received, registered and effective ... The features of social life that 'got in the way' of this were either to be treated as 'noise', interference, or as irritating inconveniences in the measurement process.
>
> McQuail, 1997, p.89

By contrast, the cyclic model acknowledges that audiences are embedded in a social context which shapes their engagement with media and that they engage in an active task of interpreting or decoding media messages which parallels that of constructing or encoding messages.

The features of social life which previously 'got in the way' become the focus of the analysis. The media message is no longer treated as a stimulus – a package of meaning whose contents are inflexible and obvious – but rather as a text whose meaning is polysemic, negotiable, to be interpreted (cf. **Bonner, 2005; Gillespie and Toynbee, 2006**). As the Italian semiotician (an analyst of cultural signs, meanings and sign systems) Umberto Eco (1979, p.5) explains: 'The existence of various codes and subcodes, the variety of socio-cultural circumstances in which a message is emitted (where the codes of the addressee can be different from those of the sender) ... result in making a message ... an empty form to which various possible senses can be attributed.'

This is not to say that audiences are all-powerful, however. Both Hall (1980) and Eco (1979), working in the critical rather than the liberal–pluralist tradition, anticipate strong limits on the process of decoding. Particularly, Hall describes a powerful media industry dominating the encoding process, together with a normative social and material context heavily constraining the interpretative activities of the audience. But these are empirical matters, as we see below.

3.3 Case study: the soap opera

Television is a prime example of the taken-for-granted. Its meanings appear unavoidable, they seem to exist 'in' the programmes and leap out at us when we watch. But social scientists work to defamiliarise the familiar, so we can see how 'reality' is socially constructed through the considerable interpretative effort which goes into making sense of events, meanings and situations in everyday life. In seeking to analyse what Elihu Katz (1980) terms 'viewers' work', audience researchers take seriously the idea that the media message is a text. In so doing, they draw on theories developed in the field of literary criticism to understand popular culture texts such as soap opera.

I have not picked the soap opera genre at random to illustrate this argument. Soap opera has long challenged audience research, partly because of its staggering success – in terms of the longevity of its series, the size of the audiences and its huge global export markets – and partly because its audience has been one of the most vilified, soaps being widely derided as 'trashy programming' for 'mindless housewives' (recall Richard Butsch's argument, in Reading 1.1, about women and children as the audience who need protection from media harms).

In critiquing such dismissive comments about women, and seeking instead to understand the pleasures they – and, indeed, many men – find in soap operas, audience researchers set out to re-evaluate the genre (Geraghty, 1991). They have taken as their starting point the argument that media contents are complex, multilayered texts, inviting semiotic analysis – that is, an analysis of signs, systems and modes of representation that convey meanings, so that audiences are best understood as 'readers' (**Gillespie and Toynbee, 2006**). This text-reader metaphor has opened up a closer analysis of the relation between encoding and decoding in the mass communication process. How does this help?

Reading 1.3 Activity

Now read Robert C. Allen, 'To be continued ... soap operas around the world', Reading 1.3. This Reading is from the introduction to his edited volume on the global success of soap opera. What, for Allen, is distinctive about the relationship between soap opera and its viewers?

Reading 1.3

Robert C. Allen, 'To be continued ... soap operas around the world' (1995)

As literary theorist Wolfgang Iser has noted, the act of reading any narrative involves traversing textual terrain over time, as the reader moves from one word, sentence, paragraph, and chapter to the next. Or, in the case of cinematic or televisual narratives, from one shot, scene, sequence, or episode to the next. As readers or viewers we take up what he calls a 'wandering viewpoint' within the text as we move through it, looking back upon the textual terrain already covered (what Iser calls retention) and anticipating on that basis what might lie around the next textual corner (protension). Both processes occur in the gaps between words, sentences, and chapters (or shots, scenes, and sequences) – those necessary textual silences where we as readers/viewers are called upon to connect the words, sounds and/or images of the text to form a coherent narrative world.

The serial, then, is a form of narrative organized around institutionally-imposed gaps in the text. The nature and extent of those gaps are as important to the reading process as the textual 'material' they interrupt. Each episode ends with some degree of narrative indeterminacy: a plot question that will not be answered until the next episode. In the US, where daytime serials are broadcast Monday through Friday, the greatest indeterminacy is left with the viewer at the end of the Friday episode, encouraging her, as the announcer's voice used to say, to "tune in again next time" on Monday. These gaps leave plenty of time for viewers to discuss with each other both the possible meanings of what has happened thus far as well as what might happen next.

[...]

Non-serial popular narratives tend to be organized around a single protagonist or small group of protagonists and to be teleological: there is a single moment of narrative closure (obviously involving the protagonist) toward which their plots move and in relation to which reader satisfaction is presumed to operate. The classic example of this type of narrative is the murder mystery, in which the revelation of the murderer at the end of the story absolutely determines the movement of the plot. By contrast, the serial spreads its narrative energy among a number of plots and a community of characters, and, what is even more important, sets these plots and characters in complex, dynamic, and unpredictable relationship with each other. Because serials cut between scenes enacting separate plot lines, the viewer is prompted to ask not only 'Where is each of these plot lines going?', but also 'What might be the relationship between different plot lines?'

It is at this point that we need to distinguish between two fundamentally different, but frequently conflated, forms of television serial: what I call 'open' and 'closed' serials. US daytime, British, and Australian serials are open narrative forms. That is to say they are the only forms of narrative (with the possible exception of comic strips) predicated upon the impossibility of ultimate closure. No one sits down to watch an episode of one of these programs with the expectation that this episode might be the one in which all individual and community problems will be solved and everyone will live happily ever after.

In a sense, these serials trade narrative closure for paradigmatic complexity. Just as there is no ultimate moment of resolution, there is no central, indispensable character in open serials to whose fate viewer interest is indissolubly linked. Instead, there is a changing community of characters who move in and out of viewer attention and interest. Any one of them might die, move to another city, or lapse into an irreversible coma without affecting the overall world of the serial. Indeed, I would argue that it is the very possibility of a central character's demise – something that is not a feature of episodic series television – that helps to fuel viewer interest in the serial.

US daytime soap operas are 'open' in another sense as well. Events in a daytime soap are less determinant and irreversible than they are in other forms of narrative, and identity, indeed ontology itself, is more mutable. For example, generally, when a character dies in a fictional narrative (assuming we are not reading a gothic horror tale or piece of science fiction) we expect that character to stay dead. In soap operas, it is not unusual to witness the resurrection of a character assumed to be but not actually dead, even after the passage of years of intervening story.

[...]

Another distinguishing feature of open serials, particularly US daytime serials, is their large community of interrelated characters. More than half of all US daytime serial episodes are one hour in length and all are broadcast five days each week. As a result, it is not uncommon for the cast of a daytime soap to include more than thirty regularly-appearing characters – not counting a dozen or more others who have moved away, lapsed into comas, been incarcerated or otherwise institutionalized, or are presumed dead. Furthermore, the audience comes to know some of these characters quite literally over the course of decades of viewing. In the nearly forty years that actress Charita Bauer played the role of Bert Bauer on *The Guiding Light*, her character evolved from young bride to great-grandmother. Viewers of *Coronation Street* have followed events in the life of character Ken Barlow since he was introduced in the show's first episode in December 1960. Thus, the community of soap opera characters shares with the loyal viewer a sense of its collective and individual history, which, in some cases, has unfolded over decades both of storytelling and viewing: the viewer who began watching *The Guiding Light* in 1951 as a young mother caring for infants might herself now watch with her grandchildren.

[...]

It is not uncommon to hear people who don't watch open serials complain that 'nothing ever happens' in them. 'Why bother watching every day or even every week', they puzzle, 'when you can keep up with the plot by watching an episode a month.' This complaint is grounded in two fundamental qualities of open serial narrative, but it also reveals an equally fundamental misunderstanding of how these narratives function and the nature of the pleasures they might generate. It is true that no story event will push the open serial narrative any closer to ultimate closure. It is also true that, compared to other types of popular narrative, the emphasis in soap operas is on talk rather than action. But, as we have seen, events in open serials take on meaning for viewers not so much in relation to their place in a syntagmatic chain but rather in terms of the changes in the paradigmatic structure of the community those events might provoke: if, after twenty years, Jason's father is revealed to be Ralph, then Jason must call off his engagement to Jennifer who is now revealed to be his half-sister, and he must come to terms with the fact that Jeremy, his nemesis, is also his half-brother! But, because he is not a regular viewer, the soap opera critic is ignorant of this complex paradigmatic structure and its history. Soap operas are to him merely so much syntagmatically inconsequential talk. To him, little changes from year to year in the soap opera community; to the competent viewer, however, each episode is loaded with important adjustments or possible alterations to that world.

Reading source
Allen, 1995, pp.17–20 ■ ■ ■

Allen claims that, in soap opera, the text anticipates what its reader (the viewer) already knows and what she wants to be shown next, guiding the viewer in certain directions according to conventions familiar to both text and reader. But the text also leaves open some opportunities – through a structured series of 'gaps' – for the viewer to think her own thoughts, draw her own inferences, assert her own preferences. To theorise this active role of the reader or viewer, Allen introduces some concepts from literary theory – particularly Wolfgang Iser's 'implied reader' (in the text) and its contingent relation with 'real' or 'empirical' readers (in the audience). He draws on Umberto Eco's distinction (1979) between open and closed texts to argue that some texts invite readers to insert their own knowledge and interests while other texts work hard to eliminate this, being more directive in determining what meanings readers get from the text. Try Activity 1.5 to see how this works.

Activity 1.5

Think about a soap opera you are familiar with. Compared with a situation comedy or romance, what 'contract' does the genre establish with its audience? Imagine how a particular recent storyline could be variously interpreted by different audiences, depending on character preferences or responses to the moral dilemmas portrayed. What difference does it make if you have watched for two weeks, two years or twenty years?

If you do not watch soap operas, watch a couple of episodes and identify the kinds of knowledge – about characters, about ongoing narratives – that are taken for granted and that you may find confusing because you have not watched before. Start a conversation about the current storyline with a friend who watches this soap and notice what they are interested in and whether they interpreted the episodes as you did. ■ ■ ■

Allen contrasts the syntagmatic dimension of the text (the sequence of events as they unfold) with its paradigmatic dimension (the set of possibilities from which any particular character, event or outcome is selected). Allen uses this idea to suggest that the sequencing in a soap opera is fairly predictable, although there are always gaps (especially, 'the cliff-hanger') for viewers to guess what will happen next. This predictability is what the person who does not watch soap operas complains about. However, the paradigmatic dimension is full of competing options – who will overhear the secret, how will they react when it is discovered, who will they tell, will the viewer remember that X once had an affair with Y. And this, for Allen, is what gets the regular viewer so involved and what makes the narrative so absorbing and satisfying.

The key idea here is that audiences are 'written into' media texts themselves. But audience researchers are not just interested in 'implied audiences', particularly as the audience implied by or addressed by the text may or may not be the audience which actually interprets it. In other words, our original question of how audiences respond to the media has been radically reframed as a question of how implied audiences relate to empirical audiences. In asking how real people think and act in relation to particular texts, researchers have developed a range of methods for exploring the process of interpretation or decoding.

In the *Export of Meaning* project, Tamar Liebes and Elihu Katz (1990) investigated one particular thesis of media power, the idea of Americanisation or cultural imperialism. This thesis was epitomised for many by the unexpected global success of the American prime-time soap opera, *Dallas* (USA, CBS, 1978–1991). Commentators argued that powerful media were imposing a particular (that is, American, consumerist, Christian) value system on the world. So, having conducted a textual analysis (an investigation into the way in which a text is structured and organised to convey certain meanings and carry particular themes) to identify the implied reader, Liebes and Katz showed an episode to small friendship groups from a range of diverse cultural settings in Israel. They listen carefully for the ways in which people approached the programme spontaneously, inviting them to 're-tell' the episode as if to someone who had missed it, and analysing the social interaction in front of the screen as people collectively decoded the episode.

The researchers' analysis of the text had suggested that *Dallas* centred on 'primordial themes' – lineage, inheritance, sibling rivalry, property, sex and marriage. Yet the empirical audience study found that viewers of different social and cultural backgrounds generated different interpretations. For example, Russian Jews were more likely to make ideological readings responding to the moral and political themes underlying the narratives. Americans focused more on the personalities and motivations of the characters to make their readings coherent (Allen's paradigmatic dimension). Moroccan Arabs instead emphasised event sequencing and narrative continuity (Allen's syntagmatic dimension). And while each group's reading was clearly constrained by the text, each also engaged with the openness of the text to draw on their diverse cultural resources, resulting in divergent readings of the 'same' programme. What is less obvious is how to theorise these cultural resources: Liebes and Katz's groups vary in terms of ethnicity, nationality, religion and social class, and it is not clear which factors make a difference in the groups' decoding of different aspects of the text.

This project is widely cited as countering the idea of cultural imperialism – showing how audiences may actively resist dominant media messages. As David Morley (1993, p.17) notes, 'local meanings are so often made within and against the symbolic resources provided by global media networks'. And, more generally, Klaus Bruhn Jensen (1993, p.26) argues that 'reception analysis offers insights into the interpretive processes and everyday contexts of media use, where audiences re-articulate and enact the meanings of mass communication. The life of signs within modern society is in large measure an accomplishment of the audience' (see Chapter 4 for further discussion of serial narratives and transnational audiences).

3.4 Consolidating the audience reception approach

A range of audience reception studies have explored how audiences interpret and use different media, mainly focusing on television genres. Audience interpretations or decodings have been found to diverge depending on viewers' socio-economic position, gender, ethnicity, and so forth (see Figure 1.7), while the possibilities for critical or oppositional readings are anticipated, enabled or restricted by the degree of closure encoded into the text or genre.

For example, Morley's study (1980) of audience decodings of the British current affairs magazine show of the time, *Nationwide* (UK, BBC, 1969), found audiences to diverge as a function of their socio-economic and labour market position. Predictably, given that Morley explored understandings of the news, audience decodings were politically framed. In focus groups, bank managers and schoolboys made the most normative readings, consistent with the ideologically dominant assumptions which structured the programme. Trainee teachers and trade union officials made politically inconsistent, ambivalent or negotiated readings. Other groups – for example, trade union shop stewards – took an oppositional position, using the resources of the text to construct a critical reading quite unintended by it. A few viewers were alienated from the text as it did not afford them a reading congruent with their own cultural position (for example, black further education students). This division of audience reception into dominant, negotiated and oppositional positions, as proposed by Hall (1980), has guided much subsequent research.

Figure 1.7 *They might all be watching the same programme, but are they having the same experience or coming to the same conclusions about it?*
Source: Journal of Communication, 1990, vol.40, no.1, p.73

To take another example – this time showing how reception studies on children have advanced beyond the 'effects paradigm' – Patricia Palmer's *The Lively Audience* (1986) showed the importance of age, gender and family circumstances. Hence, 'with the development of an understanding of narratives, of story and character, older children make more complex demands on their favourite TV shows' (Palmer, 1986, p.121). After the age of eight or nine, children prefer more realistic and complex programmes instead of the cartoons or toy animal shows they liked earlier. More importantly, they interpret shows differently as they learn to make subtle judgements about genre expectations, the sequencing of narratives, the realism of what is portrayed and the relation between the drama and their own lives. But this does not mean they simply copy televised events or display shared media experience. Rather – as we saw in Ellen Seiter's work in Reading 1.2 – they use media to define their identities, to negotiate friendships through role play and to work out rules for social interaction in the playground.

We have, then, three arguments for the active engagement of audiences with the media. Firstly, audiences must interpret what they see even to construct (or decode) the message as meaningful and orderly, however routine this interpretation may be. Secondly, the experience of viewing is socially and culturally located, so that viewers' everyday concerns, experiences and knowledge become a resource for the interpretative process of viewing. Thirdly, audiences diverge in their interpretations, generating different readings of the same media text. These differences may be anticipated by an open text, though at other times they are reading 'against the grain' of a closed text. Interestingly, sometimes viewers are playful, reflexively self-conscious in their critical or creative approach to the conventions of the text. Audience creativity and heterogeneity are not unlimited, however, for viewers' are constrained by their position in the social structure. Hence, viewers diverge in their interpretations and uses of media according to their gender, ethnicity, political and class identities, age, personal experience, nationality and other factors.

In consequence, audience researchers have come to agree on several points. Firstly, one should not make assumptions about how audiences will perceive a text from knowledge of the text alone – and so media analysis should combine studies of production, text and audience rather than study each separately (see **Evans and Hesmondhalgh, 2005**). Secondly, one cannot talk of the audience in the singular or, indeed, of the singular meaning or impact of particular media contents – and so audiences must always be located within specific everyday social contexts. Thirdly, media power is a two-way interactive process, even though many of the cards remain in the hands of the media producers and even though audiences are more constrained by their own circumstances than free to read anything they like into a text – and so the myth of direct media effects and of passive vulnerable audiences should be laid to rest at last.

4   Where next for active audiences?

4.1 Critical responses to audience reception research

In parallel with the developing arguments, methodological explorations and emerging findings of audience reception studies, there have been various criticisms of this work.

Activity 1.6

By now you may have thought of some questions or doubts about this work on audience reception. Perhaps you know about other research that would argue in support of or against the findings of reception studies. Take a moment to think of these. Does the empirical research outlined above seem to you to fit the cyclic model of communication well? Is it perhaps also compatible with the linear effects tradition? ■ ■ ■

The research community has held a lively debate regarding the theoretical and empirical claims of reception studies, as follows.

■ *Identifying the implied reader.* How confidently can we identify the dominant meanings (Stuart Hall's, 1980, 'preferred reading') in media texts? Analysis of audience response rests on a prior analysis of media texts and genres. If we cannot reliably identify the textual gaps, the degree of openness or closure, the conventions of the genre, and so on, then how can we know when the text is guiding the reader and when the reader/viewer is being creative or resistant?

■ The *limits of audience activity.* Many are concerned that audience research has exaggerated the extent of audience activity, overestimating the power of the audience compared with the power of the media. John Fiske's (1992) celebration of the 'sovereign viewer', faced with the 'unlimited semiosis' (or 'semiotic democracy') of the text (that is, the power, creativity and freedom of the audience to make and take meanings), attracted many counter-claims pointing to structural limits on audience diversity and, more important, on the audience's resistance to ideology or cultural imperialism.

■ *The problem of contextualisation.* Research has looked for various demographic and contextual factors shaping viewers' orientation to the media. But these hardly encompass the complexities of everyday life. So, should the moment of reception be contextualised in what some writers call 'the whole way of life'? It seems that the more research explores contexts of media use (rather than the context of production, in order to avoid 'media-centrism'), the less attention is paid to the moment of reception or to the media text, while in charting individual variability within the audience, we lose sight of social analysis.

■ *Competing theories.* 'Audience reception theory' masks key differences in theoretical origin and orientation. It draws on social constructivist social psychology (asking how people make sense of social life), on feminist media studies (re-evaluating the marginalised or ridiculed media often enjoyed by women) and on anthropological or ethnographic studies of everyday contexts of mass consumption, to name but some traditions. And despite the interconnections between literary (Eco, 1979; Iser, 1978; Allen, 1995) and critical (Hall, 1980; Morley, 1980, 1993; Seiter, 1999) approaches, the differences also matter.

■ *The end of the audience?* It is apparent that most research centres on television viewers and on well-established genres – soaps, news and children's shows, for example. But television is changing, diversifying and, most importantly, converging with new media to create a complex media-rich environment. Is this the end of the mass audience or will the lessons of mass audience studies continue to be relevant in the new media environment?

There are no simple answers to be had, for research generates many new questions along the way. So, these important criticisms set the agenda for the next stage of audience research. I will end on the last issue, bringing the history of the audience (as described by Butsch, 2000 and McQuail, 1997) up to date by considering how the changing media environment challenges the concepts and methods developed thus far to understand media audiences.

4.2 Changing contexts, changing media

Audience researchers are faced with a moving target as once-'new' media become familiar and ever-newer media emerge (see Figure 1.8). Television is changing, diversifying, becoming increasingly segmented, globalised, narrowcast and fan-based. The home contains multiple sets, each with multiple channels, converging with other information and communication technologies – with telephony, radio, computing and even print. Much of this convergence is mediated by the internet. As a result, the activity of viewing to which we have devoted so much attention is converging with reading, shopping, playing games, going to the library, writing letters, and so forth. And it occurs anytime, anyplace, anywhere.

We do not know how to describe the audience for new media. 'Audience' fits the activities of listening and watching. New information and communication technologies open up more active and diverse modes of engagement with media – playing, surfing, searching, chatting and downloading. So, rather than each new medium replacing what went before, in practice we find an accumulation of modes of 'audiencing' (Fiske, 1992) – as we add listening to reading, viewing to listening, surfing to viewing, and so on.

We could say 'users' – media users, users of the internet – but this is rather individualistic and instrumental, losing the idea of a collectivity which is central to 'the audience'. After all, mass communication has always been communication from the one to the many; however, on the internet, most obviously, communication is increasingly one-to-one or peer-to-peer, so we must now ask, rather than assume, how far mediated

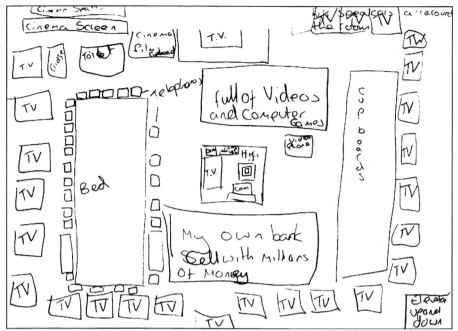

Figure 1.8 *A 10-year-old boy's drawing of the bedroom of the future*
Source: from Sonia Livingstone, *Young People and New Media*, 2002

communication leads to a shared or communal understanding. Also, 'user' does not necessarily relate to communication at all, for it applies just as well to users of the washing machine or toaster. In other words, the more we focus on varieties of media technologies, the more audience research shifts away from questions of reception and moves into asking questions about the consumption of goods or services.

Even assuming we continue to use the term 'audience', along with 'readers', 'fans' and 'viewers' as appropriate, we should bear in mind the historically different notions of 'audience'. Abercrombie and Longhurst (1998) identify three broad phases in audience history:

1 the 'simple audience' – face-to-face, direct communication, in public, often highly ritualised – as in the theatre or political meeting;

2 the 'mass audience' – highly mediated, spatially, even globally, dispersed, often in private – as in the newspaper readership or television audience;

3 the 'diffused audience' – strongly dispersed and fragmented, yet at the same time embedded in or fused with all aspects of daily life; characterised by routine and casual inattention and yet always present – as in the 'always on' internet connection which multi-tasks with working from home, watching television, shopping on line, participating in chat rooms or fan cultures.

According to Abercombie and Longhurst (1998), although these phases are historically sequenced, new phases add to rather than replace older phases, resulting in three simultaneous contemporary modes of audience experience. So, while people still form part of simple and mass audiences, the diffused audience raises some new questions. As Abercrombie and Longhurst (1998, pp.36–7) say, 'the qualities and experiences of being a member of an audience have begun to leak out from specific performance events which previously contained them, into the wider realms of everyday life' – linking leisure with work, education with entertainment, the public realm of the community with the private domain of the home.

Activity 1.7

List the media your grandparents' and parents' generations grew up with at home. Compare this with the media you yourself grew up with and then with those of children today. What are the similarities and differences? How do you think these make a difference to childhood and to the audience? For example, do they change the things that people – such as parents, children and friends – share in common? Do they make it easier to pursue individual tastes? ■■■

Some changes turn out to be fairly predictable. For example, media typically start out as household possessions and then are gradually transformed into cheaper, smaller, more mobile personal possessions in media-rich households. Consider the transformation of the telephone into the mobile phone, the wireless into the transistor radio, the household television into the portable or bedroom set, the desktop computer into the laptop. What are the consequences of such changes? We might speculate as follows.

- The multiplication of personal media (personal stereo, mobile phone, laptop computer) seems to encourage the social process of *privatisation* (the 'bedroom culture' of young people, for example), undermining the participation in a shared culture and public space which national media arguably once supported.

- The diversification of media contents – multiple television channels, the World Wide Web, musical subcultures – seems to encourage the social process of *individualisation* (or perhaps 'sub-culturalisation'), transforming the culture from one in which parents socialise children according to well-established traditions to one in which each new generation feels free (even, is required) to invent their own lifestyle, their own 'project of the self', using the resources of the media (see Thompson, 1995).

- Since many of these new media and media contents are transnational in their scope, it seems that audiences are increasingly *global* whereas previously they were mainly national or local. Do audiences share more with others across the globe than with their next door neighbours?

- The *interactivity* of new media, especially the internet, is something we have yet to theorise. New interactive technologies put the interpretative activities of the audience or user at the very centre of media design. On the internet, for example, there is no text beyond the home page without an active reader clicking, selecting, ignoring or contributing to the site, making the text–reader metaphor of reception studies particularly apt.

- So, what are the emerging genres of new media and how do these open up, guide or close down audiences' interpretations, indeed their active creation of the dynamic flow of new media texts (the path through the Web, the to-and-fro of chat, the outcome of the online game, the intertextual mixing of different media contents)? And how does the social context – particularly as people blur learning and leisure, information and communication, production and reception – shape engagements with media?

These questions require empirical investigation rather than *a priori* assumptions about audiences. It should be clear from this chapter that audiences are often unpredictable and diverse, so that predictions about audiences which are 'read off' from media technologies or texts are hazardous, even foolhardy. Hence, we must avoid asking the familiar questions about the 'effects' of new media as were asked of old media. And we must resist assumptions from the public and policy makers, which assume media impacts on a vulnerable, decontextualised and homogenised audience. Rather, we need to examine carefully how new and old media are being used together, across diverse social contexts, in order to understand how they become embedded in – both shaping and shaped by – our everyday lives and symbolic world views.

Further reading

Abercrombie, N. and Longhurst, B. (1998) *Audiences: A Sociological Theory of Performance and Imagination*, London, Sage. This book gives a good and timely overview of the past 50 years of audience research and argues that we need a new conception of audiences better suited to changing media and social relations.

Brooker, W. and Jermyn, D. (2003) *The Audience Studies Reader*, London, Routledge. This collection brings together key writings exploring questions of reception and interpretation, reprinting forgotten pieces and combining key essays with new research.

Dickinson, R., Harindranath, R. and Linné, O. (1998) *Approaches to Audiences – A Reader*, London, Arnold. This is a very comprehensive volume of work on audience research from different perspectives.

Livingstone, S. (1999) 'New media, new audiences', *New Media and Society*, vol.1, no.1, pp.59–66. This special issue offers insights into changing practices of audiences and users of new media and raises important methodological questions.

Tulloch, J. (2000) *Watching Television Audiences: Cultural theories and methods*, London, Arnold. This book is a survey of work on the audiences for different TV genres. It provides students and academics not only with an understanding of audience theories but also of the different methodologies used to research different types of audience.

References

Abercrombie, N. and Longhurst, B. (1998) *Audiences: A Sociological Theory of Performance and Imagination*, London, Sage.

Allen, R.C. (1995) *To Be Continued ... Soap Operas Around The World*, London, Routledge.

Ball-Rokeach, S.J. (1985) 'The origins of individual media-system dependency: a sociological framework', *Communication Research,* vol.12, no.4, pp.485–510.

Bandura, A., Ross, D. and Ross, S.A. (1961) 'Transmission of aggression through imitation of aggressive models', *Journal of Abnormal and Social Psychology,* vol.63, no.3, pp.575–82.

Blumler, J.G. and Katz, E. (eds) (1974) *The Uses of Mass Communications: Current Perspectives on Gratification Research*, Beverly Hills, CA, Sage.

Bonner, F. (2005) 'The celebrity in the text' in Evans, J. and Hesmondhalgh, D. (eds) *Understanding Media: Inside Celebrity*, Maidenhead, Open University Press/The Open University (Book 1 in this series).

Butsch, R. (2000) *The Making of American Audiences: From Stage to Television, 1750–1990*, Cambridge, Cambridge University Press.

Cantril, H. (1940) *The Invasion from Mars: A Study in the Psychology of Panic*, Princeton, NJ, Princeton University Press.

Carey, J.W. (1989) *Communication as Culture: Essays on Media and Society*, London, Unwin Hyman.

Cohen, S. (1972) *Folk Devils and Moral Panics: The Creation of the Mods and Rockers*, London, MacGibbon & Kee.

Drotner, K. (1992) 'Modernity and media panics' in Skovmand, M. and Schroder, K.C. (eds) *Media Cultures: Reappraising Transnational Media*, London, Routledge.

Eco, U. (1979) *The Role of the Reader: Explorations in the Semiotics of Texts*, Bloomington, IN, Indiana University Press.

Evans, J. and Hesmondhalgh, D. (eds) (2005) *Understanding Media: Inside Celebrity*, Maidenhead, Open University Press/The Open University (Book 1 in this series).

Fiske, J. (1992) 'Audiencing: a cultural studies approach to watching television', *Poetics,* vol.21, no.4, pp.345–59.

Geraghty, C. (1991) *Women in Soap Operas*, Cambridge, Polity Press.

Gerbner, G., Gross, L., Morgan, M. and Signorielli, N. (1986) 'Living with television: the dynamics of the cultivation process' in Bryant, J. and Zillman, D. (eds) *Perspectives on Media Effects*, Hillsdale, NJ, Lawrence Erlbaum.

Gillespie, M. and Toynbee, J. (eds) (2006) *Analysing Media Texts*, Maidenhead, Open University Press/The Open University (Book 4 in this series).

Hall, S. (1980) 'Encoding/Decoding' in Hall, S., Hobson, D., Lowe, A. and Willis, P. (eds) *Culture, Media, Language*, London, Hutchinson.

Iser, W. (1978) *The Act of Reading: A Theory of Aesthetic Response*, Baltimore, John Hopkins UP.

Jensen, K. (1993) 'The past in the future: problems and potentials of historical reception studies', *Journal of Communication,* vol.43, no.4, pp.20–8.

Katz, E. (1980) 'On conceptualising media effects', *Studies in Communication,* vol.1, pp.119–41.

Katz, E. and Lazarsfeld, P.F. (1955) *Personal Influence: The Part Played by People in the Flow of Mass Communication*, New York, The Free Press.

Lasswell, H.D. (1948) 'The structure and function of communication in society' in Bryson, L. (ed.) *The Communication of Ideas*, New York, Harper and Row.

Liebes, T. and Katz, E. (1990) *The Export of Meaning: Cross-Cultural Readings of 'Dallas'*, New York, Oxford University Press.

Livingstone, S.M. (1996) 'On the continuing problems of media effects research' in Curran, J. and Gurevitch, M. (eds) *Mass Media and Society* (2nd edn), London, Edward Arnold.

McQuail, D. (1997) *Audience Analysis*, London, Sage.

McQuail, D. and Windahl, S. (1993) *Communication Models*, London, Longman.

Morley, D. (1980) *The Nationwide Audience: Structure and Decoding*, London, British Film Institute.

Morley, D. (1993) 'Active audience theory: pendulums and pitfalls', *Journal of Communication,* vol.43, no.4, pp.13–19.

Palmer, P. (1986) *The Lively Audience: A Study of Children Around the TV Set*, London, Allen and Unwin.

Parliamentary Office of Science and Technology (1993) 'Screen violence', *The Psychologist*, August, pp.353–6.

Pearson, G. (1983) *Hooligan: A History of Respectable Fears*, London, Macmillan.

Rowland, W.R. (1983) *The Politics of TV Violence: Policy Uses of Communication Research*, Beverley Hills, CA, Sage.

Schramm, W., Lyle, J. and Parker, E.B. (1961) *Television in the Lives of Our Children*. Stanford, CA, Stanford University Press.

Seiter, E. (1999) *Television and New Media Audiences*, New York, Oxford University Press.

Thompson, J.B. (1995) *The Media and Modernity: A Social Theory of the Media*, Cambridge, Polity Press.

The media sensorium: cultural technologies, the senses and society

Tony Bennett

Contents

I Introduction

In a book that perhaps did more than any other to put the role of the media on the agenda of public debate in the 1960s, Marshall McLuhan and Quentin Fiore argued that 'the medium is the massage'. What they meant by this was that it was not so much the content communicated by the media that mattered, but *how* they communicated that content and, in doing so, how they worked *on* us, massaging and shaping our capacities in various ways with marked consequences for the organisation of social relationships. Here is how they summarised their claims:

> All media work us over completely. They are so pervasive in their personal, political, economic, aesthetic, psychological, moral, ethical, and social consequences that they leave no part of us untouched, unaffected, unaltered. The medium is the massage. Any understanding of social and cultural change is impossible without knowledge of the way media work as environments.
>
> McLuhan and Fiore, 1967, p.26

A key aspect of the way in which media work as environments, they went on to argue, consists in the different ways in which they involve our senses and shape the relationships between them: 'Media, by altering the environment, evoke in us unique ratios of sense perceptions. The extension of any one sense alters the way we think and act – the way we perceive the world. When these ratios change, men (sic) change' (McLuhan and Fiore, 1967, p.41).

They were not the first to make such points. To the contrary, they drew freely on the work of a large number of scholars who had demonstrated the consequences of different media for the organisation of our sensory and, thereby, our social lives. McLuhan and Fiore, however, went a few steps further in suggesting that this perspective could account for the major transformations that have characterised different phases of human history. This was especially true of McLuhan who, in an earlier book, *The Gutenberg Galaxy* (1962), had spelt out in some detail the case for viewing the invention of print as the key to the distinctive course of western history since the early modern period. Preliterate cultures, McLuhan argued, depended primarily on face-to-face forms of communication in which all the senses – sight, smell, touch, taste and hearing – were simultaneously in play. Early forms of literacy, in which most reading took the form of reading out loud in a variety of social and public contexts, similarly involved seeing, speaking and hearing. Print culture, by contrast, abstracted the eye from the other senses and subjected it to a distinctive form of training by obliging it to follow each letter and each word, in their sequential toil across the page, then on to the next line, and so on. The social consequences of this were, in McLuhan's assessment, pretty well unlimited. The abstraction of the eye from other sensory and tactile forms of involvement paved the way for perspective art and for abstract numerical forms of calculation that proved crucial to the development of modern states and markets. Print, in encouraging silent and solitary reading, also played a key role in the development of modern forms of private life. And, unlike manuscript culture, in which each letter is unique, the uniformity of print provided a model of visual repetition for the development of standardised forms of commodity production.

McLuhan advanced these arguments from the perspective of what he viewed as another, equally significant transformation in the way media affected the sensory environment in which social relations are shaped and conducted. The new age of what he called electric technology – initiated by telegraphy and subsequently developed by radio and television – substituted new forms of all-round sensory involvement for the isolation and abstraction of the eye that had characterised print culture and, for McLuhan, the cinema too. Such media did not just re-attach the eye and the ear; they also, McLuhan argued, created the possibility for returning to the forms of interactive involvement characterising preliterate societies but on a global scale. Echoes of this – his idea of a global village – can still be heard in contemporary over-hyped assessments of the possibilities of the internet as a new 'global commons' in which all can participate in public debates on equal terms. Indeed, the stress on interactivity and the new possibilities of point-to-point communication opened up by the new media have created a context in which McLuhan's ideas have once again been drawn on in public debate on these issues (Robins and Webster, 1999, pp.72–4).

The reception of McLuhan's ideas within media studies has been more cautious. On the one hand, there is broad agreement that the issues he points to are important ones that need to be taken into consideration in any account of the relationships between media and power. For, however we construe it, the power that media exert can only be exercised via the ways in which they work on, with and through us, and this must include a consideration of the different ways in which they relate to, connect with and involve our senses. However, McLuhan's accounts of the differences between one media age and another tend to be overdramatised and fly in the face of the evidence. This is the conclusion reached by Elizabeth Eisenstein, for example, in her assessment of McLuhan's account of the social and cultural consequences of the introduction of print (Eisenstein, 1979). McLuhan has also been accused of advocating a one-way technological determinism by placing too much stress on the ability of media technologies to shape sensory attributes and social relationships without considering how those technologies are themselves shaped by social and cultural factors. Indeed, some would go further to argue that it is not just a question of understanding the interactions of technologies, culture and society. Technologies themselves have to be understood as cultural forces. This has been especially true of those media theorists who have argued that media should be understood as *cultural technologies* – that is, as technologies that are made up of a complex interplay between technical, social and cultural factors – if their influence on the sensory organisation of social life is to be adequately understood. The primary purpose of this chapter is to introduce this perspective of media as cultural technologies and explore some of its implications for our understanding of the relations between media and audiences.

This chapter aims to:

■ examine the different ways in which a range of contemporary and historical media construct and organise distinctive forms of sensory response;

■ outline the concept of cultural technology and illustrate this by examining the relations between the media and the senses;

■ consider the ways in which the media, by shaping sensory activity, also play a role in organising and shaping distinctive social relationships;

■ consider the respects in which the relations between the media and the senses have given rise to distinctive political and civic concerns.

2   The media and the ratio of the senses

Let us start by clarifying what we mean by 'media sensorium'. The term 'sensorium' is in fact quite an old one. It has its roots in the seventeenth century when it referred to the seat of sensation in the brain of humans or animals. Since then its usage has become generalised to refer to 'the whole sensory apparatus' (*New Shorter Oxford English Dictionary, 4th edition, 1993*). The media sensorium, then, refers to the interface between the media and this 'whole sensory apparatus'.

A necessary starting point for these concerns is to get some sense of the different forms of sensory participation that are associated with different media. We can make a good deal of headway here by just standing back from our everyday experience of the media and thinking about it in sensory terms.

Activity 2.1

Make a list of the different media that you use regularly and note for each of these:

- which senses they involve;
- which of these senses is the most important, and how the different senses are related to each other in typical patterns of use;
- the social relationships that are involved: is this something you do by yourself? With others? If so – with whom? And in what contexts? ■ ■ ■

Let us consider some of the more obvious points first. Radio, for example, involves only hearing and, in this respect, differs from cinema and television, both of which involve sight and sound. But then it is not just that the radio involves hearing, it also constitutes a historically distinctive kind of hearing in which, to cite the title of a famous study of radio, what is heard is an 'unseen voice' (Johnson, 1988). Setting aside experience of mystical revelation and the confessional, radio has made possible an entirely new form of listening in which – rather than being co-present to one another, thus allowing for verbal messages to be interpreted in the light of visual clues – speaker and listener are separated. All the radio listener can hear are disembodied voices transmitted from another place (Figure 2.1). Listening to the radio can also be quite a different activity depending on the circumstances in which it takes place – listening by oneself in the car, for example, as opposed to listening as a family or group. Different kinds and degrees of sensory participation are also involved depending on whether we have the radio on as background noise or for something we specifically want to listen to – the news, for example. Whichever of these is the case, however, radio also has the ability to make people who are not co-present to one another while listening (they may, indeed, be as far apart as Hong Kong and the Orkneys) feel that they are nonetheless a part of the same audience. Radio, in this way, has brought about an entirely new set of social relations among listeners.

Similarly, if cinema and television both involve sight and sound, they do so differently. Typically, although not always, the experience of the spectator in the cinema is one of being isolated in a crowd as the darkness in the auditorium cuts out lateral interaction among the audience to focus his or her attention on the screen, in an environment in which sound and image are usually perfectly aligned. While many people (teenagers and older people, for example) watch television alone, television viewing is more usually a group experience, whether at home or in the pub, with typically a good deal of communication taking place between the members of the audience. Sound has a greater independence from the image than is typically the case with cinema – so that one can,

Figure 2.1 *'Women's domestic work made more enjoyable by the companionship of the wireless'*
Source: ABC Archives

for example, listen to the news or a documentary on television, without necessarily viewing it, and make sense of it in ways that would not be true of listening to a film soundtrack without seeing the film.

Since the introduction of remote control consoles and, more recently, digital television, touch is also now a part of the ways in which audiences experience, relate to and interact with television. Reading, quite clearly, primarily involves the eye – except, of course, for Braille where reading depends on touch. But touch can be involved in sighted forms of reading too. McLuhan argues that this was especially true of the manuscript culture of the medieval period when reading – which also often included tracing the fingers across illuminated and frequently heavily embossed manuscripts – involved a good deal of tactile involvement in the text (see Figure 2.2). While this is now a diminished aspect of the activity of reading it has not entirely disappeared. The pleasure in reading 'high quality' fashion magazines, or *haute cuisine* recipe books, comes partly from the texture of the glossy paper. When contrasted with the 'coarse' feel of, for example, a daily newspaper, this quality of touch reinforces the sense of distinction – of being distinguished from 'the masses' – that is a part of the primary message of such magazines.

There is also a good deal of difference between reading silently for oneself and reading aloud for others – or being read to. Indeed, it is on precisely this difference that McLuhan builds many of his main historical arguments. Prior to the development of printing, most people had access to what was then the key text of western culture – the Bible – only indirectly. Available only in Latin and in manuscript form, access to the scriptures was possible only via the priesthood whose authority depended on their monopolistic claim to read, decipher and interpret the word of God. The invention of printing; the standardisation of the Bible and its translation into the vernacular that this made possible; and growing literacy – these all, McLuhan argued, made it possible for each individual to read the Bible in solitary isolation, thus heralding the birth of individual conscience, which played such a key role in the Reformation.

Figure 2.2 The Adoration of the Magi, *an early fourteenth-century illuminated manuscript from the psalter of Robert de Lisle*
Source: By permission of The British Library (Arundel 83 f.124)

So, McLuhan has a point: the media do 'massage' our senses in different ways and, as we can see from the brief range of examples discussed so far, this matters. However, while his work has been useful in drawing attention to these issues, it has proved less helpful in enabling us to understand them. This is mainly because the one-sided technological determinism underlying his work detracts attention from the respects in which any technology has itself to be understood as socially and culturally organised. It is in view of this that our concern, in the next section, is to introduce the perspective of *cultural technology* to illustrate how the 'ratio of our senses' associated with different media involves a shaping of our sensory capacities that is just as much social and cultural as it is technological. We do so by looking at some episodes in the early history of film and at the role played later by the introduction of sound in the development of cinema as a distinctive cultural technology. We then look more closely at how the organisation of the relations of looking associated with the cinema is connected to social relationships of particular kinds – so much so that these might be called *socio-sensory relationships*. Here we consider how the lighting codes associated with mainstream western cinema have contributed to racialised ways of seeing. We then finally consider the ways in which debates concerning the influence of the media on the senses have been related to debates about the media, politics and citizenship. In particular, there is a concern that modern media of mass communication tend to promote only distracted forms of attention and involvement, as opposed to the fully attentive forms of participation that many critics suggest ought to be the aim of media in democratic societies. We shall look more fully at these debates when considering the relations between the media and public spheres in Chapter 3.

3   The media as cultural technologies

We shall stay with McLuhan for just a little longer to look at some of the things he had to say about film. To the surprise of many of his critics, McLuhan viewed film and television as radically different. While television belonged to the electronic age, he saw film as still a part of the organisation of the senses that had been fostered by print technology. Here are some of the things he had to say about film.

> If the movie merges the mechanical and organic in a world of undulating forms, it also links with the technology of print. The reader in projecting words, as it were, has to follow the black and white sequence of stills that is typography, providing his own sound track.
>
> McLuhan, 1964, p.303

Movies, as a non-verbal form of experience, are like photography, a form of statement without syntax. In fact, however, like the print and the photo, movies assume a high level of literacy in their users and prove baffling to the nonliterate. Our literate acceptance of the mere movement of the camera eye as it follows or drops a figure from view is not acceptable to an African film audience. If somebody disappears off the side of the film, the African wants to know what happened to him. A literate audience, however, accustomed to following printed imagery line by line without questioning the logic of lineality, will accept film sequence without protest.

McLuhan, 1964, p.304

Like the oral Russian, the African will not accept sight and sound together. The talkies were the doom of Russian film-making because, like any backward or oral culture, Russians have an irresistible need for participation that is defeated by the addition of sound to the visual image. .... For with silent film we automatically provide sound for ourselves by way of 'closure' or completion. And when it is filled in for us there is very much less participation in the work of the image.

McLuhan, 1964, p.306

Activity 2.2

Identify those aspects of these arguments that you find convincing and those that you find unconvincing, giving your reasons for both. ■ ■ ■

It is clear, first of all, that there is a good deal of stereotyping going on here in McLuhan's description of African and Russian audiences as 'backward', and in his failure to distinguish between different types of audiences in both contexts. And you might also have spotted how McLuhan often seems to want both to have his cake and to eat it. While print, he tells us, reduces any sense of participation by detaching the eye from the ear, the talkies are also said to be anti-participatory although they evidently reconnect seeing and hearing. But the root of both of these difficulties is that McLuhan does not distinguish between *film* and *cinema* – for while the former is a particular assemblage of different pieces of technical equipment (cameras, projectors, lighting equipment), cinema is a particular *cultural technology* in the sense that it effects a particular ordering of the relationships between these pieces of equipment and the codes of film production, as well as organises the particular conditions in which audiences receive, and engage with, films. In what follows we shall explore this distinction further by looking at the early history of film exhibition, prior to the development of cinema. Contrary to McLuhan's suggestions, this both involved sound and produced an effect – one of shock – that is not easily reconciled with McLuhan's description of the linear sequencing of print technology. We then look at the introduction of sound recording to see how this more formalised organisation of the relationships between sound and vision altered the ways in which cinema shaped the reception of film.

The US film theorist Miriam Hansen helps us get at the distinction between film and cinema when she notes that, although public film screenings began in the mid-1890s, it was not until a decade later – crucially between 1907 and 1917 – that the codes of classical cinema began to emerge and develop. This involved a number of processes. First, it involved the development of specialised and, especially into the 1920s, respectable contexts, often modelled on the theatre, for the exhibition of film. Before this time, Hansen notes, spectators' relationships to film were strongly influenced by the early popular entertainment contexts in which they were typically shown. These included 'vaudeville and variety shows, dime museums and penny arcades, summer parks, fair grounds, and travelling shows' (Hansen, 1991, p.29). And in all of these contexts, as we shall see, film screenings were accompanied by a veritable cacophony of sounds: films may have been silent, but their exhibition rarely was. The later development of specialised contexts for film screenings provided a setting in which a whole new and distinctive set of relations between audience and film could be produced. This was accomplished through the development of new conventions of editing and narrative that transformed what were hitherto diversely constituted audiences into *film spectators*. Hansen, in her study of film spectatorship in early American cinema, identifies three key ways in which this new relation of the film spectator to the screen was produced, prior to the introduction of recorded sound.

First, she argues, 'classical cinema offered its viewer an ideal vantage point from which to witness a scene, unseen by anyone belonging to the fictional world of the film, the diegesis' (Hansen, 1991, p.23). Through a variety of filming conventions – the abolition of direct-to-camera shots, for example – the spectator was placed outside the fictional frame of the diegesis, and given a privileged vantage point in relation to the film as a whole that was denied to characters within the film.

Second, new conventions of film editing provided a type of narration that seamlessly linked each shot to the next one within the framework of a cumulative narrative carrying the spectator through the film. This meant that the spectator was knitted into the film as a part of its organisation rather than seeing the film, as had been true earlier, as part of another kind of exhibition context – a fairground booth or vaudeville theatre.

Third, as film reception became increasingly standardised along these lines, 'the moviegoer was effectively invited to assume the position of this ideal spectator created by the film, leaving behind ... an awareness of his or her physical self in the theatre space, of an everyday existence troubled by social, sexual, and economic discrepancies' (Hansen, 1991, p.23).

With this in mind, let us now go back to the 1890s and look at how film was first seen and experienced before any of these aspects of later cinema were developed.

Reading 2.1 Activity

Now read the following extract from Tom Gunning, 'An aesthetic of astonishment: early film and the (in)credulous spectator' (Reading 2.1), and answer the following questions:

- On what grounds does Gunning dispute accounts of the 'shock effect' of early film couched in terms of the naïvety of the spectator?
- What does Gunning mean when he says that the spectator's astonishment is due less to the speed of the train than to the force of the cinematic apparatus?
- What are the distinguishing features of what Gunning calls 'the cinema of attractions'?
- How and why was this cinema at odds with contemporary norms of detached and contemplative spectatorship?

Reading 2.1

Tom Gunning, 'An aesthetic of astonishment: early film and the (in)credulous spectator'

Terror in the aisles

> The damming of the stream of real life, the moment when its flow comes to a standstill, makes itself felt as reflux: this reflux is astonishment.
>
> Benjamin, 1977

In traditional accounts of the cinema's first audiences, one image stands out: the terrified reaction of spectators to Lumière's *Arrival of a Train at a Station* [France, dir. Lumière, 1895]. According to a variety of historians, spectators reared back in their seats, or screamed, or got up and ran from the auditorium (or all three in succession). [...]

The first audiences, according to this myth, were naïve, encountering this threatening and rampant image with no defences, with no tradition by which to understand it. The absolute novelty of the moving image therefore reduced them to a state usually attributed to savages in their primal encounter with the advanced technology of Western colonialists, howling and fleeing in impotent terror before the power of the machine. This audience of the first exhibitions exists outside of the willing suspension of disbelief, the immediacy of their terror short-circuiting even disavowal's detour of 'I know very well [...] but all the same'. Credulity overwhelms all else; the physical reflex signalling a visual trauma. Thus conceived, the myth of initial terror defines film's power as its unprecedented realism, its ability to convince spectators that the moving image was, in fact, palpable and dangerous, bearing towards them with physical impact. The image had taken life, swallowing, in its relentless force, any consideration of representation – the imaginary perceived as real. [...]

Although I have my doubts whether actual panic took place in the Grand Café's Salon Indien, there is no question that a reaction of astonishment and even a type of terror accompanied many early projections. I therefore don't intend to simply deny this founding myth of the cinema's spectator, but rather to approach it historically. We cannot simply swallow whole the image of the naïve spectator, whose reaction to the image is one of simple belief and panic; it needs digesting. The impact of the first film projections cannot be explained by a mechanistic model of a naïve spectator who, in a temporary psychotic state, confuses the image for its reality. But what context does account for the well-attested fact that the first projections caused shock and astonishment, an excitement pushed to the point of terror, if we exclude childlike credulity? And, equally important, how could this agitating experience be understood as part of the *attraction* of the new invention, rather than a disturbing element that needed to be removed? And what role does an illusion of reality play in this terrified reception?

Only a careful consideration of the historical context of these earliest images can restore an understanding of the uncanny and agitating power they exerted on audiences. This context includes the first modes of exhibition, the tradition of turn-of-the-century visual entertainments, and a basic aesthetic of early cinema I have called 'the cinema of attractions', which envisioned cinema as a series of visual shocks. [...]

While contemporary accounts of audience responses, particularly unsophisticated viewers, are hard to come by, the very mode of presentation of the Lumière screenings (and of other early film-makers as well) contains an important element which served to undermine a naïve experience of realism. It is too infrequently pointed out that in the earliest Lumière exhibitions the films were initially presented as frozen images, projections of still photographs. Then, flaunting a mastery of visual showmanship, the projector began cranking and the image moved. Or as Gorky described it, '[...] suddenly a strange flicker passes through the screen and the picture stirs to life.' [cited in Leyda, 1960, p.407].

While such a presentation would seem to forbid any reading of the image as reality – a real physical train – it strongly heightened the impact of the moment of movement. Rather than mistaking the image for reality, the spectator is astonished by its transformation through the new illusion of projected motion. Far from credulity, it is the incredible nature of the illusion itself that renders the viewer speechless. What is displayed before the audience is less the impending speed of the train than the force of the cinematic apparatus. [...]

This [...] sudden transformation from still image to moving illusion, startled audiences and displayed the novelty and fascination of the cinématographe. [...]

The audience's sense of shock comes less from a naïve belief that they are threatened by an actual locomotive than from an unbelievable visual transformation occurring before their eyes, parallel to the greatest wonders of the magic theatre. [...]

The aesthetic of attractions

> There came a day when a new and urgent need for stimuli was met by the film. In a film, perception in the form of shocks was established as a formal principle.
>
> Benjamin, 1968

While these early films of on-coming locomotives present the shock of cinema in an exaggerated form, they also express an essential element of early cinema as a whole. I have called the cinema that precedes the dominance of narrative (and this period lasts for nearly a decade, until 1903 or 1904) *the cinema of attractions*. The aesthetic of attraction addresses the audience directly, sometimes, as in these early train films, exaggerating this confrontation in an experience of assault. Rather than being an involvement with narrative action or empathy with character psychology, the cinema of attractions solicits a highly conscious awareness of the film image engaging the viewer's curiosity. The spectator does not get lost in a fictional world and its drama, but remains aware of the act of looking, the excitement of curiosity and its fulfilment. Through a variety of formal means, the images of the cinema of attractions rush forward to meet their viewers. These devices range from the implied collision of the early railroad films to the performance style of the same period where actors nodded and gestured at the camera ... or where a showman lecturer presented the views to the audience. This cinema addresses and holds the spectator, emphasising the act of display. In fulfilling this curiosity, it delivers a generally brief dose of scopic pleasure.

And pleasure is the issue here, even if pleasure of a particularly complicated sort. When a Montpellier journalist in 1896 described the Lumière projections as provoking 'an excitement bordering on terror', he was praising the new spectacle and explaining its success. If the first spectators screamed, it was to acknowledge the power of the apparatus to sweep away a prior and firmly entrenched sense of reality. This vertiginous experience of the frailty of our knowledge of the world before the power of visual illusion produced that mixture of pleasure and anxiety which the purveyors of popular art had labelled 'sensations' and 'thrills' and on which they founded a new aesthetic of attractions.

References

Benjamin, W. (1968) 'On some motifs in Baudelaire' in Arendt, H. (ed.) *Illuminations*, New York, Harcourt Brace.

Benjamin, W. (1977) 'What is Epic Theatre?', *Understanding Brecht* (Bostock, A., trans.) London, New Left Books.

Leyda, J. (1960) *Kino: A History of the Russian and Soviet Film*, London, Allen & Unwin.

Reading source

Gunning, 1989, pp.31–7 ▪ ▪ ▪

Gunning argues that the shock effect of early film was not based so much on the naïvety of spectators as on the new and remarkable nature of the moving images on the screen. But the key point to take from this reading is that the experience of early film audiences was not simply an automatic effect of the technical properties of early forms of filming and film projection. These had their consequences, to be sure, but only when considered alongside the distinctive aesthetic properties of early films (as 'a cinema of attractions' – a cinema based not on narrative, but primarily on a consciousness of the nature of the film image), the exhibition contexts in which they were shown and the expectations engendered by other turn-of-the-century forms of visual entertainment.

Further consideration of the question of sound will help to amplify this point. Although recorded sound was not introduced until 1926, film screenings before this were in fact accompanied by a variety of acoustic effects. These were, however, often context specific, varying from one exhibition context to another, thus lacking the forms of standardisation and repetition, as well as the synchronisation of sound and image, that recorded sound made possible. They also usually had their roots in the variety of pre-cinematic contexts in which films were first exhibited, just as the subjects of films were derived from earlier forms of entertainment. Vaudeville acts, comic skits and sight gags, dances, erotic scenes, highlights from popular plays or operas, melodramatic episodes, re-enactments of tales of the Wild West, tableaux from passion plays, trick films drawing on the tradition of magic shows, news or actuality films featuring wars, sensations, murders and disasters, scenes of everyday life: these, Miriam Hansen argues, were typical subjects for early films. Reflecting this, the exhibition contexts for early film screenings often drew on the ways of organising looking, and of connecting seeing and hearing, that characterised earlier forms of popular entertainment. These included live musical accompaniments modelled on those of the variety theatre or music hall, factual commentary, the hype of the fairground barker, behind-screen sound effects, and the simulation of particular sound environments. Hansen records the case of Hale's Tours, which, from 1904, toured American cities projecting scenic views, taken from a moving train, in a booth that was designed like a railroad car complete with 'simulated sways and jolts, clickety-clack and brake sounds' (Hansen, 1991, p.32).

It is just as important to note that early film screenings were usually accompanied by lots of noise from the audience: cat-calls, whoops of astonishment, running commentaries, as well as rude and comic interjections. This lack of sonic decorum on the part of early film audiences was one of the reasons why film was viewed with apprehension by a range of moral and cultural reformers, as well as local and national governments, in the early twentieth century. Along with the development of the nickelodeon theatres, as the first custom-built film exhibition contexts, came the fear that their dark and secluded interiors would result in sexual misconduct and promiscuity. While these concerns were generally shared internationally, there was an added aspect to them in New York – still the centre of the American film industry at this time – where nickelodeon audiences were seen as being dominated by immigrants from the crowded tenements of lower Manhattan. Viewed, in racist terms, as inferior to white Americans, immigrants were also regarded as sources of dirt, disease and contagion, as well as a political threat in view of their often strong associations with European traditions of socialism and communism (Uricchio and Pearson, 1998; Griffiths, 2002).

In the midst of all these anxieties, there was the additional concern that the meanings of films – how audiences might interpret and engage with them – were relatively undetermined. For how the soundless moving images of film might be interpreted could well vary from one exhibition context to another depending on the kinds of interpretative clues that were provided. It was quite common, for example, for film exhibitions to be accompanied by lectures that would aim to direct the audience to decipher the meaning of the moving images correctly. The difficulties here, however, were obvious, as the same film might be seen and interpreted quite differently depending on whether the lecture accompanying it were given by an authoritative expert in an official context (a screening in a church hall, say) or by a socialist agitator at a film screening in one of the many immigrant political and cultural societies that flourished in New York's Lower Eastside.

Classical or narrative cinema developed as a response to these anxieties. This was understood as a cultural technology that organised the relations between sounds and moving images, between screen and spectator, between spectators within the auditorium and between film exhibition and other entertainment forms in distinctive ways. As such, it had many aspects. Some were industrial, including, beginning in 1908–9, the development of voluntary codes of industry self-regulation and censorship aimed at making film, in the words of the slogan of the US-based Motion Picture Patents Company, 'Moral, educational and cleanly amusing'. Some were cultural, especially the development of the codes of narrative cinema through which sequences of images were edited together to tell a continuous story. And some were technical, including the development of sound recording and techniques for laying a soundtrack on the film stock that would synchronise sound and image. It is, however, in the intersections between these that we can best understand the formation of cinema as a cultural technology whose technical components are just as much cultural as its cultural aspects are technical.

Steve Neale's discussion of the consequences of the introduction of sound recording illustrates this point nicely. The introduction of sound, Neale argues, made it possible for sound and vision to be more closely co-ordinated with one another through the synchronisation of dialogue with the image of the actor. Take the 'lip-synch', for example (the synchronising of sound to moving image). This played a key role in bringing sound into the film frame and thereby subordinating it to the image. But this also meant that sound was incorporated into the narrative structures of film, reducing the possibility of any jarring relationship between off-screen sound and on-screen image. This served to deepen the spectator's immersion in the filmic narrative. The 'lip-synch' also contributed a stronger and more individualising delineation of character.

In this respect, alongside other aspects of sound film, 'the degree of *presence* and psychic individualism provided by the voice ... finally completed the evolution of the conventions of narrative film' (Neale, 1985, p.95).

Let us stand back from the details of this argument and take stock of the more general position we have been developing concerning the nature of media as cultural technologies. This concept has been developed in the context of criticisms of technological determinism: the view that media histories are essentially determined by the purely technical properties of different communications technologies. 'New technologies,' Raymond Williams writes in an influential summary of this position, 'are discovered, by an essentially internal process of research and development, which then sets the conditions for social change and progress' (Williams, 1974, p.13). According to this view, technological change is a process driven purely by technical considerations, one change leading to another in a series of purely logical next steps. As such, it is unaffected by social and cultural considerations; indeed, social and cultural change is seen as something that can be largely accounted for as a set of responses to technological change.

The perspective of media as cultural technologies, developed as a corrective to this, argues, to the contrary, that every technology has to be seen as itself being shaped – and shaped from within – by social and cultural considerations. There is, from this perspective, no such thing as a purely technical history of technologies since every technical option is always culturally informed. As we have seen from Steve Neale's discussion, what seem to be purely technical decisions about recorded sound in fact turn out to be intimately affected by all sorts of cultural presuppositions, just as they give rise to equally distinctive cultural consequences. The forms of recording and mixing that accord a priority to voice and dialogue in relation to other sound, and the matching of sound to image via the 'lip-synch', are now things we tend to accept as natural, as routine aspects of the habits of listening and viewing that we spontaneously adopt when going to the cinema. Neale (1985), however, shows that there was nothing inevitable about any of these choices. Rather than being dictated by technical requirements, they are the outcomes of complex relations between technical possibilities and the specific social and cultural contexts in which media are used and developed. The implications of these choices, once taken, are, in turn, never purely technical: the ordering of the relations between sound, image and audience that the introduction of the soundtrack effected was part and parcel of the new and distinctive cultural regulation of the spectator associated with the codes of narrative cinema.

The concept of cultural technology, then, provides a means whereby the relations between technical, social and cultural factors can be investigated without assuming that any one of these is more important than the others or that they can be clearly separated from each other. 'At a basic level,' Jonathan Sterne argues, 'a technology is a repeatable social, cultural and material process (which is to say that it is all three at once) crystallised into a mechanism or set of related mechanisms' (Sterne, 2003, p.376). But if technologies thus crystallise habits, or certain ways of doing things, they also serve to promote them. This means that they need to be seen as both affected by human practices and as affecting such practices. It is to a further elaboration of this argument that we turn in the following section. Here, in considering the ways in which the media, in shaping the senses, also shape social relationships, we shall connect our earlier discussion concerning the 'media sensorium' to the question of media power. In doing so, we also change focus slightly: for what we shall look at here concerns less the relations between the senses associated with particular media than how the media organise one sense in particular: that of sight.

4   Shaping the senses, shaping society

We shall start here by looking at a painting – *The Magic Lantern*, by the eighteenth-century artist Paul Sandby (see Plate 1 in the colour section).

Activity 2.3

Look closely at the two servants at the extreme left- and right-hand edges of this painting. Can you see anything distinctive about the relationship of these two figures to the way in which the distribution of light is organised in this picture? ■ ■ ■

Now compare your own thoughts with what Richard Dyer has to say about the picture:

> At either side of the image there are two figures of contrast. On the right there is a white woman, a nurse cuddling a baby. The light from the lantern screen barely illuminates those watching it, and she is even further than they from the screen, yet she is luminescent with lighter clothes than everyone else and light from no source above striking the top of her bonnet. She is a figure of (maternal) virtue and/or of desirability. On the left there is a male servant, who looks as if he is of African descent (a common enough practice in wealthy households at the time). He is completely dark, apart from

one dot of an eye and a little illumination from a candle held close
to his waist. His left side is silhouetted against the light of the
screen, an aesthetic play on his skin/hue and the colour of light. The
white woman, albeit lowish in status, has no need of the light to be
lit up. The black man, directly in front of the screen and holding a
candle, still does not pick up the light, is still opaque. His candle,
though, does enlighten a book he is carrying, a treatise on light by a
Dr Taylor. The two servants (the white nurse, the black houseboy)
do not look at the screen, but across the paper at each other, with
desire. The figure of dark, physical, unenlightened desire looks across
at the (responsive) figure of illuminated desirability, while the well-to-
do whites look on at their slide.

Dyer, 1997, p.141–2

Notice that Dyer's discussion of this painting does not take account of
the role of the ornamental mirror in distributing the reflected light of
the magic lantern projection into the right of the picture frame. But
this does not detract from his conclusion concerning the way in which
the use of light in this painting effects a particular ordering of racial
relations. Dyer's discussion of the painting is offered as a summary and
distillation of his argument about how the use of light and lighting in
visual arts and media has operated as a cultural technology to promote
racialised ways of seeing by visually privileging whiteness. Before we
can come to this, however, we need to see how, and why, for Dyer the
question of lighting is no more a purely natural or technical process
than the question of sound is for Neale. There are, Dyer argues, six
elements to be taken into account in analysing film and photography as
'technologies of light' (1997, p.85). They are:

1   the *lighting*, in the sense of the light that is thrown at the subject of
     the image – be it the natural light of the location or light that is
     projected or filtered by using a range of technical devices (lenses,
     reflectors, etc.);

2   the properties of the *subject*, that is, the ways in which people and
     things of different colours absorb and reflect light differently;

3   the film or photographic *stock* and, depending on its chemical
     properties, its variable ability to register distinctions between light and
     shade, to enhance some colours at the expense of others, etc.;

4   the *exposure*, including length of exposure time and the size of the
     aperture through which light passes before it is registered on the film
     stock;

5   the *development* of the stock and, depending on the processes used, the
     modulation of light qualities this can effect;

6 *projection* and the different qualities of light that are achieved depending on the projector used, the conditions in the auditorium, and, indeed, whether the final form is film projection, video or DVD.

While recognising that each of these elements sets limits to the nature of the light quality that can be achieved, Dyer also argues that social and cultural factors can intervene in each and every one of these elements in myriad ways. His specific concern, however, is with the ways in which they have done so, in the history of classical cinema, to privilege whiteness. Accepting that black and white skins reflect light differently (roughly speaking, white skin is about twice as reflective as black skin), Dyer argues that what he calls 'movie lighting' – that is, the forms of lighting that were developed in Hollywood from the 1920s and that have since become dominant through the industry – has accentuated this by taking the white face as its touchstone. That is, while film stocks, camera exposures, projectors and location lighting could all have been developed in many different directions, the forms of their use and development that have become habitual – and have become a cultural technology in Jonathan Sterne's sense – are ones that have the idealised representation of whiteness as their primary aim. The development of film stock, according to Dyer, was primarily motivated to overcome the difficulty that early film stock was insensitive to red and yellow and so – without the addition of thick white make-up – was unable to render the whiteness of the white face. Similarly, the introduction of colour – a technical possibility from 1896 – was delayed until the mid-1930s owing, in good measure, to the difficulties of rendering white flesh tones on the first versions of colour film stock. Getting the white face right – but never the black face – was similarly, Dyer shows, the acid test of competence evident in manuals of photography and cinematography until well into the 1950s.

With this background in mind, then, let us now look more closely at how Dyer examines a specific aspect of lighting in film and photography – the use of overhead light. In doing so, we shall be particularly concerned with the ways in which the codes and conventions of overhead lighting have been influenced by more general cultural assumptions about the relations between light and dark in western culture (for a detailed discussion of semiotic concepts of 'codes' and 'conventions', see **Gripsrud, 2006** and **Bonner, 2005**). We shall also be concerned with the ways in which these codes effect a particular racialisation of ways of seeing and with how these connect with assumptions about the relations between 'race', gender and sexuality.

Reading 2.2 Activity

Now read the following extract from Richard Dyer's book, *White* (Reading 2.2), and attempt to answer these questions:

- Dyer argues that 'in the movies there is always light from on high'. How is this achieved? And in what ways does it reflect the use of light in earlier traditions of European painting?

- Why is light from on high 'superior light'? And how is its superiority connected to racialised ways of seeing?

- What does Dyer mean by 'the glow of white women'? How is this glow achieved? How does Dyer assess its consequences in relation to notions of both racial supremacy and codes of heterosexuality?

Reading 2.2

Richard Dyer, 'Light of the world'

Light comes from above

While the idea of life as a transparency, though we are habituated to it, represents a remarkable perceptual leap, the idea that light comes from above may seem uninteresting. Surely, after all, in its natural forms – sunlight, moonlight, starlight – it does? This is undeniable, but consider two points. It is only since the eighteenth century – and only commonly since the late nineteenth – that artificial lighting has come from above. And it is only in Northern countries that middle-of-the-day overhead light is regarded as the optimum time for being about; in the South it is the low slanting (but still, granted, overhead) light of morning and evening by which things and people are most often seen. Yet in the movies there is always light from on high. [...]

Both theatre and photography had, by the end of the nineteenth century, established the use of overhead lighting (though according to Nicholas Vardac it was not until 1917 that Belasco 'managed to eliminate the distortion of footlighting' altogether (1968: 119)). Film adopted the convention. Initially, natural sunlight was used (with interiors shot on open-roofed sets) but this was soon modified (diffused by the use of sheets, gauzes and so on) and/or supplemented by artificial lighting. Up to 1919 the latter were generally placed just above the performer's head (Salt 1983: 141); even this constitutes a relatively high position (compared to footlights or table lamps), but movie lighting proper placed it much higher. [...]

Movie lighting drew on nineteenth-century traditions of using and representing light that were explicitly indebted to North European painting, above all to Rembrandt and Vermeer, painting rediscovered in this period (Slive 1962). This had provided, through its emphasis on domestic portraiture as opposed to classical and biblical subjects, a venerable model for photography in its bid for profitable respectability, something very clear in figures who were soon recognised as early masters of photography, such as David Octavious Hill and Robert Adamson (Rembrandt) and Henry Peach Robinson (Vermeer). Similarly in the theatre, Belasco and Appia, even though their work in many ways moved in opposite directions (towards naturalism and anti-illusionism respectively), had both seen the Dutch and Flemish masters as their masters, and both made extensive use of overhead lighting. Lighting in film, once it was not just using available sunlight, also drew on North European painting, partly through taking over the conventions of photographic portraiture, partly under the influence of Belasco (directly and tellingly on Cecil B. DeMille (Baxter 1975: 101)) and partly in the rather separate development of a film lighting style in the Scandinavian countries (in tune with the flowering of a distinctive style in the arts based on the observation and reproduction of the qualities of Nordic light (see Kent 1987)), a development that was in turn taken up by Hollywood.

From the late 1910s on, it became usual to refer to the ideal for lighting the movies as 'North' or 'Northern' light: 'I've always used his [Rembrandt's] technique of north light – of having my main source of light on a set always coming from the north' (cinematographer Lee Garmes, quoted in Russell 1973: 45). North light is defined by Barry Salt as 'the kind of light that comes into a room in daytime through a large north-facing window, or some arrangement that produces an identical effect with artificial means' (1983: 329). It is soft, white and steeply slanted. Even the move to suffuse sunlight in the early movies can be seen as a wish to reproduce the softness of Northern light, and it is central to the development of three (and more)-point movie lighting. More recently, it may also be achieved by bounced light using quartz or an umbrella light (ibid.: 329–330).

However effected, this light has certain implications. It is, literally and symbolically, superior light. The North, in ethnocentric geography, in the map of the world that became standardised in the process of European expansion, is above the South. It is still most common to think in terms of going up North, being down South and so on. This is also the region of North Europeans, the whitest whites in the white racial hierarchy. [...] the North is an epitome of the 'high, cold' places that promoted the vigour, cleanliness, piety and enterprise of whiteness. White people come off best from this standardised Northern light, such that they seem to have a special affinity with it, to be enlightened, to be the recipient, reflection and maybe even source of the light of the world. [...]

Following Belasco, pools of light were used for scenes of spiritual devotion and conversion (Gunning 1991: 182, 187). One of the earliest examples of the expressive use of light in film, that is, going beyond general, overall illumination, is the vision of Eva as an angel in *Uncle Tom's Cabin* (Figure 2.3). Both the ray of light in which Eva appears and the 45° slanted light coming through the window are in fact painted on the set. The example – famous as an example of literally painting light and also because of the runaway commercial success of the film – could not be more germane ethnically: Eva is the last word in white purity even before she joins the angels, themselves figures of central importance in the construction of ideal white womanhood. [...]

Figure 2.3 Uncle Tom's Cabin *(USA, 1903)*

The glow of white women

So far I have been arguing that the aesthetic technology of the photographic media, the apparatus and practice *par excellence* of a light culture, not only assumes and privileges whiteness but also constructs it. Finally I want to look at an extreme instance of this, the use of light in constructing an image of the ideal white woman within heterosexuality.

A passage in *Uncle Tom's Cabin* (1852) describes a visual effect that has become standard in photography and film:

> Eva came tripping up the verandah steps to her father. It was late in the afternoon, and the rays of the sun formed a kind of glory

behind her, as she came forward in her white dress, with her
golden hair and glowing cheeks.

Stowe, 1981, p.401

Idealised white women are bathed in and permeated by light. It streams
through them and falls on to them from above. In short, they glow.

They glow rather than shine. The light within or from above
appears to suffuse the body. Shine, on the other hand, is light
bouncing back off the surface of the skin. It is the mirror effect of
sweat, itself connoting physicality, the emissions of the body and
unladylike labour, in the sense of both work and parturition. In a
well-known Victorian saw, animals sweated, and even gentlemen
perspired, but ladies merely glowed. Dark skin too, when it does not
absorb the light, may bounce it back. Non-white and sometimes
working-class white women are liable to shine rather than glow in
photographs and films. [...]

The development of an image of the glowing human being can
be traced in European art. One index of it is the means for
representing haloes. In medieval art, these are gold, very material,
silhouetting the head; since the Renaissance, they have seemed to
radiate from the head, in turn suffusing it with a glow. Rudolph
Arnheim discusses the way in which in Rembrandt's work, objects
(including people) receive the impact of light from without, but at
the same time 'become light sources themselves, actively irradiating
energy. Having become enlightened, they hand on the message'
(1956: 314–15). This is the perception that was carried over into
movie lighting. [...]

The angelically glowing white woman is an extreme representation
precisely because it is an idealisation. It reached its apogee towards
the end of the nineteenth century and especially in three situations
of heightened perceived threat to the hegemony of whiteness.
British ideological investment in race categories increased in
response to spectacular resistance to its Empire, notably the Indian
Mutiny of 1857 and the Jamaican revolt of 1865 (Miles 1989: 83).
The Southern US ideal of womanhood intensified in the period
after the Civil War, with the defeat of official racism and slavery
and the supposed rise of Negro lawlessness. The celebration of the
Victorian virgin ideal in the cinema, in stars like Lillian Gish and
Mary Pickford (Figure 2.4), was part of a bid for the
respectabilisation of the medium, a class issue but indissociable
from ethnicity in the USA in the early years of the twentieth
century, in the form of both mass immigration of non-Nordic
groups to the USA and the huge internal migration of African
Americans from the scattered, rural South to the concentrated,
urban North. (May 1983, Hansen 1991).

Figure 2.4 *Nelson Evans' photograph of Mary Pickford (circa 1917)*
Source: BFI Stills, Posters and Designs

References

Arnheim, R. (1956) *Art and Visual Perception*, London, Faber and Faber.

Baxter, P. (1975) 'On the history and ideology of film lighting', *Screen*, vol.16, no.3, pp.83–106.

Gunning, T. (1991) *D. W. Griffiths and the Origins of American Narrative Cinema*, Urbana/Chicago, IL, University of Illinois Press.

Hansen, M. (1991) *Babel and Babylon: Spectatorship in American Silent Film*, Cambridge, MA, Harvard University Press.

Kent, N. (1987) *The Triumph of Light and Nature: Nordic Art 1740–1940*, London, Thames and Hudson.

May, L. (1983) *Screenings out of the Past: The Birth of Mass Culture and the Motion Picture Industry*, Chicago, IL, University of Chicago Press.

Miles, R. (1989) *Racism*, London, Routledge.

Russell, S.A. (1973) *Semiotics and Lighting: A Study of Six Modern French Cameramen*, Boston, MA, UMI Research Press.

Salt, B. (1983) *Film Style and Technology: History and Analysis*, London, Starword.

Slive, S. (1962) 'Realism and symbolism in seventeenth-century Dutch painting', *Daedalus*, summer, pp.469–500.

Stowe, H.B. (1981) *Uncle Tom's Cabin; or, Life among the Lowly*, Harmondsworth, Penguin (originally published 1852).

Vardac, A.N. (1968) *Stage to Screen: Theatrical Method from Garrick to Griffith*, New York, Benjamin Blom (originally published 1949).

Reading source
Dyer, 1997, pp.116–27 ■ ■ ■

For Dyer, the codes of 'movie light' are just that: a set of lighting set-ups, exposures, techniques of make-up and processes of film development that have become sedimented as normal, as habitual, taken for granted – prior to the interventions of black film makers – as much by audiences in their viewing practices as by film producers and photographers. The use of overhead lighting in theatre and photography had been established by the end of the nineteenth century. Film lighting also drew on the conventions of lighting established in North European painting. It is described as 'soft, white and deeply slanted' and images of white people are seen to benefit from this standardised Northern light. Given this, a part of Dyer's concern is clearly to disrupt these socially powerful, but changeable and contestable, ways of making films. But he is also concerned to challenge and change us as spectators. Dyer shows that the codes of 'movie light' are the outcomes of very specific histories, and that our own practices, as audiences seeing within those codes, shape our sensory capacities in ways that make us complicit with – bind us into – racialising social processes. His aim is to challenge our habits as they have been shaped and formed by these aspects of mainstream cinema. As such, his concerns connect, albeit in a distinctive way, with a longer history in which questions concerning the relationships between viewing habits and the media have been posed as a matter for more general concern. This is a history in which new forms of media have been accused of numbing their audiences into passive forms of inattentiveness and distraction with marked consequences for the ways in and extent to which they are then able to engage in political and civic life. It is to a consideration of these arguments that we turn next.

If the apparatuses of photography and film have 'seemed to work better with light-skinned peoples,' Dyer argues, this is 'because they were made that way, not because they could be no other way' (1997, p.90). This sense of 'it could have been, and could become different' is central to the perspective of media as cultural technologies. As we have seen, following Sterne (2003), any technology is a matter of things that could have been otherwise before settling, for a time, into habitual patterns. This is a notion he captures by suggesting that what technologies tend to do is 'to "sediment" social relationships' – that is, to temporarily fix particular ways of doing, seeing, thinking, feeling and interacting.

5   Regulating the senses: media and the politics of vision

It will be useful to broach the issues we shall consider here by looking at another painting – George Seurat's *Cirque* (see Plate 2 in the colour section). We shall look at this through the theoretical and historical framework of analysis provided by Jonathan Crary who sees it as a commentary on late nineteenth-century spectatorship (Crary, 1996). He notes the strong resemblance between the painted scene and an image produced by Emile Reynaud for his *Praxinoscope à Projection* (Figure 2.5) – a device for projecting moving images that Reynaud later developed into the *Théâtre-Optique* (Figure 2.6). The latter device, first used at the Musée Grevin – a wax-work museum in Paris that also featured popular visual entertainments – offered the first projection of moving images from film. These were, however, animated images, unlike the moving photographic images of Louis and Auguste Lumière's demonstration of cinematography in 1895. But they remained popular throughout the 1890s, attracting thousands of paying customers on a weekly basis. Crary's point is not that Seurat was necessarily familiar with the circus scene from Reynaud's *Praxinoscope à Projection*, or that he had necessarily seen the *Théâtre-Optique* at the Musée Grevin – although both are highly probable. Rather, his contention is that these visual technologies and the contexts in which they were exhibited formed part of a more broadly based public discourse about the nature, conditions and consequences of new forms of spectatorship in late nineteenth-century France. These had preoccupied Seurat in earlier paintings so they are reasonably interpreted as being of concern to him in *Cirque* too. It is, then, Seurat's depiction of the circus audience that most engages Crary's attention.

Figure 2.5 *A circus scene from Emile Reynaud's* Praxinoscope à Projection

Figure 2.6 *Emile Reynaud's* Théâtre-Optique

Activity 2.4

Before we see what Crary has to say about this audience, take a look at Seurat's *Cirque* (see Plate 2 in the colour section) for yourself.

■ What are its distinguishing characteristics?

■ How do the members of the audience relate to the circus performance? How do they relate to one another?

■ Can you see any similarities between Seurat's depiction of this audience and the way the audience is portrayed in the 1892 exhibition of Reynaud's *Théâtre-Optique*? ■ ■ ■

Crary's main point is to note the audience's withdrawal from, and seeming lack of interest in, the circus scene. He interprets this as, like the cinema, a scene of live movement but one that has been stilled, caught, as it were, in freeze-frame. The members of the audience either talk to one another or watch the scene in a state of numbed distraction from it as if, as Crary puts it, 'the specific content displayed to them is a matter of absolute inconsequence' (Crary, 2001, p.273). This audience, like the audience for Reynaud's *Théâtre-Optique*, is distracted – they are not watching with alert interest.

This idea of the distracted attention of the audience for popular visual media recurs whenever the social impacts of new visual media are explored, and is usually regarded as a matter for concern. We find it, for example, in contemporary concerns about the 'couch potato' whose inertness before the screen represents a modern form of the distraction of which Crary speaks. Mike Michael, noting a dictionary definition of the couch potato as 'one who is addicted to watching television and does this while lying on the couch, as inert and braindead as a potato', goes on to quote from a 1996 *Daily Telegraph* feature article in which the couch potato is described as follows: 'He sits back on the sofa, his face vacuous and dumb, and stares at the television screen, and shovels popcorn, crisps, chocolates into his agape mouth while programmes reel by. Occasionally he aims the remote control at the screen, randomly selecting another channel' (cited in Michael, 2000, p.106).

As a figure of inert and distracted passivity (Figure 2.7), Michael argues, the couch potato condenses a number of contemporary social, political and cultural concerns. He (for it is usually a he) represents (i) *the unhealthy body* and, as such, a drain on the national health system, (ii) *the unproductive body*, the work-shy dole-cadger transfixed in front of the box rather than getting out to do a decent day's work, and (iii) *the uncultured body*, sliding into a passive reception of whatever is on the screen rather than engaging actively and intellectually in cultural pursuits. The couch potato, finally, also represents *the uncivic body*, turning to television for solitary entertainment at the price of active involvement in the public sphere.

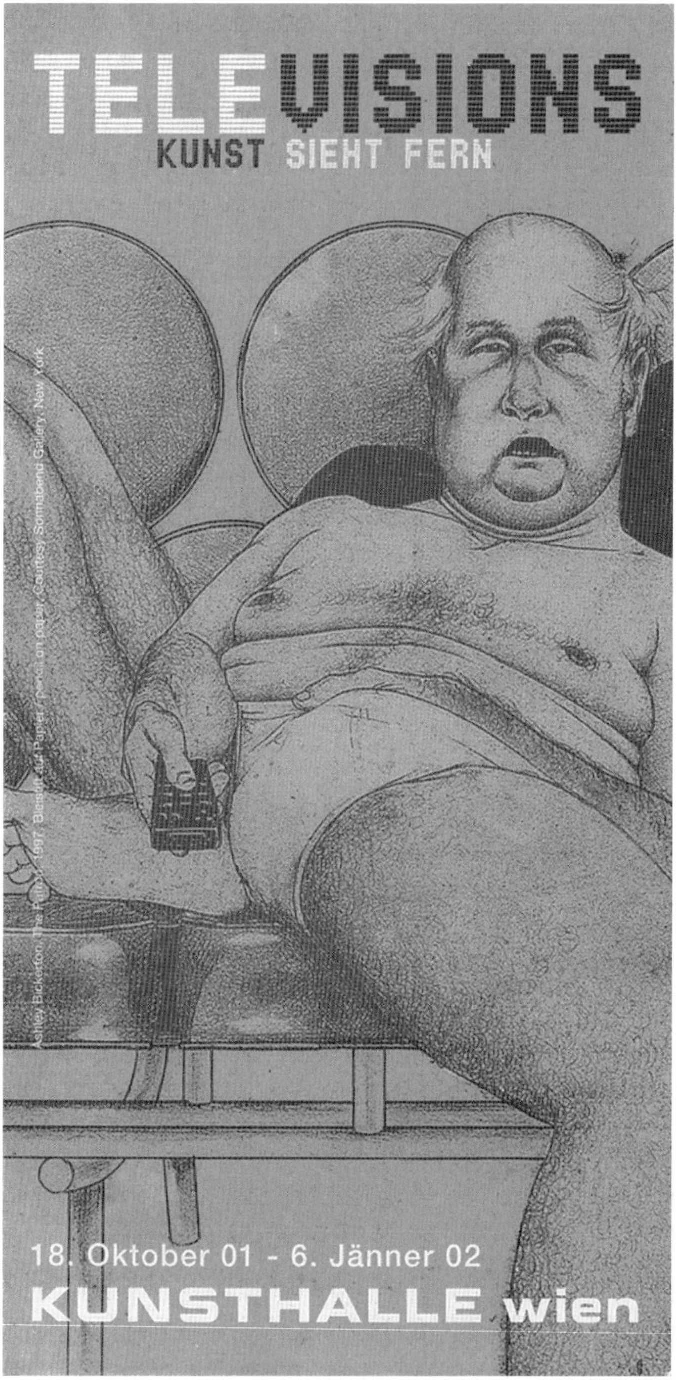

Figure 2.7 *The image of a couch potato from a poster for a cultural festival entitled* Televisions Kunst Sieht Fern *(or Art Watches Television) in Kunsthalle, Vienna, 2002* Source: Sonnabend Gallery, New York

It was in relation to early cinema that the concern was first aired that modern forms of spectatorship constituted a distracted form of attention. It will therefore be worth looking more closely at the context in which these concerns first surfaced by returning to the cinema of attraction that we looked at in Reading 2.1, but broaching this from a different perspective.

Now read the following extract from Ben Singer, 'Modernity, hyperstimulus, and the rise of popular sensationalism' (Reading 2.3). You will probably find this a little more taxing than the earlier readings, so take your time with it and use the following questions as a guide to the key issues to focus on.

- What does Singer mean by 'a neurological conception of modernity' (for 'modernity' read 'modern life' or the condition of being modern)?
- What part is played in the new intensity of sensory stimulation associated with modern life by (i) new forms of city life and (ii) new forms of commercial amusement?
- What relations does Singer see between this new intensity of sensory stimulation and the forms of distraction associated with cinema and other forms of popular visual culture?

Before starting this reading, however, you might find it helpful to note that the three thinkers that Singer names at the start of his discussion – Georg Simmel, Siegfried Kracauer and Walter Benjamin – all played a major role in developing early twentieth-century German accounts of the distinctive qualities of modern life.

Ben Singer, 'Modernity, hyperstimulus, and the rise of popular sensationalism'

With the recent interest in the social theories of Georg Simmel, Siegfried Kracauer, and Walter Benjamin, it has become clear that we are also dealing with a fourth major definition of modernity. These theorists focused on what might be called a *neurological* conception of modernity. They insisted that modernity must also be understood in terms of a fundamentally different register of subjective experience, characterized by the physical and perceptual shocks of the modern urban environment. [...] Modernity implied a phenomenal world – a specifically urban one – that was markedly quicker, more chaotic, fragmented, and disorienting than in previous phases of human culture. Amid the unprecedented turbulence of the big city's traffic, noise, billboards, street signs, jostling crowds, window displays, and advertisements, the individual faced a new intensity of sensory stimulation. The metropolis subjected the individual to a barrage of impressions, shocks, and jolts. The tempo of life also became more frenzied, sped up by new forms of rapid transportation, the pressing schedules of modern capitalism, and the ever-accelerating pace of the assembly line.

[...]

Looking backwards [...] one is struck by the extent to which Kracauer and Benjamin were tapping into an already widespread discourse about the shock of modernity. Social observers in the decades around the turn of the century were *fixated* on the idea that modernity had brought about a radical increase in nervous stimulation and bodily peril. This preoccupation can be found in every genre and class of social representation – from essays in academic journals to aesthetic manifestos (such as Marinetti's and Leger's) to middlebrow commentaries (such as the ubiquitous discussions of neurasthenia) and cartoons in the illustrated press (both in comic magazines such as *Puck, Punch, Judge,* and lowbrow sensational newspapers such as New York's *World* and *Journal*).[1]

[...]

The illustrated press offers a particularly rich trace of the culture's fixation on the sensory assaults of modernity. Comic magazines and sensational newspapers scrutinized the chaos of the modern environment with a dystopian alarmism that, in varying degrees, characterized much of the period's discourse on modern life. Many cartoons represented the new landscape of commercial solicitation as a type of horrific, aggressive stimulus (Figure 2.8). Others, portraying dense, chaotic mobs of pedestrians, keenly illustrated (fifty years in advance) Benjamin's (1968, p.174) suggestion that 'fear, revulsion, and horror were the emotions which the big-city crowd aroused in those who first observed it' (Figure 2.9).[2] A 1909 illustration in *Life* magazine entitled 'New York City, Is It Worth It?' represented the metropolis as a frantic onslaught of sensory shocks (Figure 2.10). [...]

A number of illustrations dealt specifically with the harsh transformation of experience from a premodern state of balance and poise to a modern crisis of discomposure and shock. A 1900 cartoon in *Life* entitled 'Broadway – Past and Present,' for example, contrasted a pastoral scene with a twentieth-century view of a trolley car bearing down on terrified pedestrians (Figure 2.11). In the background, billboards advertise a sensational newspaper called the *Whirl* and Sunday shows of boxing movies. The serenity of the 'savage's' life in the past accentuated the true savagery of the metropolitan present. The collision between two orders of experience – premodern and modern – also figured in numerous images representing actual collisions between horse-drawn carts – the traditional mode of transportation – and their modern-day replacement, the electric trolley (Figure 2.12). Such

Figure 2.8 *'How we advertise now'*, Punch, 1887

Figure 2.9 *'A quiet Sunday in London; or, the day of rest'*, Punch, 1886

Figure 2.10 *'New York City: is it worth it?'*, Life, 1909

pictures conveyed an anxiety about the perilousness of life in the
modern city and also symbolized the kinds of nervous shocks and jolts
to which the individual was subjected in the new urban environment.
[...]

Modernity transformed the texture not only of random daily
experience but also of synthetic, orchestrated experience. As the urban
environment grew more and more intense, so did the sensations of
commercial amusement. Around the turn of the century, an array of
amusements greatly increased the emphasis placed on spectacle,
sensationalism, and astonishment [...] Modernity ushered in a
commerce in sensory shocks. The 'thrill' emerged as the keynote of
modern diversion.

BROADWAY—PAST AND PRESENT.

IN THE SIXTEENTH CENTURY.   IN THE TWENTIETH CENTURY.

Figure 2.11 'Broadway – past and present', Life, 1900

The thrill took many forms. Beginning around 1895, as we have seen, sensational newspapers began flooding their pages with high-impact illustrations of anything strange, sordid, or shocking. The Coney Island amusement complex opened in 1895, and other parks specializing in exotic sights, disaster spectacles, and thrilling mechanical rides soon proliferated across the country. These concentrations of visual and kinaesthetic sensation epitomized a distinctly modern intensity of manufactured stimulus.[3] Vaudeville, which also emerged as a major popular amusement in the 1890s, epitomized the new trend toward brief, forceful and sensually 'busy' attractions, with its random series of stunts, slapstick, song and dance routines, trained dogs, female wrestlers and the like. Gaudy burlesque shows and 'dime museums' (housing sundry curiosities, freak shows, and, occasionally, short

Figure 2.12 *'Horse smashed cable car window',* New York World, *1897*

blood-and-thunder dramas) also took on greater prominence around the turn of the century, as did a variety of mechanical dare-devil exhibitions, such as 'The Whirlwind of Death' and 'The Globe of Death,' in which a car somersaulted in midair after hurling off a forty-foot ramp (Figure 2.13). The editors of *Scientific American*, [...] aptly summarized the essential objective of all these varieties of popular sensationalism: 'The guiding principle of the inventors of these acts is to give our nerves a shock more intense than any hitherto experienced.' [4]

[...]

The rise of the cinema culminated the trend toward vivid, powerful sensation. From very early on, the movies gravitated towards an 'aesthetics of astonishment,' in terms of both form and subject matter. The thrill was central, for example, to the early 'cinema of

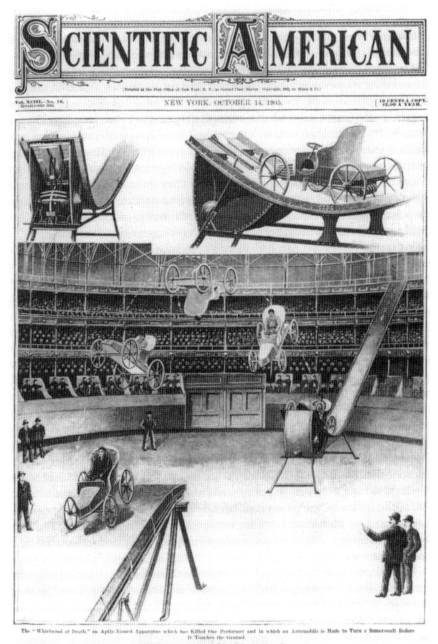

Figure 2.13 'The whirlwind of death', Scientific American, 1905

attractions' (to use Tom Gunning's (1989) term for spectacle-centred films before the rise of narrative integration around 1906) and to powerful suspense melodramas such as Griffith's Biograph thrillers of 1908 and 1909 (*The Fatal Hour, An Awful Moment, The Lonely Villa,* among others).[5] Action serials in the early teens, such as *The Perils of Pauline* and *The Exploits of Elaine*, elaborated every form of physical peril and sensational spectacle in explosions, crashes, torture contraptions, elaborate fights, chases, and last-minute rescues and escapes.[6.] It is not surprising that the modernist avant-garde, drawn to modernity's affective intensity, seized upon these serials, and upon the cinema in general, as an emblem of modern discontinuity and speed.

Notes

1   An example of an academic essay is Howard B. Woolston, 'The Urban Habit of Mind,' *The American Journal of Sociology* 17, no.5 (March 1912): 602–614. Stephen Kern offers a stimulating and eclectic survey of contemporaneous literary and artistic discourses about speed, fragmentation, and modernity (such as the Cubist and Futurist manifestos) in *The Culture of Time and Space, 1880–1918* (Cambridge: Harvard University Press, 1983), especially chapter 5. On neurasthenia, see Kern (chapter 5); Tom Lutz, *American Nervousness, 1903: An Anecdotal History* (Ithaca, N.Y.: Cornell University Press, 1991); James B Gilbert, *Work Without Salvations: America's Intellectuals and Industrial Alienation, 1880–1910* (Baltimore: Johns Hopkins University Press, 1977), pp.31–43. George Beard's *American Nervousness* (New York, 1881) is generally considered the seminal discussion of neurasthenia.

2   It is no coincidence that social theorists began focusing on mob psychology around the turn of the century. Two key works, among many popularizations, were Gustave Le Bon, *Psychologie des foules* (1895) and Gabriel Tarde, *Opinion and the Crowd* (1901). A representative popularization is Gerald Stanley Lee, *Crowds: A Study of the Genius of Democracy and the Fear, Desires, and Expectations of the People* (London: Methuen, 1913). Quotation from Walter Benjamin, 'On some motifs in Baudelaire,' in *Illuminations*, ed. Hannah Arendt (New York: Harcourt Brace, 1968), p.174. All further citations of Benjamin are from this collection.

3   John F. Kasson *Amusing the Million: Coney Island at the Turn of the Century* (New York, Hill and Wang, 1978); Richard Snow, *Coney Island: A Postcard Journey to the City of Fire* (New York: Brightwaters Press, 1984); Andrea Stulman Dennett and Nina Warnke, 'Disaster Spectacles at the Turn of the Century,' *Film History* 4 (1990): 101–111.

4　'A hundred ways of breaking your neck', *Scientific American*, 14 October 1905.

5　Tom Gunning explores aspects of sensationalism in early film in 'An aesthetics of astonishment: early film and the (in)credulous spectator,' *Art and Text*, 34, (spring 1989): 31.

6　On sensational melodrama and the action serials, see [Singer's] article 'Female power in the serial-queen melodrama: the etiology of an anomaly,' *Camera Obscura* 22 (January, 1990): 91–129, and [Singer's] chapter on serials in Geoffrey Nowell-Smith, ed., *A History of the Cinema, 1895–1995* (Oxford: Oxford University Press, 1995).

References

Benjamin, W. (1968) 'On some motifs in Baudelaire' in Arendt, H. (ed.) *Illuminations*, New York, Harcourt Brace.

Gunning, T. (1989) 'An aesthetics of astonishment: early film and the (in) credulous spectator', *Art and Text*, vol.34, pp.31–45.

Reading source

Singer, 1995, p.72–91　■ ■ ■

In looking more closely at the issues this reading raises it will be useful to begin by noting that it connects well with our starting point in this chapter – the relation between the media and the senses – but also goes beyond it and, indeed, questions some of the terms in which these issues have been posed so far. Singer argues that different aspects of modernity – city life, new visual media, the organisation of industrial production – 'prompted a kind of reconditioning of the individual's sensory apparatus' (Singer, 1995, p.2). Modern living involved an increase in sensory stimulation, in its intensity and shock effect, that incites nervousness. The reading suggests that what matters is the relationship between the media and distinctive mental or psychological kinds of perception or attention, and the ways in which the body is socially organised and regulated. It is not just the senses that emerge as being socially and historically malleable and subject to training, rather it is the articulation of the relations between the senses and other capacities – the whole perceptual, sensory, neurological and physiological organisation of the individual (or what Walter Benjamin (1969) calls 'the human sensorium').

The second point we should note concerns the respects in which the accounts of distraction that Singer draws on – particularly that of German film theorist, Siegfried Kracauer (1987) – form part of a historical contrast in which the disjointed, over-stimulated, jaded, abstracted, trance-like forms of sensory engagement associated with cinema spectatorship compare unfavourably with earlier, more attentive and fully engaged sensory relations to cultural life. The perspective of Walter Benjamin is a little different. He argued that the forms of technological reproducibility of the image and sound associated with photography, film and the phonograph entailed the destruction of the 'aura' of the work of art that had earlier been associated with its irreducible individuality. However, he saw real possibilities for a new democratic relation to culture arising out of the distracted attention of the cinema-goer. Here is how he puts the matter:

> Reception in a state of distraction, which is increasingly noticeable in all fields of art and is symptomatic of profound changes in apperception, finds in the film its true means of exercise [...] The film makes the cult value recede into the background not only by putting the public in the position of the critic, but also by the fact that at the movies this position requires no attention. The public is an examiner, but an absent-minded one.
>
> Benjamin, 1968, pp.240–1

Writing, like Kracauer, in Germany in the 1920s and 1930s, Benjamin saw in this absent-minded distraction the possibility for a new mode of mass participation in cultural life, bypassing the authority of the cultural critic, which, if worked on and transformed, would give rise to a more relaxed, cool and contemplative relation to works of art than those forms of emotional intensity that had earlier characterised the experience of its aura. Be this as it may, Benjamin's account still forms part of a commonplace historical contrast: what Rutsky calls 'reception in a state of distraction' (Rutsky, 2002, p.283) is counterposed to an earlier period when the forms in which works of art and culture were produced and distributed both required and enabled non-fragmented and holistic forms of sensory and intellectual involvement on the part of their audiences.

There are two difficulties here. The first is that drawing the historical lines separating a past, in which the senses are organically interrelated, from the sensory alienation and distraction of the present has proved to be something of a moveable feast in media studies. For Kracauer and Benjamin the key division was between film, photography and the phonograph and the period prior to the development of these techniques of mass reproduction of images and sounds. In more recent versions of similar arguments, however, cinema is contrasted favourably with television in view of the forms of concentrated viewing it is said to require, as opposed to the inattentive distraction which, in such accounts, defines television as such. This was especially true of much of the film theory associated with the journal *Screen* in the 1970s and 1980s: a focused and concentrated gaze was imputed to cinemas, with a more casual glance said to characterise television viewing. For John Ellis, for example: 'The regime of viewing TV is thus very different from the cinema: TV does not encourage the same degree of spectator concentration. There is no surrounding darkness, no anonymity of the fellow viewers, no large image, no lack of movement amongst the spectators, no rapt attention' (Ellis, 1982, p.127–8).

Views like this, John Caldwell argues (1995), have inhibited an adequate recognition of the distinctive styles of what he calls 'televisuality' – that is, stylistically exuberant and excessive codes of production in which the stylistic possibilities of television are exploited to the full. As broadcasting has given way to narrowcasting and mass audiences been replaced by niche ones, he suggests, highly concentrated, active and knowing forms of television and video viewing have been promoted through which young elites have developed a sense of their own cultural distinctiveness.

The second and more general difficulty consists in the terms in which such contrasts are drawn wherever, in time, they happen to be placed. This is the basis on which Jonathan Crary takes issue with both Kracauer and Benjamin. Rather than seeing modern forms of distraction as 'a disruption of stable or "natural" kinds of sustained, value-laden perception that had existed for centuries', he sees the emergence of distraction as a problem in late nineteenth-century thought as 'an *effect*, and in many cases a constituent element, of the many attempts to produce attentiveness in human subjects' (Crary, 2001, p.49). This concern with attentiveness was, in its turn, the result of a radical change in the way in which the sense of sight and practices of seeing were conceived. Around the middle of the nineteenth century, subjective accounts of vision began to replace the 'rational optics' that had dominated European thought during the seventeenth and eighteenth centuries. According to 'rational optics', most influentially elaborated by the French philosopher René Descartes, seeing was much less a physical matter of the senses than a rational matter of the mind registering and interpreting the images registered on the retina – much like the position of an observer within a *camera obscura* (Figure 2.14) which often served as convenient summary of this account of vision. This detachment of vision from the body meant that it was seen as objective: we all see the same world in the same way.

The period from the 1830s on, by contrast, witnessed what Crary calls the subjectivisation of vision (Crary, 1996). As a result of a number of developments in scientific thought, and especially the emergence of 'physiological optics', seeing was no longer regarded as a rational disembodied process but as profoundly influenced by the eye's corporeality – that is, its nature and function as a part of the body's physiological processes. As a consequence of this, what had hitherto been

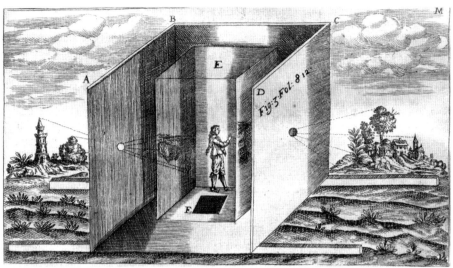

Figure 2.14 *Camera obscura, 1646*
Source: Crary, 1996

thought to be objective, came to be regarded as subjective: perceptions of colour were, according to Johann Wolfgang von Goethe (1749–1832, German poet, playwright and scientist), affected by physiological processes rather than being determined by objective properties of light and could thus vary from individual to individual. Once this door to subjective variation in the ways we see the world had been opened, there were no limits. If sight could vary owing to variations in the physiological make-up of the perceiver, then, since the physiological constitution of individuals could be affected by climate, diet and social conditions, there seemed to be no end to the ways in which seeing might vary. These, then, are among the reasons why, as Martin Jay has argued, sight, which had been a trusted source of rational perception in the eighteenth century, came to be widely denigrated in nineteenth- and twentieth-century thought as illusory and unreliable (Jay, 1994). Yet, at the same time, the demands of new forms of mass industrial production and city life, not to mention the requirements of citizenship in mass democracies, all placed a premium on accurate and focused forms of attention.

The conjunction of these two factors – the one undermining the reliability of vision while, at the same time, the other placed a premium on reliable and focused attentiveness – resulted in a plethora of attempts to standardise and regulate vision. Psychological experiments were designed to established norms for 'correct' vision; optical devices codified visual space in ways designed to train the eye into standardised and homogeneous form of perception; and, as the work of Michel Foucault (1977) has shown, social spaces – in schools, factories, hospitals, prisons, and theatres – were designed in ways that aimed to regulate the practices of observers, compelling their attentiveness to the lesson, the task in hand, etc. To put the matter in this way suggests a different way of looking at the relationship between early cinema and the issue of audience distraction than the one Singer proposes. It suggests that, rather than seeing the cinema as necessarily producing new forms of distracted inattentiveness, the more interesting issue is why cinema audiences came to be seen in this light and how this view of them affected early cinema as a cultural technology. For its development was affected both by its perception as a site of popular and perceptual disorder and by attempts to compensate for and correct this.

6 Conclusion

It will be useful, in concluding, to review the implications of the perspectives developed in this chapter for our overall understanding of the relations between media, audiences and meanings. And a good way of doing this is to think about their relationship to what we have learnt about approaches to audiences in Chapter 1.

Activity 2.5

Recalling your work both for Chapter 1 and for this chapter, in what ways do you think the perspective of the 'media sensorium' might (i) qualify or challenge, or (ii) usefully complement and extend the approaches to media audiences you are now familiar with? Note down your responses before reading further. ■ ■ ■

Many of the approaches introduced in Chapter 1 either assume or imply that media–audience relationships primarily concern the content of media messages. Take, as a couple of examples, Harold Laswell's sender–message–receiver model and Stuart Hall's Encoding/Decoding model. Both of those are essentially concerned with audience understandings or interpretation of meanings. Of course, there is no discounting the importance of these concerns. But they do suggest a view of audiences as essentially disembodied, as if their relations to the media take place without their eyes, ears, noses and fingers being particularly involved in the matter. One aspect of the approaches reviewed in this chapter, then, is that – in common with much contemporary social theory – they stress the importance of viewing what we do as audiences as being just as much *embodied practices* as are our other social actions.

Now let us think about the new media and compare the ways in which new media reorder the relations between the senses and the new forms of social interaction they make possible. Look back at your answer to Activity 2.1. How, now, would you want to add to this with new media like the internet specifically in mind? ■ ■ ■

One obvious example of new media reordering the relations between the senses and social interaction is the mobile phone, which has introduced into our daily lives – on buses and trains, in restaurants and shops – the sometimes disconcerting phenomenon of people who share the same social space talking and listening to others who are physically distant, avoiding any interaction with those who are nearby. Digital television also opens up new sensory possibilities. It brings about a much closer association between touch and sight and, like the internet, brings about distinctive relations between looking and reading. The camcorder has opened up quite new relationships between seeing and being seen, making it possible for millions of disconnected individuals to become voyeuristically engaged in the everyday lives of others. Think of the increasing use of PowerPoint presentations in lectures in which saying and showing, listening and seeing, merge to become almost indistinguishable. Our ability to listen to extended lectures without a visual supplement may well soon become a thing of the past. All of these, then, are telling signs that the ratio of our senses – the degree to which we draw on them and use them in relation to one another – is constantly being reorganised as a result of the influence of new media and the uses we make of them.

Further reading

Dyer, R. (1997) *White*, London, Routledge.

McLuhan, M. and Fiore, Q. (1967) *The Medium is the Massage*, London, Penguin Books.

Neale, S. (1985) *Cinema and Technology: Image, Sound, Colour*, London, Palgrave Macmillan.

Robins, K. and Webster, F. (1999) *Times of the Technoculture: From the Information Society to the Virtual Life*, London, Routledge.

Williams, R. (1974) *Television: Technology and Cultural Form*, London, Fontana.

References

Benjamin, W. (1968) 'The work of art in the age of mechanical reproduction' in Arendt, H. (ed.) *Illuminations*, New York, Harcourt Brace.

Bonner, F. (2005) 'The celebrity in the text' in Evans, J. and Hesmondhalgh, D. (eds) *Understanding Media: Inside Celebrity*, Maidenhead, Open University Press/The Open University (Book 1 in this series).

Caldwell, J.T. (1995) *Televisuality: Style, Crisis, and Authority in American Television*, New Brunswick, NJ, Rutgers University Press.

Crary, J. (1996) *Techniques of the Observer: On Vision and Modernity in the Nineteenth Century*, Cambridge, MA, MIT Press.

Crary, J. (2001) *Suspensions of Perception*, Cambridge, MA, MIT Press.

Dyer, R. (1997) *White*, London, Routledge.

Eisenstein, E.L. (1979) *The Printing Press as an Agent of Change* (2 volumes), Cambridge, Cambridge University Press.

Ellis, J. (1982) *Visible Fictions: Cinema, Television, Video*, London, Routledge and Kegan Paul.

Foucault, M. (1977) *Discipline and Punish: The Birth of the Prison*, London, Allen Lane.

Griffiths, A. (2002) *Wondrous Differences: Cinema, Anthropology, and Turn-of-the-Century Visual Culture*, New York, Columbia University Press.

Gripsrud, J. (2006) 'Semiotics: signs, codes and cultures', in Gillespie, M. and Toynbee, J. (eds) *Analysing Media Texts*, Maidenhead, Open University Press/The Open University (Book 4 in this series).

Gunning, T. (1989) 'An aesthetics of astonishment: early film and the (in)credulous spectator', *Art and Text*, vol.34, pp.31–45.

Hansen, M. (1991) *Babel and Babylon: Spectatorship in American Silent Film*, Cambridge, MA, Harvard University Press.

Jay, M. (1994) *Downcast Eyes: The Denigration of Vision in Twentieth-Century French Thought*, Berkeley and Los Angeles, CA, University of California Press.

Johnson, L. (1988) *The Unseen Voice: A Cultural Study of Early Australian Radio*, London, Routledge.

Kracauer, S. (1987) 'The cult of distraction: on Berlin's picture palaces', *New German Critique*, no.40, pp.91–6.

McLuhan, M. (1962) *The Gutenberg Galaxy: The Making of Typographic Man*, London, Routledge and Kegan Paul.

McLuhan, M. (1964) *Understanding Media*, London, Sphere Books.

McLuhan, M. and Quentin F. (1967) *The Medium is the Massage*, London, Penguin Books.

Michael, M. (2000) *Reconnecting Culture, Technology and Nature: From Society to Heterogeneity*, London, Routledge.

Neale, S. (1985) *Cinema and Technology: Image, Sound, Colour*, London, Palgrave Macmillan.

Robins, K. and Webster, F. (1999) *Times of the Technoculture: From the Information Society to the Virtual Life*, London, Routledge.

Rutsky, R.L. (2002) 'Pop-up theory: distraction and consumption in the age of meta-information', *Journal of Visual Culture*, vol.1, no.3, pp.279–94.

Singer, B. (1995) 'Modernity, hyperstimulus, and the rise of popular sensationalism' in Charney, L. and Schwartz, V.R. (eds) *Cinema and the Invention of Modern Life*, Berkeley and Los Angeles, CA, University of California Press.

Sterne, J. (2003) 'Bourdieu, technique and technology', *Cultural Studies*, vol.17, nos.3–4, pp.367–89.

Uricchio, W. and Pearson, R.E. (1998) 'Corruption, criminality and the nickelodeon' in Fullerton, J. (ed.) *Celebrating 1895: The Centenary of Cinema*, London, John Libbey.

Williams, R. (1974) *Television: Technology and Cultural Form*, London, Fontana.

Plate 1 *The Magic Lantern*, by Paul Sandby (see Section 4, Chapter 2)

Plate 2 *Cirque*, by George Seurat (see Section 5, Chapter 2)

Plate 3 A Hindu nationalist politician (BJP party) masquerades as Lord Rama during the 1991 election campaign, exploiting popular religious sentiment and symbolism generated by the Indian TV epics (See Section 5, Chapter 3)

Plate 4 The Indian TV epics drew upon popular images of Hindu Gods (such as the one above of Lord Krishna) in representing the deity on screen. Such images use iconographic conventions, developed over centuries, making them instantly recognisable to audiences (see Section 4.2, Chapter 4)

Media publics, culture and democracy

David Herbert

Chapter 3

Contents

1 Introduction

Much of our knowledge and understanding of the world is acquired via the media. These media are, at least in some senses, increasingly diverse. Consider the number of sources available via the internet, or the increase in television channels accessible via cable and satellite. The media also make previously remote locations ever more widely accessible, at least until the roving media eye moves on. So we rely on the media for our knowledge of the world and the media bring us more of the world to consider. By presenting us with more, it potentially increases our 'universe of concern' – the things we know about and hence can care about. But, because our capacity to watch and listen is limited, the increasing range of media available requires us to make choices about our media sources, even before we turn on, tune in or log on to them. For this reason, as media sources diversify, one possible effect is that we increasingly choose to attend to what we like and ignore what we do not like, shrinking instead of stretching our universe of concern.

This chapter examines some of the political implications of this kind of a media world. Firstly, what does media diversification mean for democracy, if democratic politics depends on an informed public that can debate issues of common concern? Secondly, how might changes in media impact on democracy? If the nineteenth century was the era of the newspaper and telegraph, the twentieth that of film then broadcast radio and television, the early twenty-first seems characterised by the internet and new forms of television transmission. In other words, how do these changes in media influence the formation of the informed publics?

This chapter aims to:

- explore the relationship between audiences and political ideas of 'the public';
- examine the interaction between television, audiences and publics in three national case studies (USA, India and Israel), assessing the political impact of television in each;
- demonstrate how culturally distinctive responses to television impact on processes of democratisation.

As we have seen in previous chapters (and this should be a basic assumption of any book on 'audiences'), it is not enough just to look at the effects of the media as if this were a one-way process from media to audience. Rather, it is necessary to consider audiences as active and selective interpreters, who not only feed their preferences into media production through market research, but also actively engage with and use media for a variety of purposes.

An important background issue here is the influence of culture on media consumption/use. If audiences are seen as 'active', the role of culture in shaping media influence is emphasised. This is because audiences draw on whatever local or national cultural resources are to hand in their responses to media. This 'localising' effect of media consumption needs to be balanced with a consideration of the possible homogenising effects of globalisation, and of technology as a determining influence. To get a sense of the different dynamics that may be involved here, it is important to consider the interaction between audiences and media forms in a variety of cultural contexts. Hence, after considering the effects of (and resistance to) the commercialisation of political communication in the USA, we shall examine two cases from the Middle East and South Asia.

In these two case studies we will examine how, through complex interactions with active audiences, television might have inadvertently helped to bring Hindu nationalists to power in India, and contributed to the polarisation of public opinion in Palestine/Israel. In these cases it would seem that the effect of new technologies has been to increase the influence of religion and political polarisation. This finding runs contrary to some common assumptions about modernisation and globalisation, namely that their effect would be to liberalise culture and diminish the social significance of religion. The case studies suggest that the effects of television are contingent on local cultural and political conditions, and the reactions of active audiences.

2 Defining media publics

Sociologist Leon Mayhew argues that there are three common uses of the term 'public' in the social sciences (1997, pp.137–54). The first is a notion of the 'general public' as developed in traditions of democratic theory: ' "[T]he public" refers in a broad sense to the people. The public is the electorate and bearer of public opinion, the ultimate source of legitimate governing power. The state holds only delegated power as an agent of the people and is separate from and accountable to the differentiated public' (Mayhew, 1997, p.137).

The second refers to a statistical understanding of the public as the average of individuals' views, calculated using survey data. The third refers to what might be called an 'active' model of the public as the result of people getting together to discuss or act in some way.

This third sense differs from the second because it takes seriously the effects of discussion and debate on individual opinion. It also takes seriously the effects of responsibility – of having to make real choices – based on opinions formed through debate. When people get together, physically or virtually, they influence each other in ways that cannot be understood or fully predicted just by taking a poll of each individual's opinion. As media theorist Nicholas Garnham argues, in contemporary societies much of the social interaction that influences public opinion in this third sense takes place through the media: '[M]uch of the reality of modern society, precisely because social relations are mediated ... cannot be explained in terms of individuals and a methodological individualism which sees all social phenomena as merely the sum of individual actions' (Garnham, 2000, p.130).

So in media-rich societies the kind of interaction that leads to the formation of public opinion in this third sense takes place not just through face-to-face encounter, but in a range of mediated forms such as television programmes involving public debate (see Figure 3.1). In what follows we shall consider some of the complexities of these processes.

Figure 3.1 *The BBC London web page featuring* People's Question Time
Source: www.bbc.co.uk/london/insideldn/politics/peoples_question_time.shtml

This chapter uses the term 'media public' to refer to situations in which members of a media audience become involved in debate about issues of shared concern. Examples include members of a family arguing about a controversial news item; or viewers of a television soap featuring a 'hot' issue such as domestic violence, responding by joining a Web discussion or radio phone-in debate. This understanding of media publics stresses the *process* of debate or discussion rather than political *effects* as such. Thus a media public is created when viewers of a party political broadcast argue about its content, rather than when that broadcast influences some aspect of their behaviour, such as the way in which (or whether) they vote. This distinction is illustrated in Figure 3.2.

Figure 3.2 *Initial model of formation and role of media publics*

In focusing on discussion rather than outcome, this model of media publics follows the idea of a 'public sphere' developed by the German social theorist Jürgen Habermas (1989/1962). For Habermas, it is this kind of discussion between ordinary people about matters of public concern that is the foundation of modern democracy.

Activity 3.1

Think of a recent occasion when you heard something on the news or watched a soap or documentary that you ended up discussing with someone. This might be because it concerned you or you felt a strong reaction, or just because it was of interest or a good bit of gossip.

- What kinds of things did you discuss and what was the course of the discussion?
- Did you or the person you spoke with change your mind about anything as a result of the conversation?
- Do you think you chose to talk to this person because you thought they would share your opinion or reaction?
- Would you talk to your boss or parents about the topic you chose? What difference do you think it makes to discussion if you see the person you are speaking to as having more authority or influence than you, whether, for example, because they manage you at work, are older or are some kind of an expert? ■ ■ ■

There are many issues in the media that people might want to discuss, ranging from who is next to be eliminated from the latest reality TV competition show to whether the US and UK invasion of Iraq in 2003 was justified. As members of a media audience, we quite often get involved in discussions about what we see or hear; whenever we do, we become part of a 'media public'.

A couple of questions can help us think about the kind of publics we are creating by engaging in these discussions. Firstly, how do pair or small group discussions differ from larger forums? Secondly, how does power or authority influence discussions? In response to the first question, we often choose to talk with people who share our interests or outlook, because this makes the discussion more agreeable and confirms us in our views. The increasing range of media available to cater to different tastes means that we can do this on a larger scale, arguably to the extent that it is possible to avoid discussing things with others of opposing views. Views opposed to our own may be represented in the media we choose, but in terms that we find disagreeable, so that engagement with those views can be avoided. In response to the second question, power and authority can influence discussion by making us reluctant to express our interests or views if we think another person is more expert or has influence over us, or will regard our interests as trivial.

Both these points have a bearing on Habermas's 'ideal' model of the public sphere (1989/1962). Firstly, he is concerned that public spheres include participants from different perspectives. This is because without real engagement between different views it is impossible for genuine consensus to develop, and so it will be the views of the largest or most powerful group that eventually dominate. Secondly, at least ideally, in the public sphere, distinctions of status are 'bracketed out' of discussion, so that it is the best or the most rational argument that ends up winning, rather than the most powerful person. Habermas sees this ideal as having first developed among the emerging middle classes in western European cities in the late eighteenth century.

3 Habermas: history and concept of the public sphere

According to Habermas (1989/1962), the public sphere is any space in which matters of public significance are discussed, and in which the outcome is decided by the quality of argument alone. He identifies the historical emergence of this ideal with the coffee houses, salons and table societies of late eighteenth- and early nineteenth-century London, Paris and Frankfurt (see Figure 3.3). It is important to note that he sees this ideal as only ever partly realised, and thus establishes a tension between the ideal or 'normative' public sphere and actually existing or 'empirical' public spheres.

Figure 3.3 *A William Hogarth line drawing of a London coffee house scene: a bourgeois public sphere (circa 1710)*
Source: Hulton Archive

For Habermas, the initial public sphere came into being through the circulation of newspapers (although arguably it had been prefigured by the explosion of Protestant pamphleteering 150 years earlier; Mayhew, 1997). The later decline of the public sphere followed its fragmentation after the increasing commercial domination of the newspaper industry. Developments in the twentieth century, especially the diversification and commercialisation of broadcasting that followed the advent of satellite and cable broadcasting, and the internet, can be seen as continuing this trajectory towards fragmentation, leading to the decline of any sense of a common public. Thus, today, broadcasting is fragmenting into narrow-casting to niche audiences. The internet, in spite of its massive capacity to enable communication between individuals over time and space, similarly fosters user groups structured around private interests.

A further strand to this argument is that recent changes in the form of dominant communications media, from print to radio to television and the internet, increasingly work against the development of sustained reasoned argument. Habermas sees such argument as necessary for informed political debate. Its decline results in forms of politics dominated by the sound bite, the use of symbols, and an emphasis on surface appearances and display, which he calls 'refeudalization' (Habermas, 1989/1962, p.231).

In the last twenty years, Habermas's idea of the public sphere has become increasingly influential in discussions of the media's role in relation to democracy. This is because it addresses concerns about the decline both of democratic participation (for example, voting) and of traditional organisations that mediate between the public and the government (for example, trade unions and political parties) in western societies. It does so by thinking about the basis of democracy in a fresh way, and is suggestive of alternative forms of political debate and new forums for political participation. It also addresses concerns about the growth of manipulative forms of political communication that are influenced by public relations techniques (discussed below in Section 4 as the 'New Public'). Habermas's idea of the public sphere thus offers a way of rethinking the social basis of democratic legitimacy in media-rich societies. However, it has also been subject to criticism, and hence development.

3.1 Criticism and development of Habermas's model of the public sphere

Habermas's original (1989/1962) model has been criticised for several reasons. Firstly, it has been challenged as an accurate historical account of the genesis of the ideal. For example, Habermas's account highlights the secular 'bourgeois' (middle-class) roots of the public sphere. This neglects the development of traditions of public debate in working-class, religious and inter-religious contexts. Similar public ideals and deliberative practices have arisen both in earlier periods (for example, the seventeenth-century English Puritan congregation; Mayhew, 1997) and in non-western cultural contexts (for example, in the rivalry between Christian missionary and Hindu revival groups in late Mughal/early British India; van der Veer, 1999). Arguments about historical origins of the public sphere are of interest because they suggest that the conditions of public communication that are supportive of democratic development can arise in a range of cultural settings.

The public sphere is also regarded as elitist, privileging a mode of communication unequally accessible to different social classes, women and minority ethnic groups (Benhabib, 1992). It is seen as an excessively rationalised model of public communication that favours the literate, educated and articulate. Rational discourse may have characterised the bourgeois male groups that inspired Habermas's model, but it is not the only way to conduct public debate, and it is unlikely to be reproduced in contemporary media-rich societies. The coherence of the bourgeois public sphere was contingent on limitations in communication such as the dominance of the print medium in these late eighteenth- and early nineteenth-century societies, and the restricted size and mobility of the reading public. This model becomes problematic, as we shall see in the case studies that follow, when publics become larger, more dispersed and more socially and culturally diverse.

Habermas later acknowledged the contribution of marginalised and working-class groups to the development of the public sphere by drawing upon examples of various social movements in the modern history of western societies. Three examples are particularly pertinent here. Firstly, in the nineteenth century, through the struggle of labour movements, industrial relations became part of public discussion and working-class men were included for the first time. Secondly, in the first half of the twentieth century, women's movements politicised the domestic sphere, and women joined the conversation. Thirdly, later in the twentieth century, especially from the 1960s, a variety of groups further extended the boundaries of public discussion, including groups concerned with global poverty, nuclear weapons, the environment, animal rights, and gay and lesbian movements. Through the struggles of these groups from the 'civil–social periphery', the boundaries of the public sphere have been greatly extended, both in terms of who can participate and of what is discussed.

In order to get politicians and the political elite to listen, such groups have had to use tactics and ways of communicating that do not conform to the ideal communication conditions that Habermas ascribes to the normative public sphere; that is, rational argument undistorted by unequal power relations. Because these groups lack direct or 'instrumental' power, only dramatic action will persuade the media to take up their concerns, bringing them to public attention, and hence ultimately persuading politicians to address them.

This has been called the 'sluice-gate' model of the public sphere, because issues need to be raised to a certain level of publicity through campaigns before they are taken up by the 'mass media', and hence break into the official or mainstream public sphere (McGuigan, 2002, pp.107–9). The media are central to this model, because the effects of dramatic actions (for example, Campaign for Nuclear Disarmament (CND) marches in the 1980s or Greenpeace direct actions in the 1990s) are greatly amplified by their dissemination through the 'mass media', and it is the media that determines their level of exposure. The internet further increases the possibilities for mobilisation of this kind.

Because groups on the civil–social periphery lack instrumental power to achieve their goals directly, they use what Habermas (1987) calls their 'communicative' power – they perform actions aimed at getting across a point of view and persuading others. Such action can range from dramatic symbolic acts – like climbing London's Tower Bridge dressed as Spiderman (Fathers for Justice) or bringing cities to a halt with huge demonstrations (for example, the anti-war marches of 2003) – to collecting and submitting petitions or producing pamphlets and websites.

Thus Habermas's revised (1996/1992) understanding of the public sphere retains the idea of rational and undistorted communication as the core of communicative action in the public sphere, but also recognises the necessity of less-than-ideal forms of communicative action to get issues onto the public agenda, and hence the legitimacy of groups who use such tactics, short of violence.

Critics, however, argue that this revised model still does not go far enough, because in the real world inequalities persist. Some groups will always be excluded from, or at least marginalised, within the mainstream public sphere. Hence Nancy Fraser (1992) argues that such groups need alternative spaces in which to organise and express their views: '[S]ubordinated social groups – women, workers, peoples of colour, and gays and lesbians – have repeatedly found it advantageous to constitute alternative publics' (Fraser, 1992, p.123).

From the perspective of such alternative publics, Habermas's ideal public sphere may still be seen as privileging a form of communication (rational discourse) that is unequally available to all, and may be used as a smoke-screen to conceal forms of domination. But what alternative medium of communication could be used to resolve disagreements between participants in alternative publics? The difference between Habermas and his critics can be seen in terms of a contrast between reason-oriented (Habermas) and culture-oriented (for example, Benhabib, 1992) models of the public sphere.

Habermas recognises that reason is always embodied in culture, but still places hope in the possibility that forms of reasoned communication can develop that transcend cultural differences. In contrast, for Benhabib, there is no such reasonable resolution of conflict; discourse remains tied to its cultural origins and the best that can be done is to try to create opportunities for voices from alternative public spheres to break into the mainstream. In other words, cultural background may be more important than reason in shaping how people perceive the world and act on/in it.

However, whether we think of one public sphere or many, Habermas's model at least allows us to think through how the media interact with other social institutions to create a public sphere or spheres, and influence politics. Thus Habermas's revised model (1996/1992) may be represented as shown in Figure 3.4.

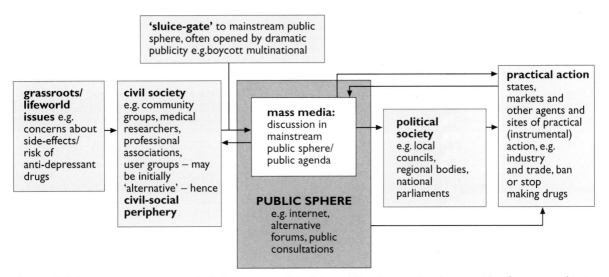

Figure 3.4 *From grassroots to practical change: a model of the public sphere, using the example of concerns about the side-effects of anti-depressant drugs*

Using Figure 3.4, answer the following:

■ Think of an example that would illustrate the arrow going from 'practical action' directly to media and vice versa.

■ Think of some other arrows you could add in to represent other links in the system.

■ Find an example of a recent controversial issue over which government or a large business was forced to reconsider its policy as a result of public protest. Based on Figure 3.4, create your own revised diagram showing different actions and actors involved in each stage of the process. ■■■

Censorship in general is perhaps the most obvious example of state influence on the media, and conversely private media owners have long been thought to exercise an unhealthy influence on government. On your diagram, an arrow leading from media to the state might indicate concerns about media owners ('press barons') having too much influence over members of a government. But there are also concerns about various newer forms of state–media interpenetration; for example, whether journalists 'embedded' with military forces end up serving the propaganda interests of the state.

There are several possibilities for further elaboration of Habermas's model. Some elements of 'civil society' (groups intermediate between the state and family) may have links into political society; for example, MPs may champion particular causes such as pro- or anti-abortion campaigns.

The actions of the state, business and industry affect the lives of everyone, so there is a direct link from the state back to all the other boxes.

Issues on the political agenda change quickly but one issue where public pressure contributed to a rethinking of government policy was genetically modified (GM) crops. The process could be represented as illustrated in Figure 3.5.

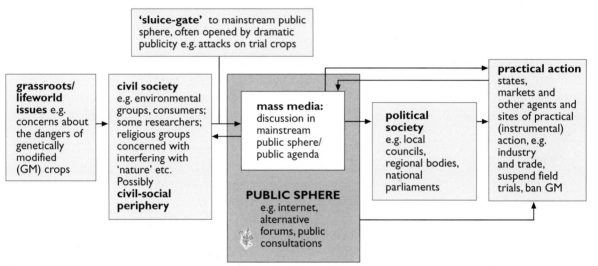

Figure 3.5 *From grassroots to practical action: a model of the public sphere, using the example of concerns about the dangers of GM (genetically modified) crops*

Using the example of GM crops, Figure 3.5 captures how issues of public concern arise, are constructed, brought to public attention, discussed and acted upon (or not) by political and other major actors. Of course, there are a lot of other influences on government and companies – not least economic influences and scientific evidence. There are also other feedback mechanisms involved: for example, between government, big business and the media, and between government, business and civil society. But this representation stresses the role of the media not just in transmitting issues from the civil society to the political centre (the arrows going from civil society to the media, and from the media to political society), but also in the construction of issues by groups in civil society in the first place (the arrow going from the media to civil society). It also shows how media publics exert influence on markets by changing demand, and on government through mechanisms such as public opinion polls (both represented by the arrow from civil society to states).

This example has drawn us into considering the role of the media in political communication, and this issue takes centre stage in our first case study.

4   Political communication and the influence of the 'New Public' in the USA

The USA is widely regarded as a 'lead society' in terms of the dissemination and influence of new communications technologies. On the dissemination side, such a claim is largely justified; for example, in terms of early and widespread penetration of television and the internet (Castells, 1996). But what of influence? This section will examine the influence of recent media developments on political communication in the USA. Sections 5 and 6 will then consider the influence of similar developments in the very different cultural contexts of India and Israel.

Politicians and social scientists in the USA have expressed concern at the decline of political participation and traditional mediating institutions, a decline that has been linked with the rise in media consumption (Greider, 1992). In such discussions, the media may be seen as both as villain and saviour, blamed both for the decline of political participation (media especially have been accused of creating a passive audience, see Chapter 2) and heralded as a potential site for its revival (especially by means of interactive media such as the internet). Particular concern about a decline in the quality of democracy has focused on the rise of the 'New Public'. This is defined as a public under the influence of professional communications, especially public relations or PR, techniques of political communication. These techniques draw on methods developed in commercial environments.

Before investigating the New Public, it is important to note that not all commentators agree that there has been a decline either in the quality of public debate or in the extent of popular participation in the public life of the USA. For example, Schudson (1993) argues that in the eighteenth and nineteenth centuries, the relatively higher voter participation rates were often achieved only by coercion, or in the context of some national emergency (for example, the Civil War). He also argues that political debates were often well attended only because they were the sole form of local entertainment available. They often served the purpose of reinforcing pre-existing solidarities rather than creating rational discussion, since 'ethnic and religious communities provided the basis for political allegiances' (Schudson, 1993, p.144). Elite nineteenth-century audiences were well read, but in a narrow canon, and mass audiences in that period read very little at all. However, even if the standards of rational discourse and the rates of political participation have not fallen, does this mean that the political effects of the media are benign? A brief digression, at this point, on research into the political effects of the media may help to clarify this point.

Research into the political effects of the media follows the tradition of media effects research outlined by Sonia Livingstone in Chapter 1.

Academic debate has moved from seeing the media as highly influential to not influential at all, then through to a range of more nuanced approaches that see effects as varying and always dependent on context and audience response (Croteau and Hoynes, 2003, pp.240–7). For example, research on voting preferences in elections suggests that media effects are minimal on people who have already made up their mind, but are stronger on floating voters (Germond and Witcover, 1989). Studies of how we acquire political ideas and values (political socialisation research) have found that media influence varies with the age and stage of the audience, with evidence that effects are particularly strong on adolescents (Graber, 1997). Studies that look at how audiences develop knowledge of the world and make judgements about social issues (cultivation research) have found that effects are stronger on those with high rates of media consumption (Gerbner et al., 1994), although clear results are hard to prove with any accuracy or certainty.

There is also a body of research that examines media influence on political elites, arguing that this group is both more sensitive to media sources and more influential on society than the general public. In this context, stress has been placed on the agenda-setting role of the media (Funkhouser, 1973). Here the idea of a two-step communication process is sometimes used. The first step involves communication to key opinion formers, and the second, to the general public. However, critics have questioned the agenda-setting role ascribed to the media by this model (Brosius and Kepplinger, 1990). They argue that the issues picked up by the media do not spring out of thin air, but rather have already been highlighted by groups in civil society. In this chapter, in keeping with the sociological orientation of the volume, I shall concentrate on wider publics rather than elites. Now let us return to the question of the New Public.

In a major study of the New Public in the USA, Leon Mayhew describes the phenomenon as follows:

> In the New Public, communication is dominated by professional specialists. The techniques employed by these specialists are historically rooted in commercial promotion, but, beginning in the 1950s, rationalized techniques of persuasion born of advertising, market research, and public relations were systematically applied to political communication. As this movement took flight in the 1970s and exploded into the 1980s and the 1990s, political consultants, media specialists, public opinion pollsters, professional grassroots organisers, specialists in issues research, and demographic researchers burgeoned in numbers and established increasingly specialised roles. Political consultants now specialise in fields as narrow as strategies for countering negative advertising. The experts of the New Public have

brought us ... sound-bite journalism, thirty-second advertising, one-way communication, evasive spin control by public figures who refuse to answer questions, and the marketing of ideas and candidates by methods developed in commercial market research.

Mayhew, 1997, p.4

Perhaps the most obvious concern about the management and packaging of news and political communication is that it makes it very difficult for the public to access the evidence underlying media representations. However, this problem is endemic in any highly mediated society: it simply is not possible to check the veracity of the evidence behind every claim. Mayhew accepts this, and argues that in such societies much depends on the public's trust in sources of information. He sees the situation as analogous to the move from a barter to a cash economy, where the system of trade becomes so complex that exchanging goods directly becomes unwieldy; instead, a symbolic system is developed to represent the value of goods and hence facilitate exchange, namely money.

Political claims can analogously be seen as tokens, not of possession of goods to the value of the sum on the bank note, but rather of the ability to back up a claim with evidence, or to deliver on a promise, if called upon to do so. Such rhetorical tokens buy politicians influence. In order to function properly, such claims and promises need mostly to be accepted at face value, but on the understanding that behind these 'tokens' lie arguments or means that could be 'redeemed' if necessary. The problem with the New Public is that it erodes trust in such 'rhetorical tokens of influence', with the result that there is an 'inflation of influence'. In this situation, just as cash buys less in a high inflation economy, so the claims of politicians and other sources of political influence have less and less credibility, and trust in the political system as a whole may be undermined.

4.1 Politics, media and public concerns

Mayhew sees a number of processes as responsible for this lack of trust, stressing in particular the problem of political communication becoming disassociated from underlying issues of public concern. He presents examples of four processes that result in disassociation of political communication from public concerns. Firstly, in political campaigns there is a tendency for campaign issues to become divorced from broader issues of public concern. The latter might prove 'dangerous' for politicians to discuss, and so:

Polling and pre-testing are employed to determine what messages will appeal to which constituencies ... and what packaging of these messages will prove most persuasive. The methods of political consultants are intended to discover winning strategies, and it is apparent that this mode of issue selection and campaign design tends towards public discussion on manufactured, disassociated issues.

Mayhew, 1997, p.240

One example he discusses is the way in which prison parole policy became highlighted in the presidential contest between George Bush Sr. (Republican) and Michael Dukakis (Democrat) in 1988. The case of Willie Horton, a prisoner who committed a rape while on parole from a Massachusetts prison at the time Dukakis was Massachusetts governor, was picked up through focus group work by the Bush campaign as having strong resonance for undecided voters. They therefore decided to promote it as a campaign issue, even though parole policy was not a major issue before, nor has it been since in US public policy discussions (Mayhew, 1997, p.237).

The Horton case also illustrates a second disassociational process – that of symbols substituting for substantive policy discussion. Thus the broad and complex issue of crime and the treatment of criminals effectively became reduced to arguments about the Horton case in the 1988 campaign. Thirdly, various forms of narrowcasting, such as direct mailing, also provide parties with opportunities for political mobilisation that bypass processes of public debate. Fourthly, 'spin', or 'strategic rhetorical devices to avoid answering questions or objections directly', and 're-packaging' bad news to make it seem more palatable – serves to frustrate open public discussion (Mayhew, 1997, p.237).

Is there anything that can be done to counter the disassociational effects of the New Public? Mayhew argues that it is possible to provide 'forums for the redemption of rhetorical tokens', by which he means places and 'media spaces' where the claims of politicians and experts can be tested by the public. Some such forums already exist – for example, in a UK context, television programmes such as the BBC's *Question Time* (UK, BBC, 1979 to present), where audiences can ask questions of a panel of politicians – and these could be developed further.

Different kinds of spaces for discussion are possible. In his analysis, Mayhew distinguishes 'forums', where more than one standpoint is represented, from 'platforms', where a single position dominates. He further distinguishes between diffuse forums, third-party and citizen forums, and between moderated or indirect and direct debate. Diffuse forums provide a good opportunity for broad participation, but the lack of constraints makes it easy for leaders to evade demands for the redemption of tokens. Third-party forums are organised by independent groups and provide an opportunity for different sides to present their views, together with critical comment by a third party. Standard newspaper articles often follow this format.

Citizen forums enable the general public to quiz leaders, and have multiplied with the proliferation of talk shows in recent years. The fact that the questioners are not known to the public arguably facilitates concentration on the quality of argument rather than the prestige of the speaker. However, many talk shows narrowcast to a particular constituency, or focus on issues of little relevance to public policy. Indirect debate interposes a third-party questioner between antagonists, typified by US presidential debates. Direct debate is favoured by most of the US public but resisted by candidates, presumably because indirect debate means they can avoid persistent awkward questions from actual antagonists.

Mayhew also mentions the work of organisations like the Harwood Group and the National Issues Forum that aim to foster effective citizenship by providing training in public deliberation. But while such groups show that people are keen to reconnect with public issues and work together, there is little evidence they are effective at connecting with larger forums in the political system. However, Castells (1996, p.50) reports on work in cities in Brazil and Holland that provide some evidence of what can be achieved through citizen consultation and local self-management schemes that make use of electronic communications media. Mayhew himself reports on examples of 'public journalism' in the USA and Canada, where local papers report the proceedings of public discussions sponsored by the papers (Mayhew, 1997, p.263). Newspapers, television, radio and the internet can all be involved in creating public discussion forums, as well as in 'degrading' the quality of news and discussion, highlighting the ambivalent potential of media developments.

Activity 3.3

Our case study of the New Public has focused on the USA. Now take some time to consider whether you can think of any examples from a UK or other European context of the media processes that disassociate political communication from public concerns. Can you think of any examples that seek to reconnect the two, for example by providing what Mayhew (1997) calls a 'forum for the redemption of tokens of influence' in a European context? Lastly, do you see any evidence of tensions between reason- and culture-oriented models of the public sphere in this US case study? ■ ■ ■

The four processes, outlined by Mayhew, that disassociate political communication from public concerns, are:

1 differentiation of campaign issues from underlying issues of public concern;

2 substitution of symbols for substantive discussion;

3   narrowcasting to a specific audience that already agrees; and

4   spin, either evading direct questions or concealing 'negative' news.

It is difficult to think of political examples of these disassociational processes that are not controversial; however, one example of the first process (see above) is the UK Conservative party's framing of the debate on health spending in the early 1990s. This justified the need for rationing of health resources on the grounds of ever-increasing demand, but rarely was this put in the context of actual rates of growth of demand, or levels of taxation that would be required to meet it. In the interests of balance, I also thought of the UK Labour Party's emphasis on the amount of money they spent on the health service during their second term of office under Prime Minister Tony Blair (2001–2005), rather than on levels of improvement in services.

An example of point 2 above, substituting a symbol or rhetoric for substantive discussion, is *The Sun* newspaper's headline on the day of the 1992 UK General Election, 9 April. The headline stated: 'If Kinnock wins today will the last person to leave Britain please turn out the lights.' Arguably *The Sun* influenced undecided voters against the Labour Party's leader Neil Kinnock and affected the outcome of the election (see Figure 3.6). The next day, *The Sun* claimed it was '*The Sun* wot won it' for the Tories.

Concerning forums for the redemption of tokens of influence, we have already mentioned the BBC's *Question Time* as such a forum. The increase of radio phone-in discussions and Web discussions following television broadcasts provide further examples. Interactive television and the internet clearly provide opportunities for audiences to become publics by engaging in debate with politicians and other experts. But there are concerns over narrowcasting. In particular the narrow range of constituencies that participate in such forums is likely to lead to the exclusion of many groups. 'New Labour' (the UK Labour Party under the leadership of Tony Blair) has been accused of many cases of spin but perhaps one of the most notorious and controversial was the claim that Iraq, under its former President Saddam Hussain, possessed weapons of mass destruction that could be deployed internationally by missile at 45 minutes' notice. Whatever the origins and basis of the claim, it assumed a central role in convincing UK audiences undecided about the case for the 2003 invasion of Iraq, yet its credibility has been widely challenged.

Mayhew's idea of political rhetoric as tokens of influence that require forums for their redemption might be seen as going some way towards bridging the gap between reason-centred and culture-centred models of the public sphere. It recognises the role of culture in shaping the form of rhetorical and symbolic tokens and the inevitable role of these in politics

THE SUN

Thursday, April 9, 1992   25p   Today's TV: Pages 40 and 41   Audited daily sale for February 3,651,641

PHOTO FINISH

By TREVOR KAVANAGH
Political Editor

TORY hopes rose last night as opinion polls showed they were heading for a photo finish with Labour.

A Gallup poll for today's Daily Telegraph puts the Tories on 38.5 per cent, Labour 38 and the Liberal Democrats 20.

John Major's team

also had a 0.5 lead in the same survey last week.

Labour are on 39 in a Mori poll for The Times — just one point ahead of the Tories after having a seven-point lead last week.

An ICM poll for The Guardian shows Labour and Tories both on 38 points with the Lib-Dems on 20.

The same poll last week showed Labour four points ahead.

The polls confirm that millions of voters have waited until the last minute before making up their minds. Tory leaders believe they have won back wavering supporters who were

Continued on Page Two

If Kinnock wins today will the last person to leave Britain please turn out the lights

TENNIS CHAMP ASHE HAS AIDS

From ALLAN HALL
In New York

TENNIS legend Arthur Ashe has AIDS, it was revealed last night.

The former Wimbledon champ contracted the killer virus from blood he was given during a heart operation 12 years ago.

Ashe, 48, underwent quadruple bypass surgery before screening was introduced to avoid AIDS infection through transfusions.

Star

AIDS was diagnosed late last year and Ashe has been taking the drug AZT in an attempt to hold the virus at bay.

The star — first black man to win a Grand Slam tournament — is one of nearly 5,000 people in America under death sentence through tainted blood.

Ashe, married with a five-year-old daughter, reached the pinnacle of his career in 1975 when he beat Jimmy Connors to take the men's singles title at Wimbledon.

The fitness fanatic seemed to be in his physical prime before a heart attack struck him in 1979.

He was just 36 and ranked No 7 in the world.

Ashe, son of a Virginia policeman, had his op later that year.

It left a ten-inch scar

Continued on Page 13

ELECTION DAY SPECIAL

IT'S D-day folks — the day you make the big decision about who you want to run our great country.

You know our views on the subject but we don't want to influence you in your final judgment on

who will be Prime Minister.

But if it's a bald bloke with wispy red hair and two K's in his surname, we'll see you at the airport!

Goodnight and thank you for everything.

Figure 3.6 The front cover of The Sun, 9 April 1992 that is believed to have influenced floating voters in the general election

Source: The Sun, 9 April 1992

in highly mediated societies. Yet at the same time Mayhew argues that to avoid an inflationary spiral of influence, forums are needed for such tokens to be redeemed. Without such forums trust in the political system is likely to break down.

In the USA professional commercial communications techniques have developed alongside new communications technologies, and these techniques have been deployed and developed in political contexts. The rise of the New Public thus illustrates one example of the interaction between culture and technology, with ambivalent effects for democracy. Negatively, the public has become more fractured as news media diversify and become more dominated by commercial interests, while political debate can become disassociated from issues of public concern. However, new media also create opportunities to rearticulate public concerns with political debate, and greatly enhance the possible range of forums available for redemption of tokens of influence.

India, the first mass democracy to host electronic national elections in 2004, provides a quite different cultural context in which to consider the interaction between television, audiences and politics.

5 Televised religious epic and the public sphere in India

Arvind Rajagopal (2001) recounts the development of an Indian public created by the launch of the first national television network in the late 1980s, followed rapidly by the arrival of satellite television and the dismantling of state controls by 1992. In particular, he examines the relationship between the serialisation (in a mammoth 78 episodes) of the Hindu epic the *Ramayana* (India, Doordarshan, 1987–1990), from January 1987 to September 1990, and the rise to power of the Hindu nationalist Bharatiya Janata Party (BJP) through the 1990s (see Plate 3 in the colour section), achieving a consistent period in office from March 1998 to March 2004 (Rajagopal, 2001, pp.326, 275). The study sheds light on the impact of the introduction of new media 'before the rationalization of politics and the "disenchantment of society"' (Rajagopal, 2001, p.7). In spite of official secularism, the serial was broadcast by the state television station, Doordarshan, and authorised by the ruling Congress party in an attempt to improve the party's popularity by presenting an image of a harmonious India. Instead, by creating a national 'visual vocabulary' expressive of Hindu identity it provided the BJP with a powerful cultural resource that enabled the party to transform itself from a marginal political player into the party of government.

The new national Hindu visual regime derives its power from the way the epics established deep resonances with traditional religious practices (see Chapter 4, which looks at this more closely). In a striking example of media use by an active audience, television was incorporated into these religious practices:

> In my house, my grandmother would not eat before she watched it, just as she would not eat before her daily worship. And granny would take off her slippers and bow to Ram-ji before watching with great absorption. ...
>
> The family next door used to perform their ablutions and bathe before they watched the serial.
>
> Respondent in Rajagopal, 2001, p.138

The serial was the first to reach a mass audience of up to 100 million, and in doing so it brought together diverse publics that had previously resided 'across distinct language strata, media, and socio-cultural domains', especially across the audiences of different language newspapers and radio stations (Rajagopal, 2001, p.148). The serial presented a model of a past golden age in which 'authoritarianism' and 'complete mutual recognition between rulers and subjects' were miraculously combined (Rajagopal, 2001, p.149). In doing so it exposed the elitism and exclusivity of existing pan-Indian public spheres. By presenting a religiously legitimised alternative to India's secular republic, it revealed the narrowness of the social base on which state secularism rests: 'If secularism had been declared by state fiat, the power of new communications brought home the fact that secularism existed, willy-nilly, as largely the sign and exercise of membership in a cultural elite' (Rajagopal, 2001, p.149).

Thus the epic exposed fractures in contemporary society in the mirror of a mythical past. The BJP were able to contrast this golden age with present disorder as well as to intimate the possibility of a restoration and revival of this idealised past. This enabled them, in the absence of any clear policy agenda, to create a fragile coalition across a public that was deeply divided by caste and regional differences. In assembling this coalition the BJP were also inadvertently aided by the commercialisation of Hindu symbols and discourse triggered by the series and the follow-up *Mahabharata* (India, Doordarshan, 1988–1990), which reached an even wider audience (Rajagopal, 2001, p. 375).

While critics may dismiss these events as the opportunistic and cynical manipulation of religious enthusiasm by nationalist politicians, such criticisms ignore the widening of participation in politics that resulted, as evidenced by two distinct phenomena. Firstly, there has been the rise to positions of political power by individuals of low-caste background (Dalrymple, 1999, p.10). This has been possible partly because the BJP's populist campaigning created new alliances across some caste boundaries – although it is not inclusive of all Hindu groups, such as *dalits* (people of 'untouchable' or of 'low' caste background). Secondly, in reaction to the

BJP's populist appeal, political campaigning by other parties now actively seeks to engage with a much wider constituency across the electorate (Rajagopal, 2001, p.279).

Yet arguably the price to pay for this participation has been increased 'confusion' in political life and a lowering of the quality of public discussion. On the specific question of political violence, Rajagopal reports some appalling incidents connected to the rise of the BJP, and Purnima Mankekar argues specifically that the serial, the *Ramayana*, had a communally divisive effect: '[T]he discourses of culture, self and other constructed in the *Ramayan* seemed to have enabled most Hindu viewers I interviewed to consolidate their Hindu identity, and further, to naturalise the slippage between Indian and Hindu culture' (Mankekar, 2002, p.141).

The effect of this 'slippage' is to undermine the legitimacy of Sikh, Muslim and Christian culture within Indian society. However, in this respect the social role of the serial must be seen as a small part of a complex national process; indeed, Rajagopal contends that 'the level of communal violence under a BJP government has been lower than that under [the secular Indian] Congress [Party]' (Rajagopal, 2001, p.280).

The deterioration of political debate in India seems to parallel developments in the USA. This has involved more commercially oriented campaigns focusing on simple and emotive messages communicable by the televisual medium, and shallower support for political parties leading to intensified competition for floating voters (Mayhew, 1997). In the Indian context, however, a specific feature of induction into the mass televisual age has been the increased circulation of religious discourse and symbols. Rajagopal argues that this phenomenon is likely to outlast the success of the BJP, whose support is based on a fragile coalition of deeply divided groups. Thus he concludes:

> Even in the absence of Hindu nationalist domination then, we may have in India a Hinduized visual regime, evidenced for example in commodity consumption in daily life, acting as a kind of lower-order claim than national identity and continuing to have force in politics, albeit of a more dispersed, subtle and less confrontational kind, ... whereby social energy may be accumulated and stored via allegiance to such images, to be put to use at some future moment, though in ways that would be hard to predict.
>
> Rajagopal, 2001, p.283

Thus, as in the USA, the effects of media developments on democratic participation are ambivalent. The public sphere has been extended, enabling the political participation of more people than ever before; but at the same time secularism has been compromised, and the position of non-Hindu minorities undermined.

Such contemporary empirical public spheres are a long way from Habermas's ideal, yet they have become more inclusive than Habermas's bourgeois public sphere ever was; it would seem that the culture-oriented public sphere has grown at the expense of the reason-oriented public sphere. We now turn to the third and final case study, which examines the political consequences of the interaction between television and audiences in the politically polarised context of Israel/Palestine.

6 Interpreting television news in a conflict zone: Israel/Palestine

This case study is based around Tamar Liebes's (1997) work on the reception of television news in Israel and Palestine up to 1995, when the state monopoly on television news broadcast ended. This monopoly situation is important because it shows how, even without significant diversification of news media, audience reception can make a huge difference to how the same broadcast message is understood, and can result in the ongoing transmission (to younger generations) of ever more divergent political perspectives.

The complex context of the Palestinian–Israeli conflict requires a brief historical introduction (see Figure 3.7). The origins of the current conflict can be traced back to the mid-nineteenth century and the failure of Jewish emancipation in Eastern Europe. The success of nationalist movements in establishing new nation states in Europe (for example, Germany, Italy) led some Jews to think that a national homeland was desirable and possible (Zionism). A small flow of Jewish immigration to Palestine began. The immigrants chose Palestine because of the historical and religious association of the Jewish people with this territory. By beginning of the twentieth century, the nationalist or Zionist movement had developed a powerful organisational basis.

The British Mandate (1921–48) allowed for the development of a Zionist infrastructure in Palestine that was eventually to form the basis of the Israeli state. During this period Jewish immigration greatly increased, especially in the 1930s, due to Hitler's expansion in Europe and persecution of Jews. This influx led to increasing tensions and conflict with Arab Palestinians. The end of the Second World War (1939–45), and revelation of the full horror of Hitler's 'Final Solution', led both to large numbers of surviving European Jews emigrating to Palestine, and to European and US sympathy for the Zionist cause. Britain turned the situation over to the newly formed United Nations, which suggested partitioning Palestine between Jewish and Arab zones (1947).

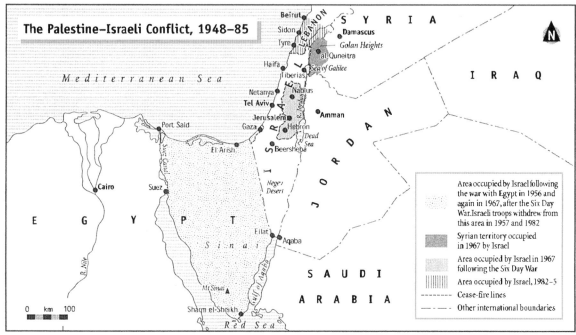

Figure 3.7 *The Palestine–Israeli conflict from 1948 to 1985*
Source: Cohn-Sherbok and El-Alami, 2002, p.2

This arrangement was rejected by the Palestinians, who, in spite of being the majority of the population, were left with a smaller share of the land. The end of the British mandate in 1948 led to the declaration of independence by Israel and to declarations of war on the new state by surrounding Arab nations. In the ensuing conflict more Palestinians were displaced, so that by the cessation of hostilities and Israeli victory in 1949, some 700,000 had fled to neighbouring countries (Shlaim, 2000). These events, known as *al-Nakhba* ('the disaster') to the Arabs, are at the root of the present conflict. In 1967, in response to security threats from neighbouring Arab countries, Israel invaded the West Bank and Gaza, bringing a further million Palestinians under their control in what became 'the occupied territories'. In 1987, following the expulsion of the main Palestinian nationalist movement, the PLO (Palestine Liberation Organisation), from the neighbouring Lebanon, the first Palestinian *intifada* (Arabic for 'uprising') began. Ended temporarily by the Oslo Peace Accord of 1993, it erupted again in 2000 following the stalling of progress towards limited Palestinian independence.

Israel is constitutionally democratic, but many rights – for example voting rights – do not apply to Arabs in the occupied territories. The media comprises a mixture of public and private producers that compares with western European norms, but the security situation, identification of the IDF (Israel Defence Force) with the Zionist cause, and a widespread consensus amongst Jewish Israelis on Zionist ideology, means that what

Liebes describes as a process of 'soft hegemony' is at work. Hegemony refers to 'the internalization of a "lived system of meanings and values" of a dominant culture through which people experience reality and see themselves' (Liebes, 1997, p.1, quoting Raymond Williams).

'Soft hegemony' is seen as entwined within a culture rather than imposed from above. Media institutions are deeply embroiled in the reproduction of cultural identities ('us') and differences ('them'). In reporting the first Palestinian *intifada*, four specific constraints tended towards the production of an 'us and them' framing of the conflict (Liebes, 1997, pp.2–6):

1   Situational/technical limitations: reporters were forced, literally, to one side or other in an armed conflict. For example, some Jewish reporters began by presenting Palestinian perspectives in the interests of balance but escalating attacks on them by Palestinians made this more and more hazardous, resulting in an increasingly one-sided view.

2   Political identifications: many journalists and publishers were active in the Zionist movement. Some commuted between their roles as journalist and politician, and political views tended to harden as the conflict proceeded.

3   Self-censorship: journalists are constrained in what they write by many factors – not least the increasingly commercialised media environment in which media organisations are controlled by a small number of private interests.

4   Political censorship: criticisms of the IDF are especially problematic, given its role as 'a central symbol in the civil religion of Israeli society', and the wide participation of Israeli citizens in the force (Liebes, 1997, p.5).

These constraints led to the production of an increasingly polarised picture of the conflict, which Liebes shows to be present across both print and electronic media. The issue addressed in the first part of Reading 3.1 is how this dominant media framing impacts on viewers' perceptions of the conflict, and how they respond to that media frame. Liebes conducted a study of family reception of the evening news at a time (before 1995) when there was just one channel showing news on Israeli television, and this often became the focus of family viewing, leading to discussion of news items. Generational patterns were a particular focus of the study.

The family featured in Reading 3.1 is one in which the parents have different views of the conflict. Thus the father is described as 'a hawk'; that is, he accepts the dominant media framing of Palestinians as hostile 'others'. In contrast, the mother is a 'dove', feeling that the media misrepresent Palestinians by focusing on the conflict. This example thus raises the question of which viewpoint is more effectively reproduced socially; that is, passed on to the children. The second part of Reading 3.1 ('How the news reinforces the attribution error of viewers') discusses why 'doves' find it more difficult than 'hawks' to transmit their view of the conflict to their children.

Reading 3.1 Activity

This exercise is based around two extracts from Tamar Liebes's study 'Reporting the Arab–Israeli conflict' (Reading 3.1). Read the extract now and jot down answers to the following questions as you read:

- What are the elements in Mrs Dekel's commentary on that night's news that could be described as 'referential' (that is, that relate to the news as 'real') and/or 'constructional' (that is, that relate to the news as a construction)?
- How does Mrs Dekel's reading of the news differ from that of her husband and daughter?
- How did television contribute to the perception of terrorism as intrinsic to Arabs, and of Arabs as 'bad', among Israeli viewers?

Reading 3.1

Tamar Liebes, 'Reporting the Arab–Israeli conflict'

The Dekels: a family profile

The Dekels (a fictitious name) are one of a subsample of families drawn from a survey of closed interviews with a representative sample of 400 Jewish families (parent and adolescent-child couples) in Jerusalem, in which we studied patterns of news viewing (including family interaction about the news), attitudes towards the news media, and political outlooks.

A subsample of 52 of those families was observed while viewing the news, commenting on it, and responding as a group to several open-ended questions we addressed to them. One of these families was the Dekel family, whom we visited at home, to join in their viewing of the evening news, and to record the subsequent family discussion, which we facilitated by occasional probing and by keeping the conversation to the news when it wandered off. Our aim was to simulate, albeit more intensively [...] everyday conversations related to the news, of the sort that might transpire often.

The Dekels are second-generation Israelis of Syrian origin. Mr Dekel is a carpenter and Mrs Dekel is an elementary schoolteacher. They have two children – Amnon, who was at the time serving in the Israeli army, and 14-year-old Yaffa.

The Dekel family may represent what the survey showed to be a dominant pattern in Israeli society. According to this pattern, although 'ideological reproduction' (of parents producing their political outlooks in their children) exists, hawkish parents stand a better chance of socializing children with a similar outlook to their own. Accordingly, in the Dekel family, while Mrs Dekel is ready to compromise with the Palestinians, her daughters are not.

In terms of attitudes toward the news, Mr and Mrs Dekel belong to the group we called 'deniers' – that is, people who believe the news is credible but nonetheless support censorship. [...] The deniers – those who believe in the news but would prefer not to see it – are people who would rather see a positive image of 'us' on the screen than worry about the check public exposure may exercise on the absolute power of the political institutions. Deniers believe that 'on stage' it is important to present harmony – preferably 'good news' – while the actual management of the affairs of the state goes on anyway, as it should 'behind the scenes'.

The Dekels: a family conversation

On the evening of our visit, at the time of the intifada, the conflict dominated the news agenda, as on most evenings. There was, however, no direct Palestinian–Israeli confrontation to be seen on the screen. Instead, the news resounded with the internal ramifications of the conflict in two contrasting trials of political extremists: one reported the conviction of an Israeli settler in the occupied territories for the murder of a Palestinian; the other concerned the continuation of a court case against a Jewish leftist newspaper team, accused of affiliation with a Palestinian terrorist organization. An item covering a ceremonial visit of the Knesset Committee for Internal Affairs to the Dome of the Rock, in the Arab part of Jerusalem, also implying a disruptive potential, represents the more consensual expression of attitudes toward the conflict in Israeli society.

Palestinians on television news are not representative: an attempt to read oppositionally

The absence from the screen of violent incidents between Israeli soldiers or settlers and Palestinian uprisers was immediately remarked upon, at the end of the broadcast, by the greatly relieved mother: 'That's already a good sign ... good news...'. That Mrs Dekel feels she has to comment first on what was *absent* in the broadcast indicates that she measures what she sees in the light of a pre-existing scheme of expectations [...] provided no doubt by the daily menu of intifada news. Labeling the missing item as 'good news' is also an expression of the mother's basic trust in the newsmakers, that is, she does not suspect them of omitting newsworthy incidents – editing out items potentially harmful for public morale, for example. Thus, in noting the absence of intifada clashes, Mrs Dekel seems to assume, the way most of us would, that if it was not on television it certainly did not happen. In other words, this would mean she is relating to the news as 'real' (or 'referential') rather than as 'constructed' [...]

However, a little later in the conversation, after the first spontaneous expression of relief had been made, Mrs Dekel brings up two more possible reasons for the omission of the intifada, in what may be regarded as a less 'naïve', more sophisticated reading. Her two remarks, which we classify as *constructional*, point to possible generic and institutional constraints in the construction of reality. The first recalls journalistic norms according to which once violent incidents have become routine (and provided the level of violence does not escalate they are no longer newsworthy). 'They (journalists),' says Mrs Dekel, 'got used to the situation ... they are not reporting much any more ...'. Her second explanation brings up the possibility of intervention of the political establishment in the workings of reporters: 'Maybe it's because it is now forbidden to take photographs, that they banned journalists from there: perhaps that's the reason.'

[...]

Substantively, the two *constructional* reasons offered by Mrs Dekel for the lack of intifada stories resemble similar conclusions reached by media scholars [...] and by political analysts in the press, and though they might have been triggered by the presence of an observer [...] the potential is still there. Nevertheless, it should not be ignored that while media scholars would be damningly critical of both routinizing violence and censoring it, Mrs Dekel, judging from everything she says, did not think that an evening with no intifada was a bad idea either way. As a compromiser who believes that news represents reality she found it difficult to argue her case if that was what reality looks like.

Unlike her mother, teenage Yaffa is quite happy at this point to take television at face value, that is as *real*. 'It (the intifada) may have calmed down', she suggests. But Mr Dekel discards the daily variations as insignificant, though still assuming a fit between the lack of coverage and the parameters of reality: 'Not every marginal incident can be broadcast on the news. Does every little thing, like if they threw a stone, have to be put in the beginning of the newscast? Not everything can be reported.'

Note how Mr Dekel adopts the anonymous, depersonalized 'they', established [...] by television's framing, to identify the stone throwers. This vagueness of the generalized 'they' is used not only to plead ignorance, or to deny contact [...], but to deny the specificity of blame and to incriminate a collectivity.

The different readings revealed in the discourse of mother, daughter, and father about the missing intifada may also be examined in light of their different political outlooks and their attitudes to authority. Mr Dekel, who expresses his belief that what is shown should be strictly controlled, is not disturbed by *not* seeing what he believes *does* exist; Yaffa prefers to stick to a naïve reading, which assumes the transparency of the news; Mrs Dekel emerges as the family's ambivalent viewer. She is relieved at not seeing the intifada which she finds emotionally stressful and ideologically problematic but, on second thought, she struggles against her own tendency to deny reality by doubting the truth of her own first reaction.

Continuing to commute between her original trust in journalists and her unease with what she sees, she is critical when considering intifada coverage on other evenings. Television, she protests, distorts reality by exaggerating Arab violence:

> It's not exactly like they are telling it; they [most viewers] think it's [like that] all the time. ... Once when they were placing explosives in Jerusalem, people from Tel-Aviv and Natanya were saying 'In Jerusalem? It's war there!' ... So I don't know, but my feeling is that it's not so serious. They are just sensationalizing [inflating matters too much].

Interestingly, Mrs Dekel is worried about the influence of television news *on others;* [...] The argument of protecting other, more vulnerable, viewers is often employed by advocates of censorship, who have full confidence in their own resilience.

Thus, Mrs Dekel would not be affected, as she knows, from her own experience, that most Arabs are law-abiding, peaceful, and hardworking. Unfortunately, this silent majority never appears on television. Her point, as it appears in the family discussion, is to convince others (notably her daughter) that not all Arabs are as 'bad' as they seem to be on television. Mrs Dekel, as it were, is trying to do no less than fight against the 'us and them' representation of the conflict.

> I think not all of them are terrorists or stone throwers, and not all of them burn tyres, and altogether they are human beings, people who want to live ... And they feel very uncomfortable. They work, these people, this family, and there are other families I know who work. They are feeling very uncomfortable in this situation. They have to get out and go to work, despite all the threats, and their children haven't been to school until now, and they want to live. And I believe them. I believe all those who say

that they would like to live with us. If there are some hotheads, it doesn't mean that they are all like that.

As is evident in this statement, Mrs Dekel is attempting the impossible. She is fighting television's stereotypes by juxtaposing them with another source of knowledge – her own personal encounters. Contrasting one's own experience with what is seen on the screen is one tactic employed by doves in their attempt to modify the black-and-white presentation of conflict.

As they seek compromise, doves have to assume that if in our camp some are good and some bad, the same must hold true for the other side. Mobilizing evidence from one's own experience as an illustration for this idea is a less analytic, more intuitive, way to make that point. It could be argued that this is trying to beat television at its own game (of personalizing processes and situations).

[...]

Mrs Dekel [...] is aware that her husband and daughter are staunch believers, comfortable in arguing that television's framing of the other side *is* representative, that is, that the Arabs *are* violent. Perceiving the news as *real,* she fears, leads them to perceive the conflict as hopelessly insoluble, and as more extreme than it really is. This perception, in turn, she senses, would cause an escalation in the real-life conflict. Being an ideological dove motivates Mrs Dekel to wish that television would show the other in a variety of roles, not only in the role of enemy. But the acceptance that this is unrealistic – that is, that everyday roles of the enemy do not make news – brings her to support censorship. The second-best thing to showing the real, multidimensional, picture is to show less hostility.

[...]

How the news reinforces the attribution error of viewers

The us-and-them rhetoric of televised conflict makes it easy for viewers to commit what social psychologists describe as the fundamental attribution error. The main claim of attribution theory, in its classic version, is that people tend to attribute their own failures to external (situational) causes, and failures of others to internal (dispositional) causes [...]

[W]e [tend to] explain other people's behaviour in the same way in which we understand the plot of a dramatic play. In both, our knowledge of the rules and roles we associate with a certain social context applies to understanding and predicting behaviour. [...]

In the case of the intifada, Israeli television's presentation constrains viewers to attribute situational reasons to the soldiers' behaviour, and dispositional reasons to protestors' [...]. Soldiers perform their role in an institutional context; Palestinians are individually responsible [...]. The process whereby television reinforced the fundamental attribution error during the intifada worked in the following way [...]. Compared to our [Israeli] side, (1) Arabs were shown almost only in their role within the script of the conflict, the most newsworthy context from the point of view of journalistic function and dramatic attributes. (2) In this script, well recognized by viewers, Arabs appeared as 'terrorists,' represented stereotypically as the stone-throwing youth, his face covered with a *kaffia,* so as not to be identifiable. Choosing to be 'faceless' in order to protect himself, also made him threatening, inhuman, almost a demonic figure. Viewers could not see him as the young person he is. (3) For most Israelis, and even more so for children, television is the only source of acquaintance with Arabs, whose image on television merges with that of 'terrorists.' (4) The 'terrorist' script portrays arbitrary violence, causing suffering to innocent victims [...]. Hardly shown is the human suffering on the Arab side and the situational or ideological context within which rioting might make sense. Thus, in terms of the attribution error, television contributed to the perception of terrorism as intrinsic to Arabs and helped viewers to think of Arabs as 'bad'.

Of course, in the context of clashes between stone throwers and the army, Israeli soldiers are seen as no less violent but 'we' are much less likely to be perceived as inherently bad. After all, (1) 'we' know ourselves not only through television – every Israeli man is a soldier himself, or the parent or son of a soldier – and we know the external context that 'justifies' our behaviour; (2) moreover, television helps by showing 'us' not only in the role of 'soldiers' but also in the private role of family members, who are victims of the violence; and (3) the ceremonies that accompany those personal tragedies are used to lend meaning to sacrifice in terms of the national ideology.

This asymmetrical picture is not so different from viewers' own perceptions. Reinforced by what is shown on television, Israelis are familiar with their own side, of course. Many are also aware, from personal experience, of the moral dissonance experienced by Israeli soldiers and the human tragedies that result from this unease. They have no personal experience with the parallel context on the other side, however. The resulting framing of the reality of the conflict is therefore, similarly to its framing on screen, dichotomized into the 'we' who are pressured by external circumstances into acting immorally, and 'they' who must be inherently bad, because that's the way they are.

Reading source

Liebes, 1997, pp.82–100 ■ ■ ■

Figure 3.8 *The aftermath of a bus bomb in Jerusalem in February 1996. The Islamic fundamentalist Hamas organisation claimed responsibility for the attack, which killed 23 Israelis*
Source: AFP/Getty Images

In the above reading, the night's news did not feature any incidents of Palestinian violence (see Figure 3.8). Mrs Dekel at first responds by describing this as 'good news', which is a referential reading, assuming that the news refers directly to reality so that if no violence is represented this means that no violence occurred. However, she then qualifies this view with two further possible interpretations. Firstly, 'They [journalists] got used to the situation ... they are not reporting it any more.' This shows awareness that the news might not represent reality because it is shaped by journalistic interests: in this case, a continued conflict ceases to be news unless there are new developments. Secondly, she suggests 'Maybe it's because ... they banned journalists.' This shows awareness that political constraints influence the news, because there is control over the movements of journalists. Thus news content is constructed in response to external constraints, as well as shaped by the bias of the reporter (an ideological constraint).

Mrs Dekel is uncomfortable with the news because, although she believes that what is reported is true, she also believes that it is only part of the truth and that the positive aspects of Palestinian life and Palestinian–Israeli interaction are neglected because they are less exciting and hence less newsworthy. She believes that this partiality will lead other Jews to have an unfairly negative view of Palestinians, which in turn will fuel the conflict. In contrast, her daughter Yaffa accepts the reality of the television presentation, responding to the exceptions to the violent images of Palestinians that her mother presents by arguing that only 'Ten percent are like that'. She is resistant to any challenges to television's representation of the situation, including her own personal experience: 'it's enough to hear about them on television'. Like his daughter, Mr Dekel accepts the televisual framing of the conflict, but he does not expect this to be strictly representative: thus while Yaffa suggests 'It may have calmed down,' Mr Dekel responds that 'Not everything can be reported.'

Mr and Mrs Dekel support censorship for different reasons. Mr Dekel supports censorship because he does not want negative images of Israeli forces to be portrayed domestically (for morale) or internationally (to maintain international support). In contrast, Mrs Dekel wants to restrict negative images of Palestinians, because she believes that these fuel the conflict. However, at another level, Mr and Mrs Dekel's support for censorship is based on the same evaluation of the news as accurate (referential readings), but both prefer not to see the different aspects of the truth that they find unpalatable. For this reason Liebes calls such viewers 'deniers'.

The first passage hints at some reasons for this. The most obvious answer is that, since the dominant television presentation presents the conflict in polarised terms, this fits better with the hawks' worldview. Doves always face the uphill struggle of pointing to evidence beyond the televisual frame, either in terms of the production of television presentations or of life beyond the world captured on camera. That this constructed television world is so persuasive – powerfully 'personalizing processes and situations' – is another reason. But the second part of the reading (on attribution errors) presents a further explanation, derived from observations of the social psychology of perception. This is the 'attribution error', which means that there is a tendency to attribute negative aspects of one's own behaviour to external and temporary sources, but the negative behaviour of others to internal and permanent sources, that is, their character. In the Israeli case, television news reinforces this by presenting mostly negative images of Palestinians as violent, while the increasing social separation of Israelis on security grounds reduces opportunities to challenge these stereotypes.

All these factors militate against doves passing on their views to their children because this requires the energy and skills continually to decode news sources. Indeed, the study concludes that 'during the intifada years, the only chance doves had to reproduce ideologically similar children was when they were highly educated' (Liebes, 1997, p.106). Among Israeli Arabs, the study found a mirror image of the Jewish sample, in which hawkish viewers of the Israeli news simply inverted the polarity of the media frame, seeing the 'truth [as] … deduced from what is absent from the screen' (Liebes, 1997, p.8). In contrast, moderates on both sides faced an uphill struggle in constructing more complex frames and hence in transmitting these to the younger generation, who have therefore tended to become more extreme on both sides.

Thus this Israeli case study illustrates some of the complexity of audience interpretation, and how this may feed back into political processes. In this case a public sphere with many of the elements of plurality associated with western democracies has been progressively polarised by conflict (see Figure 3.9). The media, or more precisely, television news, has reinforced this process not primarily through censorship by the Israeli regime, but rather through structural constraints acting on journalists that have produced a polarised presentation of the conflict and the dehumanisation of the Palestinian 'other'. This frame for viewing the conflict can be contested by both Jewish and Palestinian moderates, but these groups have difficulties in transmitting their views to the next generation, resulting in increased polarisation and its political consequences.

But what implications does this case study have for our themes of the impact of media diversification and changing media forms on the creation of shared publics? And how does it relate to the tensions we have explored between culture-oriented and reason-oriented models of

Figure 3.9 *Palestinian boys search through the rubble of a Palestinian house in the Gaza Strip, bulldozed by Israeli forces*
Source: Abid Katib/Getty Images

the public sphere? The case study shows that, due in part to attribution error, audiences can reach utterly different readings of a common source, even prior to significant media diversification. Our other case studies suggest that polarisation is likely to increase further once a wider range of sources is available. It also suggests that the sense of immediacy created by television is misleading, because images can be read in quite different ways. Furthermore, the conversation of the viewers illustrates the extent to which reason is shaped by culture and individual interpretation, as viewers produce quite sophisticated and reasoned but utterly different analyses of a common source.

7 Conclusion: technological convergence, media diversification and media publics

The spiritual and cultural reservations that the Oriental peoples may have toward our technology will avail them not at all. The effects of technology do not occur at the level of opinions or concepts, but alter sense ratios or patterns of perception steadily and without resistance.

McLuhan, cited in Starrett, 1998, p.87

The suicide warriors who attacked Washington and New York on September 11, 2001, did more than kill thousands of civilians and demolish the World Trade Center. They destroyed the West's ruling myth.

Western societies are governed by the belief that modernity is a single condition, everywhere the same and always benign. As societies become more modern so they become more alike. ... Being modern means realising *our* values – the values of the Enlightenment, as we like to think of them.

Gray, 2003, p.1

These two quotations present different perspectives on the central issue that has been examined in this chapter: the kind of effects that increasing exposure to globally shared communications media will have on the formation of media publics and hence on the prospects for democracy. Both authors convey the idea that exposure to modern media will produce cultural convergence, but while early media theorist Marshall McLuhan supports this idea because of the powerful sensory effects of technology, philosopher John Gray argues that the events of '9/11' (the terrorist attack on the USA on September 11 2001) have dramatically proven this view false.

Our case studies suggest that each is partly right and partly wrong. McLuhan is right that the introduction of new media into non-western cultures has had effects that are not mediated through the filter of rational argument. Rather, new circuits of meaning that have challenged traditional authorities and created new and chaotic public spheres have developed; for example, the challenging of traditional caste loyalties by Hindu populism in India. In highly mediated societies, hierarchical structures of authority are more difficult to sustain, and authority comes to rest in the media product and its mobilisation.

However, the Indian case study also shows that 'the medium is not the only message' (Starrett, 1998, p.93, referring to McLuhan's famous phrase 'the medium is the message'). For in India new media have enabled an intensification of competition based around indigenous religious symbols and discourse, rather than producing a secularisation of public life. So Gray, too, is both right and wrong. Contrary to Gray's assertions, societies do become more alike in some ways (for example, in the problems expanded public spheres cause for maintaining the monopolies of dominant elites), but Gray is right that this does not necessarily entail a convergence of liberal values.

While societies are becoming more alike in their media interconnectedness, this convergence is not replicated culturally or ideologically. The example of Israeli television shows how, in a conflict situation, a television programme designed in part to promote ideological convergence can have the reverse effect because of the dynamics of audience response, a divisive effect that has deepened across the generations.

But the New Public in the USA suggests that western public spheres, like those in Asia and the Middle East, are also becoming more chaotic as well as more populist. Indeed, the disassociation of political discourse from public concerns by substituting symbols for policy discussion can be seen both in the USA and in India. In both cases, the range of opportunities (forums) for participation is also widening but the political sphere is becoming more fragmented and, as visual and aural media increasingly predominate over print, so, arguably, opportunities for developing public debate diminish.

The increasing interconnection of societies through the media means that we live in a world in which, in the words of anthropologist Clifford Geertz (1983, p.234) 'no-one is leaving anyone else alone and isn't ever again going to'. Yet increasing iconic familiarity – that is, in terms of the transnational circulation of cultural symbols, whether through circuits of news, advertising or markets – does not necessarily translate easily into 'multi-cultural competence', the ability to negotiate cultural difference (Jackson and Nesbitt, 1992); on the contrary, it can rather increase polarisation.

Our examination of media–public interactions in several national contexts suggests that the challenge this presents for democracy is to find ways to balance the popularising effects of increased mediation with the creation of forums for the redemption of tokens of influence, which, as the US case study shows, can take many forms. These would enable critical scrutiny of the claims of both politicians and populist discourses, and provide a crucial balance between reason-oriented and culture-oriented public spheres.

Further reading

Ginsburg, F., Abu-Lughod, L., and Larkin, B. (eds) (2002) *Media Worlds: Anthropology on New Terrain*, Berkeley and London, University of California Press. Collection of essays that examines the many uses that audiences from across the world make of new media. Case studies include the USA, Thailand, Tibet, India and China.

Mayhew, L. (1997) *The New Public: Professional Communication and the Means of Social Influence*, Cambridge, Cambridge University Press. Study of how television and the professional communications industry has influenced democracy in the USA. Examines ways to improve public debate.

McGuigan, J. (2002) 'The public sphere' in Hamilton, P. and Thompson, K. (eds) *The Uses of Sociology*, Oxford, Blackwell/The Open University. This useful essay introduces and examines Habermas's concept of the public sphere in a clear and systematic way.

Rajagopal, A. (2001) *Politics After Television: Hindu Nationalism and the Reshaping of the Public in India*, Cambridge, Cambridge University Press. Study of how television, through the Hindu epics, has influenced politics in India.

References

Benhabib, S. (1992) 'Models of public space: Hannah Arendt, the liberal tradition, and Jürgen Habermas' in Calhoun, C. (ed.) *Habermas and the Public Sphere*, Cambridge, MA, MIT Press.

Brosius, H. and Kepplinger, H. (1990) 'The agenda setting function of television news: static and dynamic views', *Communication Research*, vol.17, no.2, pp.183–211.

Castells, M. (1996) *The Rise of the Network Society*, Oxford, Blackwell.

Cohn-Sherbok, D. and El-Alami, D. (2002) *The Palestine–Israeli Conflict: A Beginner's Guide*, Oxford, One World.

Croteau, D. and Hoynes, W. (2003) *Media/Society: Industries, Images and Audiences* (2nd edn), London, Sage.

Dalrymple, W. (1999) *The Age of Kali: Indian Travels and Encounters*, London, Flamingo.

Fraser, N. (1992) 'Rethinking the public sphere: a contribution to the critique of actually existing democracy' in Calhoun, C. (ed.) *Habermas and the Public Sphere*, Cambridge, MA, MIT Press.

Funkhouser, R. (1973) 'The issues of the sixties: an exploratory study in the dynamics of public opinion', *Public Opinion Quarterly*, vol.66, pp.942–66.

Garnham, N. (2000) *Emancipation, the Media, and Modernity: Arguments about the Media and Social Theory*, Oxford, Oxford University Press

Geertz, C. (1983) *Local Knowledge*, New York, Basic Books.

Gerbner, G., Gross, L., Morgan, M. and Signorielli, N. (1994) 'Growing up with television: the cultivation perspective' in Bryant, J. and Zillman, D. (eds) *Media Effects: Advances in Theory and Research*, Hillsdale, NJ, Lawrence Erlbaum.

Germond, J. and Witcover, J. (1989) *Whose Broad Stripes and Bright Stars: The Trivial Pursuit of the Presidency*, New York, Warner.

Graber, D. (1997) *Mass Media and American Politics* (5th edn), Washington, DC, Congressional Quarterly Press.

Gray, J. (2003) *Al-Qaeda and What it Means to be Modern*, London, Faber.

Greider, W. (1992) *Who Will Tell the People? The Betrayal of American Democracy*, New York, Simon and Schuster.

Habermas, J. (1987) *Theory of Communicative Action Vol. 2: Lifeworld and System: A Critique of Functionalist Reason*, Cambridge, Polity/Blackwell.

Habermas, J. (1989/1962) *The Structural Transformation of the Public Sphere* (trans. T. Burger and F. Lawrence), Cambridge, Polity.

Habermas, J. (1996/1992) *Between Facts and Norms* (trans. W. Rehg), Cambridge, Polity.

Jackson, R. and Nesbitt, E. (1992) *Hindu Children in Britain*, London, Trentham.

Liebes, T. (1997) *Reporting the Arab-Israeli Conflict*, London, Routledge.

Mankekar, P. (2002) 'Epic contests: television and religious identity in India' in Ginsburg, F., Abu-Lughod, L. and Larkin, B. (eds) *Media Worlds: Anthropology on a New Terrain*, Berkeley and London, CA, University of California Press.

Mayhew, L. (1997) *The New Public: Professional Communication and the Means of Social Influence*, Cambridge, Cambridge University Press.

McGuigan, J. (2002) 'The public sphere' in Hamilton, P. and Thompson, K. (eds) *The Uses of Sociology*, Oxford, Blackwell/The Open University.

Rajagopal, A. (2001) *Politics After Television: Hindu Nationalism and the Reshaping of the Public in India*, Cambridge, Cambridge University Press.

Schudson, M. (1993) 'Was there ever a public sphere? If so, when? Reflections on the American case' in Calhoun, C. (ed.) (1993) *Habermas and the Public Sphere*, Cambridge, MA, MIT Press.

Shlaim, A. (2000) *The Iron Wall: Israel and the Arab World*, London, Penguin.

Starrett, G. (1998) *Putting Islam to Work: Education, Politics and Religious Transformation in Egypt*, Berkeley, Los Angeles, CA, and London, University of California Press.

van der Veer, P. (1999) 'The moral state: religion, nation and empire in Victorian Britain and British India' in van der Veer, P. and Lehmann, H. (eds) *Nation and Religion: Perspectives on Europe and Asia*, Princeton, NJ, Princeton University Press.

Television drama and audience ethnography

Marie Gillespie

Contents

1   Introduction

An anecdote circulates among students of anthropology about a tribe of nomads in North Africa whose annual migration, since time immemorial, always took place in the same season. The story goes that, with the advent of television, they became so enthralled with the US drama serial *Dallas* (USA, CBS, 1978–1991) (see Figure 4.1) that they delayed their migration in order not to miss the final episodes (Miller, 1993, p.163).

This story may be apocryphal but it signifies how the world is changing, or at least how we imagine the world is changing, as a result of the ways in which media circulate around the globe today. Television brings different cultures and ways of life into our living rooms. It portrays values and beliefs that may be different from our own, offers vicarious experience and reshapes our routines. For this tribe of nomads, as for many of us, drama serials like *Dallas* offer many pleasures and each episode leaves us with a compelling desire to discover what happens next and how the story will end.

Television is a cultural resource that can be used in empowering ways. We can use it to acquire a knowledge and understanding of ourselves, others and the world around us. We negotiate changing values, beliefs and our sense of identity in an ongoing dialogue with television stories. We interweave our talk about television with our own personal and social experiences, and the ways in which we talk about television reveal a lot about who we are, what we believe and the influence of television in our lives.

However, although television may empower us, it also exerts power over us. Television contributes to regulating identities, creating (and conflating) 'good' citizens and consumers. It constructs and promotes certain ideas, identities and lifestyles and can fix and reproduce ethnic or national stereotypes. It may just as easily reinforce power relations and social inequalities as challenge them. What its effects and uses may be are questions that are best researched empirically in particular contexts of use. In this chapter we will examine questions of media effects (what the media do to audiences) and uses (what audiences do with media), and show how these two questions belong to quite distinct research traditions.

In some parts of the world, in India and Egypt for example, state television is used as a tool of economic and political development. Television producers, quite self-consciously, promote the identities that, they believe, will support their particular vision of development. They do so without necessarily instigating democratic challenges to ruling elites, even if the outcomes of some projects contribute to processes of democratisation. In contrast, smaller countries, like Trinidad, that do not have a strong television production base, are unable to produce enough

Figure 4.1 *The Ewing clan. The main characters in the television serial,* Dallas, *which began screening on the US television network, CBS, in 1978*

of their own television programmes and so import cheap US television programmes to fill their schedules. Arguably, they also import US values and ways of life.

So how do audiences in Trinidad actually respond to US television imports? How do audiences in India and Egypt respond to state television projects aimed at national integration or modernisation? What kinds of power does television exert over us and/or through us? In what ways might we be empowered by television? And what kinds of theoretical frameworks and methods of research might help us begin to find answers to these questions?

This chapter will explore these questions through a detailed examination of three ethnographic case studies of particular audiences in Trinidad, India and Egypt. Ethnographic studies are based on lengthy participation in, and observations of, the everyday lives of people in particular places. Ethnographies of audiences are very detailed accounts of the media and cultural worlds that people inhabit, from the point of view of the audiences themselves. Ethnography is a valuable and demanding research method that enables us to explore how television experiences are embedded in everyday lives and relationships, including the wider power relationships that envelop us.

In this chapter we focus on one of the most popular forms of television – serial drama. Drama serials have, for a long time, occupied a great deal of time and space in television schedules everywhere. Alongside news and comedy programmes, they have constituted the staple diet of national broadcasting systems around the world. They encompass a wide range of types of programmes, including soap operas, and take very different national and cultural forms, despite sharing certain storytelling features. All serials recount one story, albeit with a complex interweaving of different narrative strands, over several months or even years. Drama serials thus enable regular, extended interactions with audiences and foster familiar, even very intimate relationships, with the fictional world of the drama and its characters. Drama serials construct fictional communities to which viewers can relate. Like the daily national news broadcasts, they may even contribute to a sense of belonging to a national community.

Historian Benedict Anderson argued that the simultaneous consumption of national media (novels, newspapers and broadcasting especially) plays an important role in how we imagine ourselves as members of a national community (Anderson, 1983). The modern nation, he argued, is not just a political, economic and territorial entity. It is a cultural construction, an 'imagined community'. This does not mean that it is fictitious but that, in order to develop a national identity, people have to feel a sense of solidarity with fellow nationals that they will never meet. National media provide narratives of the nation, national histories, myths and symbols, ceremonies and traditions (some of which are invented, such as the investiture of the Prince of Wales). This creates a feeling of national unity and belonging, a common sense of historical time and social experience. So national media help to forge a sense of national identity, even if such identities are far from homogeneous.

In this chapter we compare how drama serials are used and interpreted by audiences in three different national contexts. The ethnographic case studies prompt you to compare and contrast the media and social worlds of the audiences in the case studies with your own, tracing similarities and differences. A comparative approach to audiences helps us to 'relativise' our media experiences, to make familiar what at first sight might seem strange, and vice versa. We also hope to make visible television cultures and audiences from the developing world that are often invisible in western media studies and in so doing avoid ethnocentric understandings of audiences. Ethnocentricism involves a belief in the centrality or superiority of one's own ethnic or cultural group and a dislike or misunderstanding of groups defined as alien or 'other'.

In Section 2, three different theoretical models of international communications are sketched out: media imperialism, media and development and global/local models. They offer theoretical frameworks for thinking about how television operates within global and national systems of power. This prepares you to think about the different approaches to media power that we encounter in the case studies, which can be seen as: media power *over* us; audience *empowerment*; and power working in a more diffuse manner *through* us via the media. Secondly, we examine some characteristic features of television drama serials, especially the concept of melodrama and its role in the constitution of modern subjectivities and sensibilities. This will help us make sense of the various ways in which audiences respond to the serials discussed in the case studies. Finally, we look at some of the advantages and pitfalls of ethnography in general and audience ethnography in particular. This will help raise awareness of the thorny methodological issues that audience researchers face, and the need for self-reflexive approaches to the methodologies that we choose.

In Section 3, we come to the first of our three case studies. We assess the impact of transnational television circuits via a case study of how a US soap opera, *The Young and the Restless* (USA, CBS, 1973 to present), is received by audiences in Trinidad. Here we consider whether the export of US television constitutes a form of media imperialism, a form of media power over us, or a more benign process of cultural globalisation.

In Section 4, we examine how television in India was used to promote national integration, with unintended consequences. We examine the extent to which viewers' interpretations comply with or resist hegemonic forms of national and gender identities represented in the serials. Here we draw on the concept of hegemony (elaborated by Italian political theorist Antonio Gramsci, 1891–1937; Gramsci, 1971). Hegemony refers to how consent for political leadership is achieved through a struggle over which versions of social reality and identities come to dominate at any particular moment. This struggle is nowadays played out in the production and consumption of popular forms of television. Audiences may comply with dominant ideas or engage in forms of resistance and thus, it is argued, can be empowered.

Section 5 examines how melodrama was used by state television producers in Egypt as a tool of development and modernisation in order to cultivate modern sensibilities and subjectivities. Here the ethnography focuses on one female viewer and explores in some depth her engagement with Egyptian melodrama and its importance for her sense of self. The notion of 'diffused power' (which originated in the work of French historian Michel Foucault) suggests that the power of the media works through, on and with us in quite profound ways – constituting our very sense of self and structuring our emotions (Foucault, 1988). This discussion weighs up some of the advantages and disadvantages of this kind of ethnography around individual subjects.

Section 6 concludes by drawing together: the various theoretical strands (the three models of international communication), the different conceptions of audiences and of power, the methodological arguments about the strengths and weaknesses of ethnography and the status of ethnographic knowledge and evidence, and the insights gleaned about how melodramatic forms are implicated in the cultural construction of emotions and gendered subjectivities.

To summarise, the main aims of the chapter are as follows:

- to examine how television represents and promotes identities for audiences;
- to explore the identifications that audiences forge with television characters, stories and lifestyles – gendered and national, religious and global among others;
- to assess the value of three different models of international communications for understanding how television operates in, and reproduces, wider power relations;
- to raise questions about how viewers use television in different ways in their lives;
- to evaluate the strengths and weaknesses of ethnographic methods for understanding audiences and power relationships.

2　A global living room?

In the 1960s, Marshall McLuhan (see Chapter 2) claimed that television was erasing time and space differences and creating a 'global village' (McLuhan, 1964). McLuhan's predictions may have exaggerated the impact of television in bringing audiences into a global community but, as the anecdote recounted at the start of this chapter suggests, people living almost everywhere in the world cannot, and may not want to, escape television. Even if more people around the world are increasingly sharing the experience of watching the same programmes, and even though drama, the world over, has certain ubiquitous storytelling features, does that mean that television has uniform effects? An ethnographic approach to the study of audiences enables us to ascertain the effects of the global media. However, it is important to bear in mind the weaknesses of the approach (see Section 2.3) as well as the strengths before reading the case studies in Sections 3 to 5.

Activity 4.1

Think about the following questions and make a note of your responses.

- Why do you think audiences all around the world enjoy US television dramas?
- What kinds of pleasures do US serials like *Dallas*, or more recent examples such as *The Sopranos* (USA, HBO, 1999 to present), *Sex in the City* (USA, HBO, 1998–2004), *ER* (USA, NBC, 1994 to present), *OC* or *Orange County* (USA, Fox, 2003 to present) bring to audiences?
- Do you watch US drama serials and if so which ones and why?
- What might be the wider consequences of the global export of US drama around the world? ■ ■ ■

Probably you have thought of several possible answers to the questions in Activity 4.1. The appeal of a serial like *Dallas* might be explained in numerous ways: the addictive quality of the storytelling that hooks audiences; the themes of family rivalry and kinship feuds, moral and financial conflicts, sexual temptation and infidelity, power and gender relations at work and in the family, have universal appeal; the pleasures of watching people and lifestyles very different to oneself and one's own, and learning from their joys and sorrows. You might take a pessimistic view and see US drama serials like *Dallas* as eroding 'authentic' traditional cultures and customs around the world. Or we might take a more optimistic view and assume that audiences can be empowered by television. For example, the exposure of female or youth audiences to alternative ways of life and value systems may help them challenge traditional patriarchal authority or existing structures of gender and generational power.

But what theories and what kinds of evidence would help us to make a judgement about such speculations? In the next section we look at three models of international communications. These offer us different ways of thinking about the consequences of transnational flows of television for audiences. They also involve different conceptions of audiences and of the power of television.

2.1 Three models of international communication

Three models of communication have dominated the field of international media studies and are sketched very briefly below. They have different orientations but share certain features.

Media imperialism thesis

Since the 1970s one of the dominant models of international communications has been the media imperialism thesis. The term 'cultural imperialism thesis' is sometimes also used, although it encompasses not only media but other cultural systems and institutions. These include the education systems, museums and libraries, as well as the wider sets of cultural values that were, and arguably continue to be, exported as part of an Anglo–American or western colonising mission to acquire and exert power in different parts of the world. The thesis proposes that a 'new world information order', dominated by a US media empire, is creating gross inequalities in media flows, especially from the North to the South, which places 'third world' countries at a huge disadvantage (Mattelart et al., 1984).

The media imperialism thesis views television dramas like *Dallas* and *Sex in the City*, with their glitzy and glamorous lifestyles, as epitomising the crass materialistic values of US-style consumer culture. Such drama serials are seen as showcases for US consumer goods that most people in developing countries can only dream of. Such serials, it is argued, promote global homogeneity and cultural uniformity and threaten to erode the diversity and destroy the authenticity of local and traditional cultures (see Figure 4.2).

Figure 4.2 *A young Peruvian boy hawking Inca Cola: a case of US domination or the 'local' adaptation of a global brand?*
Source: Jeremy Paul postcard

The importance of this model lies in the strong connections that it makes between the development of media infrastructures in the developing world, the promotion of US foreign policy and the expansion of capitalist economies. In other words, the export of US media is seen to serve US foreign policy and commercial interests.

The thesis takes many forms. The more sophisticated versions of the model suggest that it is not so much US foreign policy or commercial interests that are exported and imposed on audiences, but more general capitalist and consumerist values. Some theorists have highlighted the deeper and longer-term ideological transformations that western media bring about. These kinds of transformations are among the most difficult to research.

A number of problems with the thesis have been identified. Firstly, it is based on an overly simplistic view of audiences as passive, vulnerable and undifferentiated. Audience research may even be seen as a waste of time since the effects of media are considered to be predictable. Secondly, it is founded on an uninterrogated model of media effects and a linear conception of the communication process (see Chapter 1) that assumes a one-way transmission of messages from sender to receiver. This ignores the complexities of the communication process and the importance of context, contingency and selectivity in the ways in which audiences use and interpret television. Thirdly, the media are seen as a monolithic locus of economic and political power and as exerting power over audiences in uniform ways. Power is exerted from above and is located in the capitalist systems of production.

It has become rather too easy to dismiss this model outright as a result of its cruder manifestations in academic work but we should not ignore the fact that there is doubtless a relationship between the power and pervasiveness of the US media and the power that the USA exerts in the world today – even if it has to be carefully theorised and researched.

Media and development

This model of communication has a longer history. It emerged in the 1950s and was based on the idea that media can be used as a tool of social, economic and political development. Of course, we cannot assume that 'development' per se is a good thing, and this model can take on very different political colours: from extreme conservatism to radical socialism. It draws, very broadly, on the 'uses and gratifications' approach to media and audiences – an approach that is more concerned with the functions of media in satisfying individual and social needs, and the activities of audiences, rather than with their effects.

Drama serials, in particular, have been used by states as tools of modernisation, from Estonia and Khazakstan to India and Egypt (Ginsburg et al., 2002), but also in the UK, where *The Archers* (UK, BBC, 1950) on BBC Radio 4 began life just after the Second World War as a way of packaging advice for farmers in an entertaining village narrative.

In 1994 *The Archers* was used as a prototype by the BBC World Service for a new Afghan radio drama *New Home, New Life* (Afghanistan, BBC World Service, 1994). A team of BBC staff were 'exported' temporarily to Afghanistan as part of the BBC's outreach and development work across the world. There they worked with local producers to produce a serial relevant to Afghanistan at that time. The soap was a success beyond all expectations. It attracted 35 million listeners or 70 per cent of the Afghan population (Skuse, 1999). The serial was so popular that the Taleban, after banning television, music, theatre and dance, was forced to drop its plans to outlaw radio. (The Taleban was in power in Afghanistan from 1994 to 2001.) The issues it tackled were forced marriages, blood feuds, landmines and opium addiction. Many see this soap as having played a vital role in assisting democratisation in Afghanistan (see Figure 4.3).

Figure 4.3 *An Afghan man with child in a refugee camp in Northern Afghanistan listening to the hugely popular Afghan version of BBC Radio 4's soap opera* The Archers
Source: Reuters

Andrew Skuse, a social anthropologist, researched the success of the soap. He suggests that the BBC was seen as more trustworthy than the national radio service. But audiences were unaware of where the programme came from; some even thought the BBC was a village in

Afghanistan (Skuse, 1999). This is a good example of how not just programmes but media expertise or 'know-how' are exported with sometimes unintended consequences. The BBC crew were instrumental in producing a format that worked and in drawing on local knowledge to tackle relevant social issues in a way that was for the most part, according to Skuse, to the benefit of the Afghan people. Today, there are many more examples of sponsorship of drama serials, not just in the developing world but in Europe too, by commercial and/or publicly funded corporations that may serve commercial and/or democratic imperatives.

Activity 4.2

Soap operas are used to raise awareness of social issues.

- Can you think of some of the social issues that the soap operas have dealt with?
- Why do you think entertainment is thought to be a better way of getting a message across than serious documentaries? ■ ■ ■

Audiences may not always respond to being preached at, so placing social problems in a narrative context can be a more palatable way of getting a message across. For example, the BBC's *Eastenders* (UK, BBC, 1985) and ITV's *Coronation Street* (UK, Granada, 1960 to present) have long tackled issues ranging from domestic violence to AIDS, teenage pregnancy and incest. They have done so, I would argue, with great success. Public awareness and discussion, for example, of domestic violence has been assisted by portrayals on soap operas. Others might argue that such projects are unnecessarily normative and paternalistic, and assume that the pro-social messages are received in straightforward ways. Despite these criticisms, the development model, though regarded as outmoded by some, has enduring significance for how broadcasters conceive of their role and how they respond to social problems and even function to promote government policies in certain areas (for example, community-based sentencing as an alternative to prison).

The media and development model, however, has been criticised for its ethnocentrism, for encouraging, rather than combating, dependency on the west. Some projects treat audiences as helpless, passive victims of multiple sources of oppression, and 'traditional' values and lifestyles as impediments to modernisation. However, the social functions and pedagogic uses of media for pro-social development are emphasised in this model as audiences are trained to become active and attentive as well as compliant.

As we will see in the case studies of India and Egypt, developing countries' state television institutions may draw on western models but do so to instigate their own programmes of social development and propagate their own visions of modernity via television. But a common strand of both western and post-colonial modernising projects is the creation of 'good' citizens and consumers.

Global/local

This model emerged in the 1980s and 1990s in a more complex media environment. It emphasises the multi-directional flows of media around the world. It is pointed out that more and more nations from the South are producing and exporting media, particularly India, Egypt and Brazil. Some see these developments as challenging (if not reversing) the media imperialism of former decades, and creating alternative transnational circuits that disrupt the hegemony of US and other western media. In this model the contradictions and tensions between global systems of production and local processes of consumption are emphasised.

Audience researchers working in this framework draw on UK cultural studies in their conceptualisations of television audiences and media power. Stuart Hall's more sophisticated circular conception of encoding and decoding (see Chapter 1) conceived of power as a two-way process. Media exercise power over audiences but audiences creatively *appropriate* and use media for a variety of purposes. Audiences may conform to, negotiate or contest media meanings. Resistance to dominant or hegemonic meanings in this model is seen as a form of audience empowerment. This Gramscian approach to audiences and power is best exemplified by the second case study of Indian audiences by Purnima Mankekar.

I cannot here capture the complexities of theories of cultural globalisation. They include liberal pluralist and critical, optimistic and pessimistic versions, as well as very different conceptions of the changes brought about by globalisation: from revolutionary and epochal to gradual transformation. Some even see globalisation as a myth, an ideological fabrication used to justify the global expansion of capitalist economies (see Mackay, 2000). Whatever our view, the globalisation of television does pose big challenges to the ways in which we define and study audiences.

Soaps are one of the most pervasive and ubiquitous forms of global television, but they have their roots in a cultural form that has a much longer historical tradition and legacy, namely melodrama. It is important that we situate contemporary soap operas in this historical and cultural context in order to appreciate the arguments presented about its role in the cultural construction of the self-centred, individualised subjects typical of modern societies. A brief word about the term 'subject' might be useful here as it combines several connotations, all of which are important and relevant. Firstly, there is the sense of a subject as someone who is subservient or subordinate to a ruler or the subject of power. Secondly, there is the sense of a human subject with individual consciousness, an independently existing person. Thirdly, theories of spectatorship in films and television studies draw on psychoanalytical theories to explain how we become human subjects. It is argued that film and television texts offer subject positions for spectators with which they can identify. Becoming a human subject is an ongoing process and media texts are implicated in these processes. Fourthly, the term is used to refer to the subjects or the people and topics of research. The term identity, in contrast, is used here in its sociological sense to refer to social identities that are constructed in opposition to 'other' identities.

2.2 Melodrama and modern subjectivity

Melodrama has long been associated with modernity. British literary critic, Peter Brooks, in his book *The Melodramatic Imagination*, argues that melodrama came to the fore at the time of the French Revolution when a crisis arose over the transition to 'modernity' (Brooks, 1976, p.15). As a genre, he claims, it focuses on 'the revelation of the moral order' in the everyday in a 'post-sacred era'. It was, he claims, central to creating modern ways of feeling and thinking about the self as an individual (Brooks, 1976, p.21). This view of modernity is derived from a 'Euro-American' conception of individuals and modernity drawing on liberal political thought. As such, it may be deemed ethnocentric and inappropriate as a way of thinking about subject formation in postcolonial societies like Egypt. Yet it provides a way into thinking about the kinds of selves that melodrama encourages.

Drama more generally, it is argued, contributes to shaping subjectivities. UK cultural studies scholar, Raymond Williams, hypothesised that our unprecedented exposure to drama on television has led to a 'dramatisation of consciousness' (Williams, 1989). Television drama has encouraged us to see our lives as narratives and to view ourselves as the key subjects in the narratives that we construct of our lives. Williams suggests that our increasing exposure to television drama is transforming our sense of self.

Many drama serials, soap operas in particular, are founded on melodrama. The term is used in a wide variety of ways in literary, film and television studies, but here we use it to refer to a cultural form and an emotional mode rather than a self-contained genre. Certain shared features are apparent across these different media: the making visible of the everyday lives of 'ordinary people'; the exploration of the most private and intimate realms of human experience; the representation of heightened emotions brought about by human suffering; the concern with the rupturing and restoration of an underlying social and moral order; the interlinking of private selves and public citizens; the emphasis on the role of fate, chance and circumstance in intervening in and destroying the hopes and dreams of individuals.

Melodramas involve a huge outpouring of emotions. The surge of emotions they set free may be socially contagious, like laughter. Melodramas may be met with irony or tears, they may elicit superficial or profound discussions, but their 'cathartic' value, the purging of fear and pity, is undisputed. The family is often the source of narrative conflict in melodramas, generating and then resolving fundamental psychic problems. Viewers work through the fears and anxieties of family problems: separation, abandonment, destruction, death and/or loss. Viewers experience pity and empathise with vulnerable and powerless characters and negotiate the never-ending struggle between good and evil on and off screen (Buckingham, 1996)

Melodramas are seen by some as a conservative or politically reactionary type of storytelling because, in their conventional forms, they tend to relegate women to the domestic and private realms of life. The close attention to emotions, some argue, trains and prepares women for the emotional labour in the family – anticipating and responding to the different emotional and material needs of family members. Others see melodrama as an inferior, debased cultural form that reinforces existing hierarchies of taste and power. They see the tears and sadness as inauthentic, false, politically disabling, infantilising, opposed to reason – a sign of 'feminine weakness' and/or that viewers have simply and unquestioningly digested the ideology of the text. Such polarised assumptions about the power of melodrama are unhelpful in the abstract. More interesting are questions about the cultural construction of emotions in specific contexts.

Television drama serials take very different forms but melodramatic stories characterise much television output (even news). In content they have widely divergent cultural and political orientations. *Telenovelas*, produced in Spanish-speaking and Portuguese-speaking countries, and broadcast there and in many other regions, differ from Egypt's equally transnational Arabic serials or the Indian 'sacred serials' we will consider shortly. *Telenovelas* have finite storylines that tend to last months rather than years, as is the case in Egypt and India. They are also highly politicised in the way in which they approach social problems. Some fall squarely into the development model and both Indian and Egyptian television producers have used *telenovelas* as a template and tool for tackling development.

The USA's open-ended, daily afternoon soap operas are more commercial. They were the original dramas sponsored by soap companies like Procter and Gamble. The target audience for *The Young and the*

Restless, the subject of our first case study, as with most soap operas, is the housewife. It has been the most popular daytime soap for sixteen consecutive years in the USA and has a global following. It revolves around the rivalries, romances, hopes and fears of the residents of a fictional community, Genoa City. Compared to other daytime US soaps, there is a greater emphasis on sex and social conflict. Such daytime soaps differ from the UK's prime-time evening soap operas with three or four episodes a week (like BBC's *Eastenders* or ITV's *Coronation Street*), and from US prime-time serials such as *Dallas* and *Dynasty* (USA, ABC, 1981–1989), which have a determinate number of episodes and are broadcast only once a week in the evening.

Television drama serials and their audiences provide us with fascinating cross-cultural, comparative material with which to analyse questions of media power and audience empowerment. But, you may well ask, how can small-scale, detailed empirical studies of particular audiences shed light on the wider structures of media and other forms of power that envelop audiences? We address this question in the next section.

2.3 Ethnography and media audiences

The term 'ethnography' comes from the Greek, *ethnos* meaning people and *graphia* meaning writing or drawing. Ethnography emerged from the disciplines of anthropology and sociology. In recent years, however, it has been adopted by a range of disciplines because it is seen as a valuable method for exploring culturally distinctive systems of knowledge, values and beliefs. Ethnographers expose the features of everyday life (habits, routines and rituals, small talk and gossip) that are taken for granted, commonplace, even trivial. They seek to understand social life through first-hand, direct experience, conducting fieldwork in particular local contexts. They use a plurality of methods and techniques to explore how we construct meaningful social worlds: they participate and observe, listen and talk to people as they go about their everyday lives.

Since the 1980s, audience researchers, particularly in cultural studies, have seen ethnography as a method that can offer rich insights into the social and cultural complexities of audiences. One of the main sources of data that audience ethnographers use is *talk*. Television talk connects and interweaves social, personal and media experiences in fascinating ways. Such commentaries should not be seen as transparent accounts of what audiences 'really think' or what they 'actually do' with television. Rather, they need to be analysed as structured ways of thinking about the world, made in particular social circumstances. The context in which statements are made may be as important to analyse as what is said. Ethnographers compare what people say and do in relation to television in different contexts. This is called *triangulation*, and it is intended to strengthen and enrich the data that is gathered because we all often say and do quite different and contradictory things.

So how does ethnography differ from other methods? You will recall how, in Chapter 1, Sonia Livingstone referred to a study of *Dallas* by Liebes and Katz (1990). This reception study, like others of its kind, focuses on the moment of encounter between text and 'reader'. The study compared and contrasted interpretations of the text by the researchers and by a range of nationally and ethnically diverse audiences. Their widely divergent readings of the same text highlight the active nature of interpretative processes. The study is also widely cited as challenging the media imperialism thesis by demonstrating how audiences might resist dominant meanings.

The problem with such reception studies, insightful and important though they are, is that it is difficult to identify with any certainty what the dominant meanings of a text are. It is arguably even more difficult in the case of soap operas where the viewer adopts a wandering point of view and no one view of reality seems to dominate. If audiences' interpretations are measured against the media analyst's, then surely this tends to privilege the analyst's reading? And is it not possible that the same person might make a range of different and contradictory readings at different times and according to social context?

Both reception studies and ethnography are valuable approaches but they elicit different kinds of data. Ethnography has more holistic ambitions. It seeks to understand audiences in the larger social, political and cultural formations in which they are enveloped. In practice, these approaches often overlap, and it is better to judge studies on their own terms, since ethnography is practised in very different ways by different researchers. Some spend as much as two years conducting fieldwork and then another year 'writing up'. Others conduct a series of in-depth ethnographic-style interviews over a period of weeks or months.

Ethnography complicates notions of audiences as either active or passive, vulnerable or powerful. Ethnographers seek to study audiences in their full sociological complexity. We operate a multi-dimensional conception of audiences that does not reduce them to citizens or consumers, but tracks how they move through and between multiple identities and social spaces, intimate and public, in and out of different texts and genres. We aim to study how audiences use media in complex and unpredictable ways and how the meanings they create are neither determinate nor complete (Gillespie, 1995).

It is important to understand the context in which any piece of research was done before we can assess it properly. Practical, material and resource constraints often dictate what is possible. It is also important to understand the relationship between the researcher and her or his subjects of research – the power relations between them, the assumptions and prejudices of both, as well as the complicities or antagonisms. These inter-subjective elements are very important to the outcome of research. Each researcher views her or his subjects through their own highly personal lens (and vice versa), rather than in any purely objective way.

Activity 4.3

Look at the cartoon in Figure 4.4. What does it suggest to you about the anthropologist and his approach to research? ▪▪▪

The anthropologist in the cartoon in Figure 4.4 has 'gone native'. It is often difficult for ethnographers to maintain a balance between involvement and distance. Some distance and an approximation to objectivity is desirable, otherwise the researcher can so closely identify with his or her subjects that she or he may lack the critical distance necessary to the analysis of data.

Anthropology and ethnographic fieldwork are not without their historical legacy or political problems. Some of these are bound up with the practices of early anthropologists and their collusion with colonialism. Anthropologists may not only identify closely with their subjects, they may also project certain qualities and attributes onto them.

Figure 4.4 *Anthropologist's diary entry: 'March 5: After several months I now feel that these lively little monkeys have finally come to accept me as one of their own'*

Activity 4.4

Take a look at the cartoon in Figure 4.5. What does the cartoon suggest about the 'primitive' people and society? What does it suggest about anthropologists? What does it suggest about their relationship? What is the joke and who is the butt of the joke? ▪▪▪

The cartoon in Figure 4.5 mocks the colonial-style encounter between anthropologists and their 'primitive' subjects. It shows how the natives anticipate and collude with the prejudices of the researchers but not without irony. The natives are faking cultural authenticity. They present themselves in accordance with the researchers' expectations as a primitive tribe, concealing their modern lives, symbolised by the ownership of the

"Quick anthropologists!"

"It's the real thing!"

Figure 4.5

television set. The anthropologists are blinded by their prejudice. They are trapped in a perceptual mind set in which they see what they want to see.

This cartoon reflects two major problems. Firstly, anthropologists have been criticised for exoticising and stereotyping the subjects of their research and producing knowledge based on ethnocentric ideas and fantasies of difference and 'otherness'. Secondly, for a long time, anthropologists conceived of cultures as bounded, static wholes inescapably linked to blood, soil and 'race'. Identities, tied to culture and territory, were often viewed as fixed and unchanging.

Ethnocentric, exotic or racist ethnographic accounts of the 'other' have been seriously challenged as anthropology, from the 1980s, experienced something of an identity crisis. The politics of doing and writing up research involve difficult questions – how is knowledge produced about the 'other', for whom and for what purposes? Does ethnography collude with existing power relations? These questions will be useful for you to remember when you come to assessing the case study material.

These questions are not easily resolved. Nowadays, with an increasing emphasis on doing ethnography closer to home, the subjects of research are often invited to participate in the research process, to talk back to the researcher and to challenge the accounts of their lives produced by ethnographers. Rather than being the subjects of research, it is more appropriate to see those we work with as interlocutors, people with whom one engages in dialogue. Ethnography is not just a method. It is as much an ethos (or an ethical framework based on reciprocity and respect) as an epistemology (a theory knowledge). The reciprocity of respect that forms the basis of all good social relationships is just as important in the research context as elsewhere.

Now we come to our first case study of audiences in Trinidad. We shall use this case study of *The Young and the Restless* to explore in more detail what media ethnography means in practice and to test the US media imperialism thesis.

3 Challenging the media imperialism thesis? *The Young and the Restless* in Trinidad

In the late 1980s Daniel Miller, a British anthropologist, was doing fieldwork in Trinidad. He was interested in exploring changing patterns of consumption and questions of modernity. Miller describes how he only came to study soap operas because for one hour every day, during the afternoon broadcasts of *The Young and the Restless* (see Figure 4.6), nobody would talk to him:

> I was reduced to watching people watching a soap opera. It seems that this anecdote could be cloned by many other contemporary anthropologists from India to Brazil. Most of my evidence comes from the manner in which the program was referred to in conversations about other topics, rather than in direct response to questions asked about watching soap operas, and it is therefore mainly concerned with the manner by which the influence of the program manifests itself in the daily lives of the communities studied.
>
> Miller, 1995, p.216

Miller's ethnographic data emerges out of conversations in natural settings and so is much less likely to be a product of the research alone

Figure 4.6 *Victoria, Ryan and Nina, three characters from* The Young and the Restless, *a US soap opera that revolves around the lives of those living in a fictional Midwestern US town, Genoa City*

or the way in which the researcher framed or loaded the questions, or interpreted the text. You may also note his use of the term 'I was *reduced* to'. There is some negativity implied in the way in which he stumbled on television, although other ethnographers take television as their starting point.

Miller, like all researchers, came to the field with certain expectations and assumptions. He expected conversations around the soap to focus on the domination of US media. Trinidad imports almost everything it consumes, not just media. The stationing of US troops in Trinidad during the Second World War, and large-scale migration from Trinidad to the USA and return migration and visits back to Trinidad, made questions of the 'Americanisation' of local life and culture very relevant. Miller conducted his fieldwork after the oil boom of the 1970s. The 1980s was a time of economic recession and widespread poverty, so viewers might have been expected to comment on the fabulous wealth of the people in *The Young and the Restless* in contrast to their own lives. Yet such topics or the USA rarely featured in conversations around the soap. Rather, they used this US soap to tackle specifically local issues and problems.

Miller's conversations and observations revealed that families, mainly women and children but some men too, watched *The Young and the Restless* on battery-charged, mobile, mini-television screens, propped up in all sorts of places – shops, garages and offices. The afternoon serial was accompanied by raucous banter, laughter and sustained commentary. And what viewers liked most about the soap was summed up by them in the word *bacchanal*. This is a Trinidadian term with distinct but related connotations. It refers to 'scandal', 'confusion' and 'truth'. Many viewers not only used the term to convey their appreciation of the soap, but also to describe the essence of Trinidadian society.

Reading 4.1 Activity

Now read the following extract from Daniel Miller's study 'The consumption of soap opera: *The Young and The Restless*' (Reading 4.1). Bear in mind that the conversations are in Trinidadian idiom. I have added explanations of terms that might be unfamiliar. Think about the following questions as you read the extract:

- How did this US-imported soap opera come to be seen as relevant to life in Trinidad?

- What lies behind this association of *bacchanal* in the soap opera with life in Trinidad?

- Does this ethnographic study confirm and/or challenge the US media imperialism thesis?

Reading 4.1

Daniel Miller, 'The consumption of soap opera: *The Young and the Restless*'

[O]ne of the most common comments about the show was its relevance to contemporary condition in Trinidad. Typical would be:

'The same thing you see on the show will happen here, you see the wife blackmailing the husband or the other way around, I was telling my sister-in-law, Lianna in the picture [*in the soap*], just like some bacchanal [*scandalous*] woman.'

'It really happening this flirtatious attitude, this one they living together, that partner working this partner, and have a date with the next one or in bed with another.'

'People look at it because it is everyday experience for some people. I think they pattern their lives on it.'

From this sense of relevance comes also the idea that there are direct lessons to be learnt from the narrative content for moral issues in Trinidad, for example:

'It teach you how husbands could lie and cheat and how a wife could expect certain things and never get it, the women always get the short end of the stick.'

'I believe marriage should be 50–50 not 30–70, the woman have to be strong she have to believe in her vows no matter what ... that make me remember *The Young and the Restless*, Nicky want her marriage to work but Victor is in love with somebody else, but she still holding on.' [...]

'With my mother in the USA she so involved you would actually think it is some of she children she is talking about.' [...]

'People in *The Young and the Restless* can't have fun like people in Trinidad, their sort of fun is boring. There's more bacchanal here than in *The Young and the Restless,* in each soap you can tell what's going to happen but around here you can't tell.' [...]

'I love Lauren, how she dresses and I identify with her.'

'I like Nicky the way she dresses, my name is Nicky too, she is a loving person.'

'Nah, when you see that show is about to start, the phone does ring. Gloria yuh watching it ... like every dress she see she say 'Oh God I want one like that', and how many yards to buy and I think she was writing on the other end.' [...]

'It is so modernized with AIDS, up to date music-wise, clothes-wise, when you look at the shoes you say this is nice this is really up to date, it's modern it's now, that why you appreciate it more, I admire the earrings, necklaces.' [...]

'What is fashion in Trinidad today – *The Young and the Restless* is fashion in Trinidad today.'

Reading source
Miller, 1995, pp.199–213 ■ ■ ■

Miller was surprised to discover that *The Young and the Restless* was not regarded as an index of US media domination, but was appropriated by viewers to explore some of the social and moral contradictions of Trinidadian society. Of all the many US soap imports this one in particular was described as 'True True Trini'. Viewers saw it as having high levels of relevance to their lives despite the US 'look' and lifestyles. They drew direct lessons from the social and moral content of the soap, debating at length the carnivalesque emotional confusion. They made comparisons between the sexual scandals revealed through soap opera and local gossip. Like many soap viewers, they perceived the realism of the soap as emotional rather than literal.

Most viewers maintained an intimate emotional involvement with the characters and their problems and yet kept enough distance to criticize implausible storylines and the like. One woman talked about the characters as if they were real. This is a common feature of soap talk that does not necessarily mean that viewers confuse media and social worlds. Rather, this blurring of the boundaries reflects the constant 'commuting' between the lives on the soap and the everyday lives of viewers.

Audiences drew on local experiences and local idioms, especially the term *bacchanal* with its equation of carnival with scandal, and gossip with exposure and truth. One of the pleasures of watching is that the soap characters and viewers, together, uncover scandals and reveal truths. Viewers attached a high moral value to exposing a scandalous truth on and off screen, but they also complained that scandals caused moral and emotional confusion.

Melodramas assume the existence of social norms and a moral order and at the same time point to the breakdown of that order; for example, through sexual temptation or the lust for power. This causes confusion and threatens chaos. Gossiping about soap life and real life is a way of reinforcing local social norms and negotiating notions of respect, respectability and reputation. Sexual scandal involves the loss of respect and reputation for women, but not for men. *Bacchanal* brings these gender inequalities and social dilemmas sharply to the fore. Soap viewers follow and judge characters in terms of *bacchanal* and weigh up losses and gains in their reputations. They explore the moral ambiguities of women's lives on and off screen – how they might affirm a social and moral code but be diverted from it.

Viewers identify less with the characters per se, than with the characters through their clothes. This often results in their copying the styles and fashions of their favourite characters. One seamstress came to see watching the soap as part of her job. Should we consider this widespread emulation of US fashion and style as confirmation of the media imperialism thesis? Does it suggest that lifestyle aspirations and identities are being shaped by US commodities showcased by this and other US soaps? Miller does not think so. He makes a nuanced argument concerning this aspect of the media imperialism thesis. In Trinidad, he argues, the cultivation of a public self through displays of clothing and style reinforces status hierarchies. He suggests that the appropriation of the fashion goods displayed on the soap enabled viewers with limited material resources to challenge local status hierarchies and existing structures of class inequality.

This is a good example of the way in which audiences may be empowered by television. Audiences exercise a kind of symbolic power. They can transform the way they look and in doing so playfully or even seriously challenge local fashion and class hierarchies. But exerting symbolic power in this context is not the same as wielding the kind of economic power that more affluent viewers have. Moreover, the emulation of fashion and style, and the ways in which these may blur with lifestyle aspirations and values, suggests that US television may indeed be powerfully influential, but in ways that are less direct, more diffuse and longer term than the media imperialism thesis suggests.

Although the study shows a far more complex pattern of local appropriation than is suggested by the thesis, we should not lose sight of the pervasiveness and cultural dominance of US media. The global/local model provides a more refined conception of power as a two-way process involving both power over audiences and audience empowerment. Analysed through the lens of the global/local model, imported television programmes generate strategies of local appropriation and resistance to domination, highlighting the active and creative nature of audiences.

The study shows that Trinidadian culture is constantly in flux and changing under different streams of influence – US media included. It underscores the crucial recognition that all cultures are impure, constantly changing and hybrid formations. Thus processes of fragmentation and hybridisation (the mixing of distinctive cultural streams) are just as strong as opposing tendencies of homogenisation and uniformity.

The global and the local are not so much opposite ends of a scale, but mutually shaping spheres. This ethnography enables us to gain insight into how viewers incorporate global television into local systems of meaning and use it to redefine local practices and identities. If this is true and if the claims of ethnography are to be justified, then let us test them in an entirely different field of observation, data and analysis. Let us therefore turn to a second case study, this time of Indian television audiences.

4 The *Mahabharat* in New Delhi

You will recall how, in Chapter 3, David Herbert explored the way in which the serialisations of the *Ramayana* (India, Doordarshan, 1987–1990) and the *Mahabharat* (India, Doordarshan,1988–1990) (see Figure 4.7) by the Indian state television, Doordarshan, were exploited by the political leaders of the Hindu nationalist party, the Bharatiya Janata Party (BJP). He argued that these serials helped to widen political participation but restricted public discourses on what it means to be an Indian. The serials encouraged viewers to equate being Indian with being Hindu and thus, contrary to the intentions of producers who hoped it would serve national integration, the serials exacerbated tensions between India's Hindus, Muslims, Sikhs, Christians and other minority religious groups. Their immense symbolic power contributed to fanning the flames of communal conflict and violence between Hindus and Muslims. (Throughout this chapter, we use the spelling 'Mahabharata' to refer to the ancient tales themselves and 'Mahabharat' for the televised version of the ancient tales.)

This case study complements and develops David Herbert's important insights into media publics. It offers an explanation of how and why these serialisations became so popular and could be put to such ideological use, something that an approach to audiences as 'the public' misses. The associated reading (Reading 4.2) is based on an extensive ethnography by the USA-based, Indian feminist anthropologist, Purnima Mankekar. It examines the extent to which female viewers in New Delhi conform to and/or contest hegemonic constructions of Indian femininity.

Figure 4.7 *An image of Lord Krishna from the Bhagavad-Gita scene of the Indian television serial the* Mahabharat *in which the concept of a 'just war' is discussed*

Source: Archivos de la Filmoteca

The *Mahabharata*

The *Mahabharata* is widely perceived as one of the foundational myths of Indian society. It is said to enshrine the philosophical basis of Hinduism and to be re-inscribed in popular Indian films and television dramas today. It is one of the longest epic poems ever written in Sanskrit and dates back to the fifth and sixth centuries BCE. The *Mahabharata* is variously translated as 'the great history of humankind' or 'the great history of the Indian "race"'. It tells the story of a long and bloody quarrel between two groups of cousins, the Pandevas and the Kauravas, over who will rule the earth/India. This epic struggle, in which the Kauravas try to destroy the Pandevas, ends in an earth-shattering war that destroys both clans and shows that the lust for power permeates everything from state politics to the family.

4.1 Indian drama serial and state development projects

The Indian epics were broadcast consecutively by the Indian state channel, Doordarshan, from 1987 until 1990 in an attempt to forge national integration and cohesion. In India the media have for long been harnessed to state modernising projects aimed at promoting communal harmony, public health, modern farming, family planning and women's status and rights.

A common theme of many Indian serials is the role of women in the family and nation. Two clearly circumscribed hegemonic representations of Indian femininity are commonly reproduced. One is based on the controlled image of femininity represented by Sita in the *Ramayana*. She is respectful of patriarchal authority, chaste, honourable, devoted, self-sacrificing and pious (see Figure 4.8). The other is based on the more rebellious image of femininity represented by Draupadi, an angry, strong independent female who challenges patriarchal authority. We shall return to pursue the implications of these images for female viewers in India in a moment.

Figure 4.8 An image of Sita from the front cover of Motherland *magazine, November 1997. Sita's image is imposed upon a map of India, thus conflating the two*

For the vast majority of Indian viewers it appears that Doordarshan's religious epics are perceived both as sacred texts and as the story of the Indian nation. Audiences found a regular port of entry into a golden age in ancient India, prior to the Mughal invasions and British colonial rule. The serials provide an apt illustration of Benedict Anderson's (1983) notion of the nation as an 'imagined community'.

Audience ratings for the religious epics broke all records in the history of Indian television. Viewing the epics became a ritualised media event. In India and across the Indian diaspora, Hindus performed purification rituals, garlanded their television sets, and observed ritual taboos as they watched. (The term 'diaspora' refers to the dispersal of peoples around the world as a result of migration.) Every Sunday morning many parts of India came to a standstill as up to 115 million people (compared with normal daily Indian audience figures of 40–60 million) simultaneously consumed a narrative of India as a Hindu nation.

Activity 4.5

Think about the following questions and make a note of your responses:

- How might we begin to explain the power and popularity of these serials?
- Does television destroy the cultural integrity or authenticity of the epics?
- Can you think of any examples of ritualised and devotional styles of viewing that you engage in (the devotional viewing of football, stars or celebrities, for example)?
- How might reflecting on our own viewing rituals inform our understanding of the effect of the epics on Indian viewers? ■ ■ ■

Various explanations might account for the popularity and power of the soaps:

- the mesmerizing power of television: the majority of Indians only acquired television sets in the 1980s and early 1990s, in many cases, in order to watch the serials, just as many Britons bought their first television to watch the coronation of Queen Elizabeth II in 1953;
- the enduring significance of these sacred narratives as the basis of Hindu beliefs, behaviour and action;
- the melodramatic ingredients;
- the reconstruction of the 'imagined community' of the nation that generated feelings of belonging at a time of great change in Indian society brought about by modernisation, globalisation and the liberalisation of markets in 1991.

The 'sacred serials' were not enjoyed by cultural critics or scholars of the Sanskrit texts. They spelt, for them, the demise of the history of diverse performance traditions, the vulgarisation and populist standardisation of the ancient texts, the marginalisation and erosion of regional and minority cultures and language differences, and the hegemonic ascension of Doordarshan's religious nationalist version of the epic.

You have also probably been able to think of many examples of devotional styles of watching television. I thought of the devotional viewing habits of my brothers when their favourite football team, Tottenham Hotspur, are playing. When they score one of their rare goals, my brothers behave as though they have had a divine vision. We might also include the devotional viewing of royal ceremonies: the coronation of Queen Elizabeth II or the funerals of Princess Diana or the Queen Mother.

4.2 Divine visions

Hindu religious worship strongly emphasises the power of vision. Colour print images of the deities are ubiquitous in homes and public places and are touched and gazed at during daily worship and acts of devotion. The iconographic conventions for portraying popular deities such as Krishna (see Plate 4 in the colour section) were strictly adhered to in the television version and did much to aid visual recognition and intimacy.

Devotees believe that the religious gaze or *darshan* (literally 'sight') helps to bring the gods inside you. In his analysis of the continuities between traditional and folk performances of the *Ramayana* and the television serialisations, Lutgendorf (1990) focuses on this concept of *darshan* or seeing in the spiritual sense. *Darshan* is perceived as a way of achieving communion or spiritual union with the deities. The deity gives *darshan* and devotees take *darshan*: one is touched by *darshan* and seeks it as a form of contact with a deity. The relationship it establishes between viewers and deity is as much tactile as it is visual, which underscores the sensory and embodied nature of television experiences (see Chapter 2). The sacred television image sanctifies the space of its presence, and to share that space is to partake of *darshan*. This explains why purification rituals are carried out around the television set, why sets are garlanded, incense is lit, *prasad*, or holy food, is eaten and prayers are offered. The experience of viewing is a devotional experience.

Viewers forged deep religious identifications with the deities on screen because of the continuities with traditional performance styles of the epics. In folk theatre performances of the epics in Indian villages, the audience is expected to focus intently on facial expression and gesture to empathise with the expression of emotion. The small screen is ideally suited to portraying such heightened emotional states. The serials make frequent use of close-ups underscored by dramatic music, techniques commonly used in film melodrama and soap operas. The narrative flow is frequently arrested to encourage the devotional contemplation of close-up shots on gods' faces, accompanied by devotional music. In such ways, audio-visual techniques of modern television drama serials are integrated into traditional folk performance styles.

Special effects are used to portray the divine intervention of gods on earth, supernatural experiences, dream sequences and miracles. These are typical of Indian films and are familiar to viewers. Scenes of great moral import, such as one where Draupadi is humiliated, are given much more dramatic and emotional emphasis than scenes that centre on a narrative puzzle. Such scenes are signalled by the suspension of narrative flow as a disembodied narrator returns to reinforce a moral point.

In the next section we examine how and why one particular scene, more than any other, was discussed and interpreted by female viewers. This is the scene in which one of the central female characters of the epic, Draupadi, is shamed publicly by her male in-laws.

Draupadi's humiliation

Draupadi is the polyandrous wife of the Pandevas brothers. Yudhishtira, the eldest of the Pandevas, is a good man but has one major weakness – gambling. Duryodhana, his evil cousin, entices him into a game of dice. He gambles and loses everything, even his wife. Draupadi becomes the property of the Kauravas. They abuse her and violate her honour by trying to strip off her sari in court. She prays to Krishna who magically appears and bestows on Draupadi a sari of infinite length. This is the main turning point of the whole of the *Mahabharata*. Her husbands have to take revenge. This is what sets off the war (of Kurukshetra) and paves the way to destruction.

4.3 Female identifications

Reading 4.2 gives us some insight into the profound emotional identification (*bhav*) with Draupadi's plight among lower middle-class female viewers in New Delhi. It demonstrates the role of the *Mahabharat* serial in the cultural construction of nationalised femininity. But it also shows how hegemonic discourses of Indian femininity are disrupted by the outpouring of emotions among female viewers that the scene evoked (see Figure 4.9). It shows how emotions do not emanate from an innate, individual source of human feelings but are culturally constructed and can be put to political use, contrary to what some cultural critics would say, who maintain sharp separations between reason and emotion, subjectivity and political engagement.

Figure 4.9 *The scene from the televised epic* Mahabharat, *in which Draupadi's in-laws attempt to violate her honour in public*

Reading 4.2 Activity

Now read the following extract from Purnima Mankekar's book *Screening Culture, Viewing Politics. An Ethnography of Television, Womanhood, and Nation in Postcolonial India* (Reading 4.2). As you do so, think about the following questions:

- How do class and gender positions inflect viewers' interpretations?
- Why is Draupadi seen as an icon both of women's vulnerability and of women's strength?
- What does this seeming contradiction suggest about viewer's interpretations?
- How do representations of gender on-screen relate to off-screen narratives of self?

- What forms do 'counter-hegemonic' readings of this scene take?
- In what ways are such resistant readings undermined by the discourses of Hindu nationalism?

Reading 4.2

Purnima Mankekar, 'Televison tales, national narratives, and a woman's rage: multiple interpretations of Draupadi's "disrobing"'

Viewers' interpretations

Viewers' interpretations of other serials seldom varied solely according to gender; the disrobing episode, however, seemed to have polarized men and women. In their conversations about the *Mahabharat*, men would talk about the war of Kurukshetra, family and state politics, and political corruption; their discussion of Draupadi's disrobing was almost invariably in terms of how it unleashed a sequence of events that culminated in the war of Kurukshetra. While women touched on other aspects of the narrative, it was the disrobing episode that they talked about at length. Some reverted to it in several conversations, and these discussions often provided a point of entry into narratives about their own lives. In fact, I found that Draupadi's disrobing enabled some of these viewers to confront and critique their own positions in their family, community, and class [...] I focus on women viewers because they, more than men, seemed profoundly moved by the disrobing and could narrate the episode and their responses to it in vivid detail and with astonishing emotional intensity for months after it was telecast. Even the most reserved and recalcitrant women would become passionate and eloquent on the subject.

[...]

All the women I spoke with saw Draupadi as an icon of women's vulnerability; for many she evoked the power of women's rage, and for some, an intimate engagement with her disrobing enabled them to rupture hegemonic constructions of Hindu/Indian Womanhood.

Draupadi as an icon of women's vulnerability

Unlike the *Mahabharat* crew, who spoke of Draupadi in terms of abstract conceptions of gender and nationhood, women viewers *intimately* identified with Draupadi and saw in her disrobing a reflection of their own struggles to negotiate an environment that they considered hostile to their dignity. Threats to their physical safety in the public spaces of New Delhi; sexual harassment at work; economic, sexual, and emotional exploitation in the family: these were the daily realities faced by the women I describe here. [...]

[...] Sushmita Dasgupta [...] lived with her large family in Vikas Nagar. She and her father were the family's primary bread-winners; her father was about to retire. Sushmita seemed to be the financial and emotional mainstay of her family, a fact that often overwhelmed her. She frequently spoke to me of her loneliness. Her cousin informed me that Sushmita desperately wanted to escape the claustrophobia of her family, to get married and start a life of her own, but her father and elder brother had become so dependent on her salary that every time a proposal came for her marriage, they found an excuse to turn it down. This, along with persistent financial anxiety, created considerable tension in the family. [...]

Apprehensive about whether her father would ever allow her to get married, terrified that she would be mistreated if she entered her in-laws' home without a dowry, Sushmita told me on two different occasions that what shocked her most about the disrobing episode was the failure of Draupadi's elders to protect their daughter-in-law. But I did not realize how deeply shaken she had been by it until one day, more than a year after the episode was telecast and about a month after the serialization of the *Mahabharat* concluded, her mother related Sushmita's reaction:

> My daughter, when she saw [what happened], cried and cried. She cried all morning. Imagine what happened to Draupadi! And in public, in front of her in-laws! A feeling came to my daughter: what will happen to me when I get married and go to my in-laws' home?

[...]

Indeed, the vulnerability of women was discussed by every single woman that I interviewed about this episode. This happened without exception – across classes, across generations, across communities. Draupadi embodied what seemed to be a crucial aspect of their understanding of what it meant to be a woman, an Indian woman living in a man's world.

[...]

But if women articulate their sense of insecurity, do they also feel *totally* helpless? Was Draupadi no more than an icon of the vulnerability of women? Was there nothing empowering in her image? I found that if Draupadi's disrobing enabled these viewers to reexperience their vulnerability, her fury at her husbands and in-laws also evoked the power of women's rage.

[...]

When [one young woman I worked with] Poonam expressed her outrage at what happened to Draupadi, [her mother] Shakuntala turned to me and said that she was terribly worried that Poonam was 'too sharp tongued.' Poonam's views on dowry terrified her even more: she frequently told her parents that she would refuse to marry anybody who asked for a dowry. And if her in-laws harassed her for a dowry after the wedding she would defy all social conventions and leave their home in anger. Shakuntala conceded that to give and take dowry was to participate in and endorse an evil that humiliated women. But if giving or taking dowry was bad, leaving the home of one's husband and in-laws in rage was worse. She said: *'This is not something women in our family do; this is not something Indian women do.'* [Our emphasis added]. Most striking in her discourse is the elision from family to nation; indeed, the two become analogous if not synonymous.

Reading source

Mankekar, 1999, pp.239–48 ■ ■ ■

Female readings of the dishonouring of Draupadi suggest, according to Mankekar, that this scene opened up a space for specifically female concerns to be expressed. Draupadi's vulnerability embodies female viewers' own vulnerabilities: their marital status as the property of their husbands and husbands' families; the predatory nature of men in public spaces in New Delhi (a place that is notorious in India for 'Eve teasing' or sexual harassment due to the large numbers of young, unmarried men from villages who flock there from rural areas in search of jobs); the difficulties that low-income families with several daughters have in providing a dowry; fears that parents might not honour their daughter with a dowry that will ensure that she will be well treated by her in-laws; the high-earning capacities of lower middle-class women; their financial exploitation by their families; fears about how their in-laws will treat them when they marry and go to live with their husband's family. These are very real fears and vulnerabilities for women in India and in the diaspora.

But Draupadi is also a symbol of female rage and strength. She is admired because she exposes and challenges the patriarchal order and rages against the failure of her husbands and in-laws to protect her honour. As a feminist ethnographer, Purnima Mankekar recognises the empowering aspects of Draupadi's story for the women she worked with. Women in developing countries, she argues, are often denied a complex subjectivity. Draupadi's rage, and the anger it provoked in women viewers, is seen as a form of empowering 'resistance' to gender oppression. This is especially so when compared to the ways in which women talk about the more docile and compliant image of Indian femininity that Sita represents. The anger of viewers resists and ruptures hegemonic discourses of Indian femininity as represented by Sita. This is seen as a sign of a developing feminist consciousness.

Purnima Mankekar argues that it is not enough to simply celebrate women's resistance to oppressive national, class or patriarchal power structures. She shows how the female viewers occupy contradictory subject positions. They may admire Draupadi and, in an ideal world, wish to be like her but still regard her as an inappropriate role model for themselves or their daughters. The fear that rebellious, independent women who choose to defy patriarchal authority will be ostracised and left without the protection of their families is pervasive and palpable, and constrains the choices available to women. Thus television images of women and the subject positions of women in real life do not translate smoothly from one to the other.

The relationship between the television images that the state wants to promote and the identities of women viewers are not straightforward, consistent or predictable. The formation of identity involves on-going processes of constant negotiation. Similarly, texts are not consumed as unitary wholes but in fragments. Particular scenes, like Draupadi's humiliation, come to have enormous resonances with female viewers. However the meanings of texts are rarely finally fixed and are contradictory and shifting.

The *bhav* or profound emotional identification, according to Draupadi's female viewers, is necessary in order to learn from the narrative. It encourages an awareness of how the position of women has not changed over the centuries. Anger at oppression is a necessary step in political awakening. The case study challenges the idea that emotional involvement and rational critical or political engagement are mutually exclusive.

The above case study approaches the question of power through Gramsci's concept of hegemony. Audiences' interpretations are judged in terms of their compliance with, negotiation of and/or resistance to hegemonic discourses of Indian femininity. It might be argued that this approach is somewhat mechanical. Women seem to embrace a form of solidarity with others, which, despite some variability, makes them seem more alike than they probably are. This is qualified by the more argumentative nature of female discussions that many ethnographers have noted around discussions of Draupadi in other cultural contexts, and the more subtle differences that emerge in talk around controversial female characters in soap operas.

The next case study takes a different approach to power. Drawing on Foucault (1988), power is not seen as having a single originating source or identifiable location. Power is seen as diffuse and contingent, localised (that is, not just in the hands of power elites) and fragmented, unstable and in constant flux. It is the outcomes of power that emerge from this state of flux that are to be analysed, rather than deploying a-priori assumptions about where power lies and how it operates.

The next case study is part of a wider investigation into media and modernity in Egypt that USA-based Egyptian anthropologist, Lila Abu-Lughod, has carried out for over fifteen years. It examines the ongoing efforts of Egyptian state television to promote national integration and create modern subjects and citizens.

5 Melodrama and modern subjectivities in Egypt

Lila Abu-Lughod explores the connections between Egyptian melodrama and modern Egyptian subjectivities. This case study involves, arguably, a more profound level of media power and influence that is, as a result, all the more difficult to research. In developing her argument she draws on Peter Brooks's (1976) arguments about the role of melodrama in the constitution of modern sensibilities, and Raymond Williams's (1989) suggestion that our unprecedented exposure to drama on television brings about the 'dramatization of consciousness'. These arguments were summarised in Section 2.2.

Lila Abu-Lughod takes both of these suggestive, if speculative, insights and relates them to Foucault's ideas about how power operates not only through institutions and discourses to cultivate modern, highly individualised selves, but also through our own choice by inhabiting certain subject positions willingly. Power is not only imposed from above but also works through us as we adopt 'techniques of the self' (Foucault, 1988, p.146) to discipline ourselves and to become the self-managing, self-regulating subjects capable of making choices, that modern states wish us to be.

'Techniques of the self' are ways of coming to inhabit subject positions through choice. Power works through us and through the interconnections between narrative, emotion, subjectivity and state authority. But for Foucault, as for Abu-Lughod, becoming a modern subject and exercising choice are not equated with greater freedom but are seen as the consequences of strategies of modern governance. Self-regulating subjects are colonised by power relations at a much more profound level. Such processes, argues Abu-Lughod, are very much in evidence among the domestic servants that she worked with in Cairo.

Reading 4.3 Activity

Now read the following extract from Abu-Lughod's 'Egyptian melodrama –
technology of the modern subject?' which focuses on Amira, a domestic
servant in Cairo, and traces the connections between her uses of
melodrama and becoming a modern subject. It suggests an idea of the self
not as given but as the subject of a narrative, something to be constructed
through individual choice and effort. Think about how you might answer the
following questions:

- In what ways does Amira's life story resemble the plot of a melodrama?
- How might melodrama be implicated in the formation of new kinds of
  modern sensibilities and subjectivities in Egypt?
- How do different belief and value systems operate in Amira's life?
- How persuasive are the arguments about the 'techniques of the self' in
  understanding how media power works through audiences?
- How does this ethnographic account compare with the others in this
  chapter?
- Why do you think Abu-Lughod puts a question mark at the end of the
  title of her piece?

Reading 4.3

Lila Abu-Lughod, 'Egyptian melodrama – technology of the modern subject?'

To illustrate how television melodrama may have come to inform
individual lives, I want to discuss the person I knew in Egypt who
was most deeply involved with television and radio melodramas; an
unmarried domestic servant in Cairo I call Amira [...]. My fieldwork
on television reception was with domestic workers in Cairo and with
women in Upper Egypt, both socially marginal groups. [...]

Unmarried and with no children, she was both freer to follow
television and more dependent on it for companionship and
emotional–social involvement than most women I worked with in
Egypt. She was somewhat isolated socially because she lived on her
own. Her mother and brothers still lived in the countryside. Her
main contacts in Cairo were an unmarried sister, with whom,
however, she had frequent conflicts, and one friend, a single woman
who had also come to Cairo from the countryside and worked as a
domestic servant. With both she watched television.

Amira was both more sentimental and more volatile than many women
I have come to know. She was often moved by the serials she watched.
When we watched television together, her explanations of particular

characters carried moral and emotional valences. But her sentimentality extended to other areas. Once when we turned on the television in 1990 and saw a clip of people in Iran crying after an earthquake, this triggered her memory of having wept 'for an hour' after the Egyptian soccer team lost the World Cup match. [...] [Her] emotional style extended beyond the world of television. She was often embroiled in conflicts and arguments – with her sister, her employers, and her neighbours.

Although I cannot argue for a direct causal link between her involvement with television serials and her emotionality, I suspect there is one. There is, however, a more obvious link between television melodrama and the ways she constructed herself as a subject. This link is through the ways she made herself the subject of her own life stories. I found it striking that of all the women whose life stories I have heard, Amira was the one whose tales most clearly took the form of melodrama. Hers was a Manichean world [one with deep divisions between good and evil] with good kind people who helped her and were generous, and greedy, stingy, or cruel people who victimized her.

One can see this in the way she constructed her story of coming to Cairo to find a better life. Amira came from a poor family and had worked on construction sites, hauling dirt and sand, for a daily wage. She wanted to go to Cairo because she saw her sisters, who had gone there to find work, coming home dressed well and wearing gold. At the age of nineteen she finally went. But she lasted only a month in the first job. The family mistreated her. [...] Each time [she was mistreated by successive employers], she found some excuse to go home to her village. Eventually she found a job with a good family as a cook and stayed with them for eight years. The themes repeat: exploited and mistreated, the innocent victim escapes until fate deals her some kind people.

It is when she talks about her brief marriage, however, that all the elements of drama crystallize. At the time of one of our conversations, at age 37, she declared that she was too old to hope for marriage. 'Who would want to marry me?' But someone had wanted to, in 1985, when she was about 30. The ease with which she told the story suggested it was a well-rehearsed one. [...]

We must ask [...] about the narrative qualities of life stories. [...] Amira's [life story] conforms more closely to the model of melodrama. Like the television dramas, the themes of her story are money, with the villain trying to cheat her out of hers, and the secret, with the truth about her sinister husband discovered too late. The melodramatic heroine, innocent and good, is wronged and victimized. Seeking a better life, symbolized by her sisters' good clothes and gold, she leaves the village and home to find herself overworked, underpaid, and hungry in a house where the food is locked up.

Seeking love, companionship, or respectability – whatever it is that marriage is supposed to bring – she finds herself betrayed.

What I think is most significant about this way of telling her life stories, however, is that through it Amira makes herself the subject, the melodramatic heroine of her own life. Perhaps inspired in part by her love of television melodrama, she has been encouraged to see herself as the subject of the emotions that sweep her, and thus as more of an individual. This view of herself puts her in a better position to be a modern citizen, something the television producers want from their melodramas. For Amira, this position is reinforced by the structures of her life: her migrant status and separation from her family, her reliance on her own labour for survival, her private apartment with its own electricity and water bills, and her subjection to the law and to taxation as an individual.

Figure 4.10 *Family watching television in Upper Egyptian village, 1993 (photo taken by Lila Abu-Lughod)*
Source: Ginsburg et al., 2002

Yet Amira's story and her life present certain complications for a straightforward narrative of coming to modern individual subjecthood as we might tell it along familiar Western lines. [...] Amira's tragic story is marked by certain absences and failures [a bad husband and a lack of family near her to support her]. [...] Amira's story, though told mostly in terms of herself as an individual moving through life, evokes the ideal she cannot have – the ideal of being a subject fulfilled and defined by kinship and family.

[...]

However there is something else of great importance in Amira's day-to-day life that does not derive from television melodrama and that in some, but not all ways, undermines the process that television encourages. [...] Amira is attracted to the new path to individual expression and respectability opened up to women in the past two decades by the movement to make Islam more central to everyday life and politics. This fact, along with the continuing centrality of kinship and the ways that Egyptian melodramas embed morality within the social, reminds us that this modern form of drama, and the forms of selfhood that it encourages, are being produced in a post-colonial nation with its own specific history and forms of modernity [...]

Religious practice organizes Amira's schedule, informs her sense of self, and colors her understanding of the world as much as work and watching television do. [...] As a result of her involvement in these religious practices [wearing *higab* or headscarf, regular mosque attendance and taking religious classes, fasting] and identifications, Amira is pulled into a community, and not the national community to which individual citizens are, according to television scriptwriters, supposed to relate themselves.

Reading source

Abu-Lughod, 2002, pp.122–26 ■ ■ ■

Global genres, like melodrama, take nationally specific forms, as we have seen in India and in Egypt. The global/local model of communications often ignores this fact and tends to underestimate the continuing significance of the national contexts of media production and consumption.

Abu-Lughod highlights how melodrama is mobilised in various ways in modernist projects of the state. Producers and scriptwriters consciously attempt to inculcate modern, secular values in audiences and create individualized citizens capable of making political and consumer choices. Yet traditional kinship systems, as well as religion, continue to define social roles. For Amira, the possible range of religious identifications opened by transnational television has increased dramatically in recent years. Her growing interest in Islam hooks Amira into the global Islamic *Ummah*, or community, and in doing so affirms her ties to Allah. But it also offers a new route to individual self-expression and respectability in Egyptian society. National identifications pull Amira in a different direction and, as in India, national identities and constructions of the 'good citizen' are gendered in particular ways. Global religious and national gendered identities co-exist in Amira (and we suppose in other women) in tension, at times complementing and at other times conflicting with each other.

Seemingly opposing belief and value systems (the traditional and modern, Islamic and secular-national, consumerist and collectivist, individualist and communitarian) are negotiated in and through melodrama. Melodrama dramatises the problems of the transition to modernity while at the same time providing symbolic resolutions to the dilemmas and conflicts experienced by modern individuals. This partly accounts for Amira's impassioned relationship to the serials. But these multiple identifications are in constant flux. They protrude and recede at different moments in different contexts in an unstable constellation of suffused power relations. 'Modern sensibilities' in Egypt, as in other post-colonial nations, thus may differ markedly from those in their western counterparts. This emphasises the continuing need for audience research that is located in national contexts but which tracks transnational forces at work in local and even individual appropriations.

Whatever the ambitions of state media projects, the social contexts of reception may undermine them. Moulding audiences is not as easy as some producers might think. As Abu-Lughod argues, states cannot control the experiences people seek outside of television watching or the everyday social worlds in which they live their lives. One of the most important contributions of ethnography is to highlight the unpredictability of audiences and the provisional nature of their engagements with media.

5.1 Narrative, emotion and state authority

Melodramas offer emotionally charged representations of the everyday social worlds in which individual subjects are the locus of turbulent inner conflict, strong sentiments and life-determining or threatening choices (**Gillespie and Toynbee, 2006**). Moral questions are firmly embedded in social relations. Amira's view of herself as the heroine of the melodrama of her life, according to Abu-Lughod, puts her in a better position to be a self-regulating individual and modern citizen. The intensity of her religious feelings, the forms of self-control in the disciplining of her body through fasting and other religious practices and her preoccupation with moral choices do not necessarily undermine, and may even support, her sense of self as a modern individual.

But what is the alternative to conceiving of one's life as narrative and oneself as the principal subject? The idea of our lives as a narrative, as a sequence of causally connected events taking place through time, has become so entrenched that it is hard to think of our lives differently. But we could see our lives as a series of haphazard, disconnected episodes with no logical or causal connection, no narrative progression, climax, resolution or overall framework of meaning – as replete with contradictions, uncertainties and ambiguities.

In seeing her life as a melodrama, Amira is encouraged to see herself 'as the subject of the emotions that sweep her and thus as more of an individual'. She may appear to have the freedom and choice of a modern individual but in reality she is sad and lonely. Her life is full of absences. She has no family to support, a brother-in-law who fails to protect her and a husband who exploited her. Her desire for love and children remains unrequited. She feels vulnerable precisely because she cannot achieve the ideal of being a subject defined by kinship and family as well as a modern individual. Melodrama may cultivate a sense of freedom and individuality which, paradoxically, serves the interests of the state better than the interests of its female subjects.

5.2 Ethnography, individual lives and the politics of research

This ethnographic account is quite different from Miller's and Mankekar's. It focuses on one individual. Might Amira simply be an idiosyncratic case, a particularly sad woman whose life does read like a melodrama? Certainly it would not be valid to make generalisations based on one case alone. But Abu-Lughod has worked in Egypt for nearly twenty years, so her analysis draws on several very valuable previous studies. By focusing on one person, she traces connections between melodrama, narrative, subjectivity and state authority. She intimates how power works in diffuse and unpredictable ways and how we come to regulate ourselves. Through the application of 'technologies of the self', we regulate our bodies, our thoughts, our emotions and our conduct as women, as citizens and as consumers. We come to inhabit subject positions through seeming acts of choice.

Abu-Lughod seeks to analyse not a programme, a narrative or even one particular kind of melodramatic serial, but a cultural form and an emotional mode. Some may object that this kind of ethnographic approach loses sight of the text altogether. But the compensation is that we get a finely articulated analysis of producers' and consumers' engagement with the genre. She tries to link, albeit tentatively, the deeper levels of subject formation to the operations of melodrama in the post-colonial setting of contemporary Egypt. This is an ambitious and difficult cultural political project marked by ambiguities and uncertainties – thus the question mark at the end of her title.

The arguments about how power works through us may be persuasive at an intuitive and abstract theoretical level; but it is difficult if not impossible to see how 'melodramatic consciousness' might operate at an empirical level. The methodological problems of researching consciousness, as Abu-Lughod herself recognises, are insurmountable.

Similarly, with notions of modern subjectivity all that one can look for are signs and meanings. But which signs and whose meanings are we looking for? We do not hear Amira's story in her own words, and even if we did, it would be hard to assess the evidence. All ethnographers select and analyse their data through their own subjective lens that is shaped by the subject positions they occupy.

We learn little of the relationship between the researcher and her subject or the actual contexts in which data was collected, so it is difficult to evaluate the empirical basis of the account. In any case this would be difficult to do in one short article (from which the reading was extracted). But this reflects a further difficulty with ethnographic accounts. They are based on detailed data but the final written account of the research can only selectively allude to that data. Although the ethnographic 'authority' of anthropologists derives from their 'being there', their evidence cannot easily be made available to the reader to scrutinise. In any case there is no pure, raw data that could be produced. All data is a construction produced by the researcher and the research context. These thorny questions of evidence and epistemology are not easily resolved.

In assessing ethnographic studies, epistemological questions need to be posed alongside questions concerning the ethics and politics of the research. Increasingly today ethnographers involve their interlocutors in the research not only out of respect and reciprocity, but also to shift the power of representation back to the subjects. What, we might wonder, would Amira make of Abu-Lughod's account of her life? Would she recognise herself?

6 Conclusion

This chapter set out to examine, via three ethnographic case studies, the place of television in everyday lives and processes of identity formation. It has highlighted the multiple identifications that audiences forge with the characters and stories of drama serials – gendered and national, religious and transnational, among others. Ethnography seeks to complicate mechanistic or essentialised conceptions of audiences, their identities and identifications. It seeks to go beyond the binaries of activity or passivity, compliance or resistance, intimacy or distance, distraction or attention that characterise much audience research, in order to shed light on the culturally specific and contingent nature of how people relate to television, and how it implicates itself in their lives in unpredictable ways. It does not bring about closure or reinforce preferred readings, but complexifies processes of interpretation and refuses to reduce complex readings to simple responses to assumed ideological messages.

The case studies have identified different ways in which audiences are addressed and conceived of as citizens and publics, consumers, users and subjects. They have shown how the serial consumption of television dramas enables regular and often very intimate emotional involvement with the characters and their worlds, and encourages ongoing dialogue and negotiations of meanings and identities to take place through everyday talk about television. We have seen how melodramas as a cultural form are implicated in the cultural construction of emotional modes and ways of conceiving self.

Three models of international communications (media imperialism, development, and global/local) were deployed in order to provide a theoretical framework. The models situated national television systems in a global context. This is a necessary starting point for any contemporary analysis of television flows that seeks to place them within wider power structures. The models suggest different ways of approaching audiences and questions of power. Taken together, the models reveal a much greater complexity in the relations between television dramas and their audiences than can any model taken alone.

Daniel Miller's study of the import of *The Young and The Restless* started out with some of the assumptions of the media imperialism model but he found that, rather than imposing US values in any direct or apparent way on passive and vulnerable audiences, this soap brought the moral, economic and social conflicts of Trinidadian society to the surface. Viewers were able to appropriate it not as a US story but as a local story. He found the global/local model provided a more useful framework of analysis. Viewed through this lens, the emulation of US fashion and style admired on the soap was seen as part of a creative process of local appropriation. However, I suggested that the appropriation of US fashions and style could just as easily be understood as part of a long-term process of 'Americanisation'. This study raises interesting questions about how ethnographic data is interpreted through both the subjective and the theoretical lens of the researcher.

This case study, drawing upon the global/local model, conceives of audiences as active and creative and concentrates on their appropriation of television to redefine 'the local'. But ethnographic studies of television audiences in local contexts need to be complemented by quantitative studies of how television circulates around the globe. Critical perspectives that illuminate the economic and cultural power of US media are needed so that we can better balance the emphasis on audience creativity and empowerment with analyses of television's power over audiences (see Downey, 2006).

The case study in Trinidad shoes how audiences are deprived of locally relevant and resonant alternatives to US and western media. Most research shows that audiences usually prefer locally or nationally produced television drama when available and of reasonably good quality. Television dramas provide a society with a way of talking to itself and tackling fundamental social problems. The best melodrama enables audiences to negotiate those tensions and provides a valve for releasing social tensions.

The global/local model helps us understand audiences' reactions to imported drama serials, but it also draws attention to the contradictions of contemporary television. 'Global' television does not mean 'universal' access to cultural goods, or uniformly negative effects. Although profound inequalities structure access to global cultural goods and the skills required to make sense of television, we have seen how audiences can and do make use of global television in unforeseeable ways. Global television is not inherently more oppressive than national and local television. These can be just as oppressive (if not more so in some cases) as domination by US or global television if poverty and patriarchy remain unchallenged. Global television can assist in processes of redefining selves and aspirations, offering alternative lifestyles and empowering role models in ways that some national television products may not.

The development model, by contrast, emphasises that national systems of broadcasting continue to play a crucial role in actively defining and promoting citizenship and national identities. Nation states are still the key political systems of the modern world even if they exist in tension with the global capitalist economy. They shape broadcasting systems and harness television to their development projects, as we saw in the case studies set in India and Egypt.

The development model is more optimistic, seeing television as a tool of modernisation in response to both national and global forces. It draws broadly on a functionalist perspective on media and audiences that emphasises the various ways in which audiences use media to satisfy a wide range of personal and social needs. This contrasts with the media imperialism model that is founded on a conception of monolithic media power and uniform effects.

But nation states in the developing world often adopt western models of broadcasting and, as part of the package, western models of development. The case studies set in India and Egypt suggest that there is no single path to development for post-colonial nations. Modern and traditional cultural forms and ways of life co-exist and are not mutually exclusive. Nor should the 'authenticity' of cultural forms, like the Indian religious epics, be seen as somehow tainted by being televised in soap operatic style. Like all cultural forms, cultures and identities, they are constantly changing and in flux and, just like the meanings of texts, never finally fixed.

Purnima Mankekar's study offers a rich and sophisticated ethnography of how television represents and promotes national and gendered subject positions. Her ethnography offers telling insights into processes of identity formation – processes made explicit in how female viewers talk about particular types of women; for example, Draupadi and Sita. This ethnography does not present a tale of hegemonic texts and passive viewers. Mankekar shows how television is a site of resistance and empowerment as well as of compliance and domination. Female viewers are not determined by texts any more than by patriarchal discourses. Viewers display complex subjectivities that are shaped by personal and social experiences as well as structured inequalities. Their deep emotional engagement with Draupadi's story and the anger it provokes causes them to reflect on women's position in Indian society past and present.

Lila Abu-Lughod offers us a compelling ethnography of a domestic servant, Amira, and her engagement with melodrama. She moves beyond notions of pleasure, resistance and domination to make connections between narrative, subjectivity and state authority. Melodrama, she argues, can be linked to the constitution of modern, individual subjectivities, encouraging individualised citizens and consumers. These arguments are tentative but they are suggestive of more profound levels of media influence.

The chapter has demonstrated that small-scale ethnographies can grapple with the operations of large-scale power systems. Through such ethnographies we can see how individual lives and subjectivities are shaped by the ways in which media exert power over us and through us. But we are also empowered in various ways by our media use. Ethnography reveals how we connect to abstract imagined entities such as nation, community, religion and culture. The ethnographies presented here are all located within the specific national, political and social contexts in which television is watched and understood. These particular and changing contexts emphasise that the role of television in viewers' lives also changes. The effects of television on our values and beliefs are not direct, predictable, uniform or constant but changing and transformative.

Ethnography is not in itself an inherently better method than others. Its success depends on how it is deployed by particular researchers – and here we have some excellent examples. Ethnography shares some of the epistemological and political problems of qualitative methods more generally: the subjectivity of the researcher; the power relations between subjects and researcher; the status of evidence and knowledge; the power and authority presumed and taken to represent others. But ethnography is more than a set of neutral tools or methods. At its best it is also an ethos based on reciprocity and respect. Above all, as the case studies show, it bears witness to the sheer versatility of our human resourcefulness and resilience in making our lives, creatively and at times playfully, from the cultural resources available to us.

Further reading

Askew, K. and Wilk, R. (eds) (2002) *The Anthropology of Media: A Reader*, Oxford, MA, Blackwell. A compilation of classic and recent media ethnographies.

Gillespie, M. (1995) *Television, Ethnicity and Cultural Change*, London/ New York, Routledge. An ethnographic monograph based on a study of British South Asian youth in Southall, London. Includes case studies of the reception of the Australian soap opera *Neighbours* and the *Mahabharata*.

Ginsburg, F.L., Abu-Lughod, L. and Larkin, B. (eds) (2002) *Media Worlds: Anthropology on a New Terrain*, Berkeley and London, CA, University of California Press. A diverse and fascinating set of case studies of national and transnational circuits of media production and consumption from an anthropological perspective.

References

Abu-Lughod, L. (2002) 'Egyptian melodrama – technology of the modern subject?' in Ginsburg, F.L. Abu-Lughod, L. and Larkin, B. (eds) *Media Worlds: Anthropology on a New Terrain*, Berkeley and London, CA, University of California Press.

Anderson, B. (1983) *Imagined Communities: Reflections on the Origins and Spread of Nationalism*, London, Verso.

Brooks, P. (1976) *The Melodramatic Imagination*, New Haven, CT, Yale University Press.

Buckingham. D. (1996) *Moving Images: Understanding Children's Emotional Responses to Television*, Manchester, University of Manchester Press.

Downey, J. (2006) 'The media industries: do ownership, size and internationalisation matter?' in Hesmondhalgh, D. (ed.) *Media Production*, Maidenhead, Open University Press/The Open University (Book 3 in this series).

Foucault, M. (1988) 'On power' in Kritzman, L.D. (ed.) *Michel Foucault – Politics, Philosophy, Culture: Interviews and Other Writings 1977–1984*, New York, Routledge.

Gillespie, M. (1995) *Television, Ethnicity and Cultural Change*, London/ New York, Routledge.

Gillespie, M. and Toynbee, J. (eds) (2006) *Analysing Media Texts*, Maidenhead, Open University Press/The Open University (Book 4 in this series).

Ginsburg, F.L., Abu-Lughod, L. and Larkin, B. (eds) (2002) *Media Worlds*, Berkeley and London, CA, University of California Press.

Gramsci, A. (1971) *Selections from the Prison Notebooks* (trans and ed. Hoare, Q. and Nowell Smith, G.), New York, International Publishers.

Liebes, T. and Katz, E. (1990) *The Export of Meaning: Cross-Cultural Readings of 'Dallas'*, Oxford, Oxford University Press.

Lutgendorf, P. (1990) '*Ramayan*: the video', *Drama Review*, vol.34, no.2, pp.127–76.

Mackay, H. (2000) 'The globalization of culture?' in Held, D. (ed.) *A Globalizing World? Culture, Economics, Politics*, London, Routledge/The Open University.

Mankekar, P. (1999) *Screening Culture, Viewing Politics: An Ethnography of Television, Womanhood and Nation in Postcolonial India*, Durham/London, Duke University Press.

Mattelart, A., Delcourt, X. and Mattelart, M. (1984), *International Image Markets*, London, Comedia.

McLuhan, M. (1964) *Understanding Media: The Extensions of Man*, New York, McGraw-Hill.

Miller, D. (1993) '*The Young and the Restless* in Trinidad: a case study of the local and global in mass consumption' in Silverstone, R. and Hirsch, E. (eds) *Consuming Technologies*, London, Routledge.

Miller, D. (1995) 'The consumption of soap opera: *The Young and the Restless* and mass consumption in Trinidad' in Allen, R.C. (ed.) *To Be Continued: Soap Operas Around the World*, London, Routledge.

Skuse, A. (1999) *Negotiated Outcomes: An Ethnography of the Production and Consumption of a BBC World Service Radio Soap Opera in Afghanistan*, PhD Thesis, University College, London.

Williams, R. (1989) 'Drama in a dramatized society' in O'Connor, A. (ed.) *Raymond Williams on Television*, London, Routledge.

The extended audience: scanning the horizon

Nick Couldry

Contents

1 Introduction

The preceding chapters of this book have developed a broad argument for rethinking what audience research should be about. In this final chapter, I want to draw together some of the strands of that argument by looking at specific ways of doing audience research differently.

Doing audience research differently means, first, operating with a different, more complex idea of what it is we are studying: the contemporary media audience. Sections 2 and 3 of this chapter develop some of the issues first raised in Chapter 1 about the changing nature of the audience and how, theoretically, we should understand it. But this theoretical shift, inevitably, has methodological implications; if our understanding of what the audience is, and does, has changed, *how* we study audiences – the particular things we look for and consider important – must change too.

This chapter aims to:

- consider the methodological issues involved in researching the contemporary audience;

- provide a case study of 'reality TV' in order to examine the social dimensions of the audience that extend beyond the original act of viewing, reading or listening to the media text;

- explore the implications of two developments in models of audience research that arise from the increasing mobility both of audiences (visits to media locations) and of the media (the domestic webcam site).

Now let us prepare the ground for the case study by examining more closely what we mean, theoretically, when we suggest that the nature of media audiences is changing.

2 What *and where* is the contemporary audience?

Consider an advertisement (Figure 5.1) that appeared on 21 February 1997 in the *G2* section of *The Guardian* newspaper. There among the advertisements for the latest film showings was a rather different type of advertisement, normally associated with the business pages: an advertisement for the sale of 750,000 shares in Wilde Films plc 'to finance an up and coming British feature film based on the play "An Ideal Husband" by Oscar Wilde'. 'The minimum investment', it continued, 'is 1,000 "B" Ordinary shares of 50p each ... ', and so on into the various technical details usually found in share offers. The first listed 'investor incentive' was not financial, but symbolic: 'to appear in the film as an extra and watch a day's shooting'. Perhaps only playfully, the intangible benefit of appearing briefly in a film was treated as a cash equivalent!

WANT TO APPEAR IN A FEATURE FILM?

Wilde Films PLC is offering 750,000 of its shares for subscription under the Enterprise Investment Scheme ('EIS') to finance an up and coming British feature film based on the play "An Ideal Husband" by Oscar Wilde. The minimum investment is 1000 "B" ordinary shares of 50p each at a price of £1 per share. *(minimum investment - £1000)*

Investor Incentives are
• *To appear in the film as an extra and watch a day's shooting* •
• *Potential tax benefits of up to 60% under the EIS* •
• *Potentially capital gains tax free after five years* •

Offer closes on 14th March 1997

For a full prospectus call 01753 ██████ **or 01753** ████████

Wilde Films PLC, Pinewood Studios, Pinewood Road, Iver Heath, Bucks SL0 0NH

Please note that (1) Levels and bases of taxation can change, (2) The above tax benefits are based on initial tax relief of 20% and deferral of capital gains tax of a further 40% (applicable to a higher rate taxpayer) through reinvestment (3) The tax reliefs referred to above are those which currently apply at the date of this advertisement, (4) The value of a relief from taxation depends on the circumstances of the taxpayer, (5) There is no recognised market for the shares in Wilde Films PLC, so that it may be difficult for the investor to sell the shares or obtain reliable information about their value or the extent of the risks to which the shares are exposed. Approved for the purposes of Section 57 of the Financial Services Act

Figure 5.1 Want to appear in a feature film? *An advertisement that appeared in* The Guardian *newspaper in February 1997*

Who were the intended readers of this advertisement? Film viewers certainly, but two more specific assumptions were being made: firstly, that they would (almost certainly) *want* to be an extra in a film and want it enough to risk a significant amount of cash for the benefit (a minimum of £500); secondly, that they would think it reasonable (or at least not completely crazy) to be publicly registered as having that desire when they applied for shares through their bank or stockbroker. We could not look for a better example of how being part of an audience is taken for granted in contemporary societies and how it is associated with, for some, a desire to perform. 'Audience-hood', in other words, is both pervasive as a cultural reference point (even in the driest of settings) and associated with more than watching television. Studying 'the audience', then, must involve observations in more than one setting and of more than one thing.

Let us make these points more specific. Recall how, at the end of Chapter 1, Sonia Livingstone argued that audience research today faces a number of challenges with which it must grapple. Those issues are complex and varied, but for our purposes here we can group them into three types: technological, social/spatial and experiential.

At the level of *technology*, we need to understand audiences' relationship to a new spectrum of media outlets: not just more media (with computing, the internet, and mobile media) but a more complex interlocking of old and new media – think, for example, of how radio is increasingly being accessed not just through the traditional radio set but through our computers and mobile phones. This is the process normally called 'convergence', although it is not the same as simplification, since the range of available media now being 'converged' has itself increased considerably. How then are the things audiences do being changed by shifts in the media technologies with which they typically interact?

The technological challenge facing audience research is linked to a *social/spatial* challenge. For, as media technologies and formats change, so do the physical and social locations of 'the audience'. This is what Abercrombie and Longhurst (1998) were arguing when, as mentioned at the end of Chapter 1, they identified three phases in the development of the audience:

1 the 'simple audience' for theatre and books before the media age (we might question whether audiences were ever 'simple' but here we can take it to mean 'simple' in the sense of co-presence of performers and audiences);

2 the 'mass audience' for the newspapers, radio, films and television of the late nineteenth and early to mid twentieth centuries; and

3 the contemporary 'diffused audience' that is almost permanently connected to one electronic medium or another, across almost every activity of social and private life.

If Abercrombie and Longhurst are partially right (we shall consider some problems in the next section) in arguing that the contemporary audience is 'diffused' across space, this raises some interesting questions: where is the best place to study what audience members do? Is it always the home, as early audience research generally assumed, or are there other important places where people perform their role as audience members? Is there only one site for studying audiences 'close-up' or is the point, precisely, to study the linkages between *many* sites in contemporary culture in order to grasp the contemporary audience?

In invoking a conception of the diffused audience, there is a risk of emphasising processes of social fragmentation: is audience activity now so various that we can no longer pull it together into an overarching account of 'what the audience does'? In this chapter, I will argue that we should not give up on the aim of building that more comprehensive account of audiences today, even if to do so we must make new connections, extending the places and activities we study in order to grasp what membership of the contemporary audience involves.

The third challenge to audience research mentioned in Chapter 1 concerns how these technological and social/spatial shifts might have affected how it feels to be part of an audience: how is the nature of audience *experience* changing? We could emphasise here the increasing individualisation of audiences' access points to media (more children in the richest countries now have their own television, computer and online connection in their bedrooms); or the increasingly global scale on which audiences are linked because of media's international flow and the internet's automatic global reach; or the new ways of engaging with media summed up in the word 'interactivity'.

If Chapter 1 challenged us to rethink audience research, later chapters have reinforced this message. In Chapter 2, Tony Bennett explored how media are not just consumed as stand-alone texts, but embedded in the whole sensory environment in which we conduct our lives. In Chapter 3, David Herbert shifted our focus and we looked at audiences conceived of as national publics who, through their viewing practices, are drawn into political processes. In Chapter 4, Marie Gillespie examined ethnographic studies of audiences in different parts of the world. She examined the ways in which audiences interpret and use television, and how television experiences shape, and are shaped by, social identities. In this chapter, I draw together and develop various strands of argument from across the book in order to rethink how we conceive of audiences today, and to map out some future directions in the study of audiences.

3 From 'diffused' to 'extended' audience

What is the 'diffused audience'? To clarify what this might mean, we need first to examine in more detail Abercrombie and Longhurst's notion of the diffused audience: what are its implications? Can we take it as a completely accurate account of the contemporary audience, or are there aspects of their conception of the audience that we should challenge?

3.1 How is the audience 'diffused'?

Activity 5.1

Go back to the Conclusion to Chapter 1 and your notes on it, and re-read the chapter's discussion of how the contemporary audience might be seen as 'diffused'. Note down what you originally understood by this term, and then any ways in which your understanding of it has been made more specific by later chapters. ■ ■ ■

As we have seen, the concept of the 'diffused audience' emerges as the final stage of Abercrombie and Longhurst's three-stage history of the audience. In fact, since their first stage (the 'simple audience') concerns the pre-media age, its relevance for media research turns principally on the shift Abercrombie and Longhurst see from 'mass' to 'diffused' audiences. We will come in a moment to what exactly we might mean by the 'diffused' audience. Firstly, we should note that Abercrombie and Longhurst develop their history as part of a larger argument about where audience research is heading. They argue (Abercrombie and Longhurst, 1998, Chapter 1) that it should move away from the analysis of ideology and the power relations between centralised media institutions and a remote 'mass' audience towards an interest in the varieties of audience-hood, where questions of domination become less central. This, they argue, is because the experience of audiences is no longer a 'mass' experience, but one deeply embedded in the varieties of individuals' own lives.

Putting that aspect of Abercrombie and Longhurst's argument to one side for now (it becomes important later), one thing immediately attractive about the notion of the 'diffused audience' is that it captures our sense that media, not just audiences, are *everywhere*. If we travel home from work, we may well be inundated with signs of the presence of media, assuming we choose to see them (we may choose to screen them out!): not only the long-familiar forms of the newspaper, the television screen seen in bars or passed in shop windows, and magazines, but perhaps news played over our personal stereo, or news and marketing updates relayed to our mobile phone or, if we live in a large town, neon displays giving the latest news headlines from a satellite news station. Media, it seems, are everywhere – not just in the corner of our living room as they used to be. The diffused nature of media today may be the most important place to start in understanding the contemporary audience. As Todd Gitlin put it:

> For all the talk, and the talk about the talk, the main truth about media slips through our fingers – the immensity of the experience of media, the sheer quantity of attention paid, the devotions and rituals that absorb our time and resources. The obvious but hard-to-grasp truth is that living with the media is today one of the main things Americans and many other human beings do.
>
> Gitlin, 2001, pp.4–5

So, if media are diffused in this sense, it seems natural to think of the audience that consumes those media as diffused as well, at least in wealthier countries (whether this argument is so compelling in other parts of the world is an important point to consider, although I do not have space to do so here).

If we concentrate on the media experiences of a wealthy country such as the UK, describing the audience as diffused has plenty of initial plausibility. It also fits well with a claim made by other writers about the direction of audience research. In a book written around the same time as Abercrombie and Longhurst's *Audiences*, the Finnish media researcher Pertti Alasuutaari introduced the idea that audience research or 'reception studies', as he calls it, has entered a 'third phase' (the first phase, incidentally, in this account was a classic analysis of how audiences decode media texts which you learned about in Chapter 1, while the second phase involved the audience 'ethnography' which you encountered in Chapter 4).

What distinguishes the current phase of audience research, according to Alasuutaari, is its more multi-dimensional way of thinking about the audience (Alasuutaari, 1999, pp.6–17). Alasuutaari's account is quite complex, but it is well summarised in the following passage:

> The third generation [of audience research] entails a broadened frame within which one conceives of the media and media use. One does not necessarily abandon ethnographic case studies of audiences or analyses of individual programmes, but the main focus is not restricted to finding out about the reception or 'reading' of a programme by a particular audience. *Rather, the objective is to get a grasp of our contemporary 'media culture'* ... the discourses within which we conceive of our roles as the public and the audience, and how notions of programmes-with-an-audience are inscribed in both media messages and assessments about news events and about what is going on in the 'world'.
>
> Alasuutaari, 1999, p.6 (emphasis added)

Alasuutaari expresses an interesting possibility: that the task of contemporary audience research is to grasp not just the direct interactions of audiences with a text, or even just the rich everyday context of those interactions, but something much bigger: the whole *media 'culture'* in which audience activity takes place and through which its wider meanings are inscribed. Joke Hermes (1999) develops the same point from the perspective of identity: we should study, Hermes argues, people's investments in many aspects of general media culture (not just the details of particular texts) as ways of constructing identity.

The point behind the historical narratives of Abercrombie and Longhurst, on the one hand, and Alasuutaari, on the other, is basically the same: that the contemporary audience is a dispersed phenomenon extending far beyond the act of sitting down to watch a particular programme. The dispersed audience allows us to think about the spatial location of audiences, while the notion of the diffused audience raises different questions about the social and power relationships between producers and consumers. However, the underlying idea that audiences and audience activities can no longer be located in the sitting room and may span a variety of social contexts, blurring the boundaries between public and private, is important to hold on to, even if there are other aspects of Abercrombie and Longhurst's account that we should challenge.

3.2 The problem of power

Through their concept of the 'diffused audience' Abercrombie and Longhurst claim something more about the contemporary audience than that it is just dispersed. It is their wider claims that we now need to consider in detail.

Reading 5.1 Activity

Now read this extract from Nicholas Abercrombie and Brian Longhurst's book *Audiences: A Sociological Theory of Performance and Imagination* (Reading 5.1) and answer the following questions:

■ What do Abercrombie and Longhurst mean by saying that 'everyone becomes an audience all the time'? Can you think of any counter-examples?

■ What do you make of their further claim that the audience's imagined relationship to production has also changed? What might be evidence for or against it? What are they implying here about the (changing) power of audiences?

■ How many people do *you* know who have been a media performer? Do you think your answer tends to support or to undermine Abercrombie and Longhurst's claim?

Reading 5.1

Nicholas Abercrombie and Brian Longhurst, 'Diffused audiences'

Further fundamental social and cultural changes have produced a very different type of audience-experience, which we will call the *diffused audience*. The essential feature of this audience-experience is that, in contemporary society, everyone becomes an audience all the time. Being a member of an audience is no longer an exceptional event, nor even an everyday event. Rather it is constitutive of everyday life. This is not a claim that simple audiences or mass audiences no longer exist. Quite the contrary. These experiences are as common as ever, but they take place against the background of the diffused audience. Indeed, as we shall show later, the three audience forms [the simple, the mass and the diffused] can feed off one another.

The notion of the diffused audience refers to several processes operating at different levels. First people spend a lot of *time* in consumption of mass media in the home – and in public. This is a media drenched society. [...]

If households are simply spending more time in the consumption of the mass media, a second and more fundamental argument is that the media are actually *constitutive* of everyday life. The media and everyday life have become so closely interwoven that they are almost inseparable. This is not just that the mass media are essentially private and directed at domestic life [...] It is a claim that the very constitution and regulation of the mundane is in the hands of the media. [...]

Television has, relatively quickly in Western societies, become integrated into the routines of everyday life. [...]

[...]

One of the effects of the intrusion of the media into everyday life is the way that formerly innocent events become turned into performances with the further result that the people involved in those events come to see themselves as performers. For example, the protests in Britain in the early 1990s in port towns against the export of live animals will have started as a simple wish to stop this trade. In a sense it was a simple performance which rapidly becomes a performance for the mass media, as press and television begin to take an interest. At that point, the protesters see themselves not only as making a moral and political point, but also as performers for a variety of audiences. [...]

In brief, the diffused audience arises from the interaction of two processes, both of which are modern. On the one hand, there is the construction of the world as spectacle and, on the other, the construction of individuals as narcissistic. People simultaneously feel members of an audience and that they are performers; they are simultaneously watchers and being watched. As Rubin (1970) puts it in talking about street political action: 'Life is theatre and we are the guerrillas attacking the shrines of authority. ... The street is the stage. You are the star of the show and everything you were once taught is up for grabs' (p.250, quoted in Schechner, 1993, p.64). Spectacle and narcissism feed off each other in a virtuous cycle, a cycle fuelled largely by the media and mediated by the critical role of performance. As with the other types of audience, performance is the key, but, unlike the other types, performance is not linked to events, but has, so to speak, *leaked out* into the conduct of everyday life.

In terms of the characteristics described in [Table 5.1], the diffused audience is clearly a very different animal from both simple and mass audiences. A crucial feature is that the distance between performers and audiences so important to performances in front of both simple and mass audiences has been more or less eliminated. Rubin (1970) puts this brutally in an essay on 'Revolution is Theatre-in-the-Streets'. 'You are the stage. You are the actor. Everything is for real. There is no audience' (p.132, quoted in Schechner, 1993, p.91). Since people are simultaneously performers and audience members, cultural consumers become cultural producers and vice versa. Being a member of a diffused audience is not necessarily to be in the position of receiving a message from a producer of messages; it is not like being *addressed* by a producer. [...] This homogenization of producers and consumers is related to the acquisition by audiences of *skills* of various kinds, the absence of which previously emphasized the distance between performers and audience. In the right circumstances, audience members use these skills to become cultural producers in their own right inside what we shall call *enthusiasms*.

Table 5.1

	Simple	Mass	Diffused
Communication	Direct	Mediated	Fused
Local/global	Local	Global	Universal
Ceremony	High	Medium	Low
Public/private	Public	Private	Public and private
Distance	High	Very high	Low
Attention	High	Variable	Civil inattention

As far as the other features described in [Table 5.1] are concerned, communication is direct and unmediated; media institutions do not interpose between performer and audience. There is little or no ceremony, for these are the practices of everyday life. Attention is generally low or variable, switching from intense concentration to relative inattention. Diffused audiences are both local and global, local in actual performance, global in that imagination – not restricted in space and time – is a crucial resource in the performance. Performances for diffused audiences are public *and* private. Indeed, they erode the difference between the two.

The potential for erosion of the distinction between private and public inherent in diffused audiences' performances suggests a general characteristic of this audience form – the breaking of boundaries. Specifically, we would argue that performance events, or media events, cannot be distinguished so well from one another and, indeed, there is a fusion of different *forms* of the media.

References

Rubin, J. (1970) *Do it!*, New York, Simon and Schuster.

Schechner, R. (1993) *The Future of Ritual*, London, Routledge.

Reading Source

Abercrombie and Longhurst, 1998, pp.68–76 ▪ ▪ ▪

Abercrombie and Longhurst argue that the relationship between audience and media industry, between media *consumption* and media *production*, is being changed, as the possibility of being on the other side of the consumption/production boundary becomes more readily imaginable by audiences. The 'diffused audience' concept represents for Abercrombie and Longhurst more than a technological convergence of the forms through which we access media; it is a convergence of social relations as well in which the once clearly demarcated social role of 'audience' (as *receiver* of media contents) becomes less obviously distinguished in everyday life from the role of the media industry (as *producer* of media contents). According to Abercrombie and Longhurst (1998, p.75), 'people are simultaneously [media] performers and audience members', with the social distinction between the two falling away.

If true, this is clearly an important claim. But does it follow automatically from the more straightforward point that the experience of being in an audience is now pervasive? This is much less certain.

We can agree that being an audience member is now an experience familiar to everyone. We can also agree that, as audiences become more 'media literate' (and most of today's television audiences, for example, will have grown up watching television, as I did), *the idea* of what it *might* be like to be a performer on television is more widespread than it once was. Certainly, this is what some American commentators have claimed, arguing, as Neal Gabler has done (Gabler, 2000) that whole dimensions of everyday life in the USA (from beauty care to crime) are now shaped by people's sense that they might appear on television some day! We should be careful about assuming that such changes in 'media culture' (to use Alasuutaari's term) are happening everywhere in the same way – and the question of *how* places might differ in this respect is a fascinating, if surprisingly under-researched, question, that we are unable to go into here. For now, let us keep our focus on the idea that some audiences might be getting used to the idea of being on the other side of the fence, becoming not the consumer, but the producer, of media, or at least part of the production process.

At this point, however, we need to pose some straightforward questions that remain unanswered in Abercrombie and Longhurst's admittedly theoretical argument, and about which Reading 5.1 Activity should have set you thinking. Is it true that everyone in today's media-saturated societies knows *both* what it is like to be a member of a media audience *and* what it is like to be a media performer? Since it seems obvious that there remain many people who have not been a media performer, should we conclude that Abercrombie and Longhurst think their argument does not depend on this factual point? If so, what are they really arguing? The point, it seems, is that, while the number of people who have *actually* been media performers remains quite low (although perhaps it increases with every year of 'reality TV', as more and more 'ordinary people' are invited onto television), it is our regular familiarity with the idea and 'look' of media performance that matters. Their proposal, perhaps, is that we are now so familiar with watching others perform (others 'like us', that is, and not just media professionals) that media performance itself has become ordinary and taken for granted, creating a *continuum* with audience viewing at one end and media performing at the other. It is this that lies behind their assertion that 'media institutions do not interpose between performer and audience' (Abercrombie and Longhurst, 1998, p.75), as well as their bigger claim that audience research in the age of the 'diffused audience' should focus much less on power.

This, however, is a much more contentious claim than merely saying the audience is dispersed. Since media institutions clearly still exist, questions remain about the power of such institutions and audiences' relation to that power. To mention 'power', and specifically the power of media institutions, raises some difficult questions which we will not be able to resolve here. It is certainly true that most contemporary accounts of power follow the French philosopher Michel Foucault (compare the discussion at the end of Chapters 2 and 4) in arguing that we cannot simply study power by looking at the assets and capacities possessed by particular people or institutions 'in power' (whether kings, governments, or corporations); instead, as Foucault (1980) insisted, we need to look at how, across social life as a whole, a huge number of activities involving everyone (including those who are not 'in power') contribute to sustaining particular power relations.

This 'dispersed' approach to power, in fact, fits well with the dispersed approach to the audience that we have been developing (as I have argued in more detail elsewhere: see Couldry, 2000, Chapter 1). It would certainly be misleading, therefore, to talk about 'media power' as if it were simply an asset that media institutions, such as television production companies, possessed; clearly, it is a society-wide phenomenon which all of us, in various ways, are involved in sustaining, not least through what we do as audience members.

But this is very different from saying that every participant in media culture (from you and me as television viewers, to newspaper journalists and commentators, to television producers such as the BBC or Endemol, the *Big Brother* production company) has the same standing, or is able to do the same things, as every other participant. I shall come back to Alasuutaari's term 'media culture' shortly, since it too needs some unpacking, but for now let us focus on how we might best understand the possible differences here between media institutions and members of the media audiences.

Firstly, there is the power which media corporations have (but audience members do not) to decide who appears in the widely circulated images and stories that we call 'media', for example *Big Brother* (UK, Channel 4, 2000 to present) or *Pop Idol* (UK, ITV1, 2001–2003): it seems odd to say this power differential has disappeared at a time when ever larger numbers compete to be seen on television. Secondly, there is the influence media corporations have (but audience members generally do not) over what information circulates widely in society, including information that is accorded the status of 'news'. It can be argued that audiences in many respects depend on media corporations for access to the socially important information we call 'news' (Thompson, 1995). This relationship of dependence does not disappear just because the experience of media consumption is dispersed.

How exactly we assess the importance of these forms of 'power' in relation to other forms of power (economic, or military, for example) is, of course, a huge question, but a helpful way of thinking about the sort of power associated with media institutions has been suggested by John Thompson in his book *The Media and Modernity*. He calls it 'symbolic power', which he defines as 'the capacity to intervene in the course of events, to influence the actions of others and indeed to create events, by means of the production and transmission of symbolic forms' (Thompson, 1995, p.17).

We do not need to consider this definition for long to realise that media, among other institutions, have power of this sort, since media activities involve, above all, 'the production and transmission of symbolic forms', such as television programmes, radio shows, newspapers or films.

The key question, however, returning to our assessment of Abercrombie and Longhurst's account of the changing relationship between audiences and media, is whether the dispersal and pervasiveness of the experience of belonging to an audience means, necessarily, that the 'symbolic power' of media institutions has been reduced. Abercrombie and Longhurst's argument, in effect, is that it does. But it is just as possible to argue in the *opposite* direction, that, in a world where media signals are everywhere (so in that sense the audience *is* 'diffused'), the differences between audience members and media performers have come to matter more, not less. The broader and more varied people's everyday engagement with media (and the less 'massified' the audience is in one sense), the greater may be the value attached to no longer being a 'mere' audience member and performing instead.

If so, in studying audiences, rather than turning our attention away from questions of power as Abercrombie and Longhurst propose, we should be building them back in to our account, even if, perhaps, in more complex ways.

3.3 The 'extended' audience

Where does this leave us? It suggests, I think, that, when we consider both weaknesses and strengths of Abercrombie and Longhurst's argument in favour of the concept of the 'diffused' audience, we can see that we might be better served by a different term. The term I propose is the 'extended' audience.

The strength of the 'diffused' audience concept was to capture how the experience of being in a media audience is both very widely shared and highly differentiated, as differentiated as the rest of our everyday lives. But its weakness was to suggest that the power dimensions of an earlier audience–media relationship have somehow been diffused or reduced. It threatens to divert us from the continuing power differentials between audiences and media institutions, which, arguably, remain as sharp as ever, and may even have been intensified by the pervasiveness of 'the audience'.

The notion of the 'extended' audience requires us to examine the whole spectrum of talk, action and thought that draws on media, or is oriented towards media. In this way, we can broaden our understanding of the relationship between media and media audiences as part of our understanding of contemporary media culture.

'Media culture', as we saw, is a term introduced by Alasuutaari (1999) to capture the huge range of ways in which we are orientated towards media and deal with them in our lives. Chapter 4 has already introduced you to some important aspects of media culture in the context of broader issues of cultural difference and cultural exchange. Here I want to keep the focus on how the idea of the 'extended' audience can contribute to our understanding of contemporary media culture, and in particular the recent media phenomenon of 'reality TV'.

4 Reality TV: a contemporary audience phenomenon

No one who watched television in Europe or North America in the 1990s and early 2000s could be unaware of the phenomenon of 'reality TV'. In the next two sections we will take a closer look at 'reality TV', in particular the *Big Brother* format introduced across many countries, which involves, in a sort of 'reality' game show, people competing to remain in a 'house' specifically constructed for the programme.

4.1 Presenting the audience's 'reality'

'Reality television' is, of course, a paradoxical phrase, because media, as representations of the world, cannot in one sense be 'reality'. The phenomenon of 'reality TV', however, makes perfect sense within the wider history of media's claims to connect us with a shared social reality ('what's going on' in our society). Recent 'reality television' has taken a variety of forms. Perhaps the most useful definition has been provided by Richard Kilborn (1994, p.423). Reality TV, Kilborn argues, involves (abbreviating his description slightly):

1   recording 'on the wing' of events in the lives of individuals or groups; or

2   the attempt to simulate real-life events through dramatised reconstruction; or

3   the incorporation of 1 and 2 in edited form in a packaged programme.

This definition captures well the formal flexibility of 'reality TV': from the mid-1990s' explosion of 'docu-soaps' in the UK (such series as BBC's *Hotel* and *Driving School*) to programmes based on reconstructions of action by the emergency services (in the UK, BBC's *999*, see Figure 5.2, and in the USA, *Rescue 911* and *Cops*), to package programmes which run together clips from surveillance footage provided by the emergency services or camcorder footage shot by viewers (in the UK, *Police, Camera, Action* and *You've Been Framed*, see Figure 5.3).

Other writers have argued for a narrower definition. For example, Jon Dovey (2000, p.71) argues that the term should be focused on programmes where the claim to represent 'reality' is at its most direct, as in footage or reconstructions sourced from the emergency services, with no obvious element of fictionality. Narrowing our definition, however, risks obscuring the flexibility of the idea of 'reality TV'. The claim to offer special access to 'reality' is compatible with many formats, including elements of fictional packaging (the 'docu-soap') or humorous

Figure 5.2 *A still from the Reality TV show, 999, showing a reconstruction of a helicopter accident. The helicopter crashed while filming a volcano site*

Figure 5.3 *Lisa Riley, presenter of the reality TV show* You've Been Framed
Source: Granada TV

commentary (*Candid Camera*), or (in reality TV's dominant development in the early 2000s) the television game show (or 'game-doc') of which the best-known example is *Big Brother*. The game-doc, while at one level explicitly a game between contestants like other studio-based games, at another level claims to show us the 'reality' of the participants by constructing long-term 'real situations' in which we can see them interact.

There is much more we could say about the historical factors underlying the rise of reality TV (see Kilborn, 1994; Dovey, 2000, for useful accounts): economic imperatives were clearly important in an era of increasing financial pressures upon, and competition between, programme schedulers, and reality TV offered cheap and (more or less) reliable ways of gaining significant audiences. We could say a lot also about the formal innovations in reality TV (see Corner, 2002). But in a book about audiences the most important thing to emphasise about reality TV as programming is the most obvious: the claim implicit in all reality TV that it presents the 'reality' of the social world, and, in particular, the 'reality' *of at least some of television's audience.*

It is true that some reality formats involve a considerable degree of distancing, showing the real lives of those precisely different from the audiences assumed to be watching them (particularly crime-based programmes which show surveillance footage). But in most reality TV everyday scenes are presented, especially work situations, from the lives of at least one sector of the presumed television audience. Reality TV in that sense appears to deliver on what Raymond Williams (with television *fictional* drama in mind) saw as the main promise of television: to provide 'images ... of what living is now like for this kind of person ... in this situation and place' (Williams, 1975, p.9). Implicitly, reality TV claims to allow parts of the audience to see *each other,* not in the controlled situation of the studio, but in everyday life. This represents a shift in the relationship (or at least in the *constructed* relationship) between audiences and the media industry, because the 'ordinary people' now presented on television are the 'ordinary people' previously assumed to be audiences only.

We would, then, expect audiences to have a complex relationship to the texts of reality TV. We will explore this both for the case of reality TV in general, and for a specific case where 'ordinary reality' is turned into a game: *Big Brother.*

4.2 Audience talk about reality TV

The classic form of audience research asked: how do audiences interpret a particular media text? This approach can be applied, in principle, to any type of media text. But when (as in the case of reality TV) the most distinctive thing about a media text is its claim to present something close to the 'real' everyday lives of its audience, then audience research must consider not just how they interpret the text as a story, but how they compare that story to their own lives. We can also expect the claims about everyday 'reality' in reality TV programmes to circulate back into everyday talk and thought more generally.

Reality TV, then, poses a particular challenge to audience research to ensure that we study the full range of ways in which its texts are put to use in everyday life, including in everyday claims about 'reality'. We need, in other words, to understand the 'extended audience' for reality TV as it operates far beyond the original viewing of the text.

The study of reality TV's audiences is relatively new, but as Annette Hill's work (Hill, 2002) highlights, a great deal of audience talk focuses on questions of authenticity. The picture of the audience we get from her work is much more complex than the often-heard crude characterisation of reality TV as 'voyeurism' might lead us to expect. On the one hand, there is considerable interest in looking for something like 'authentic' performance in reality TV, even in the apparently most constructed type of reality TV, the 'game-doc':

> Viewers watch BB [*Big Brother*] for many reasons ... but perhaps the most striking reason for watching BB is that everybody else is watching and talking about it, and everybody else is forming judgements on the contestants and how they act up for the cameras. The focus on the degree of actuality, on real people's improvised performances in the programme, leads to a particular viewing practice: audiences look for the moment of authenticity when real people are 'really' themselves in an unreal environment.
>
> Hill, 2002, p.324

On the other hand, scepticism about the 'reality' of reality TV is high, with more than 70 per cent of those surveyed by Hill questioning its authenticity, across all ages, classes and genders (Hill, 2002, p.328). If we recognise from the outset that the issue of authenticity is *inevitably* raised by programmes that claim to represent the lived reality of their audiences, then this general scepticism may not be surprising. If people are asked directly about whether they *believe* in reality TV, we might expect them, perhaps, to say 'no, we don't', because such reality programmes automatically raise questions of authenticity. But, as Hill suggests, this is not incompatible with audiences also seeking out the 'reality' amidst the construction, as in *Big Brother*. So this is not a simple scepticism either.

Reading 5.2 Activity

You should now read Annette Hill's 'Reality TV' (Reading 5.2), and answer the following questions:

- How, in Hill's interview extracts, do those interviewed judge whether material on television is constructed or not?
- Are there any contradictions in how they talk about this question?
- Hill interprets her interviewees as discussing questions of 'authenticity' – is this how you would interpret what they say in this extract?
- What evidence do these interviews provide of interviewees' sense of the importance of appearing on television?

Reading 5.2

Annette Hill, 'Reality TV'

Here is an example of the way audiences typically talk about authentic 'performances' in reality programming:

Peter It's real life, innit, I mean ...

Rick I don't think it is though... The ones on holiday are more real life than these people, I don't, I don't believe anything now, I think it's all an act but on holiday they might be acting a little bit more but because they're drunk as well it's real life, innit.

Nancy It's not real life really, is it? Cos real life doesn't happen like that?

Rick If it were real life you, you'd have to not know that the cameras were there and that's never the case with any of those programmes.

Paul If it was real life I'd be watching someone sitting down watching telly all day.

This group of adult viewers were discussing travel reality series, such as *Ibiza Uncovered*, that often feature British tourists behaving badly abroad. Variations on the word 'reality' are echoed in each turn of the conversation ('real', 'real life'), and this points to a critical examination of the truth claims of these programmes. As with other examples of audience discussion I have used [...], the authenticity of reality programming is examined in relation to the performances of the people featured in the programmes themselves. These viewers question how the talk and behaviour of the ordinary people being filmed on holiday in Ibiza can be judged as authentic given that they are under the influence of alcohol. For one viewer, the fact that British tourists are drunk is a good indication of the reality of their behaviour in the programme – the more drunk, the less control these tourists will have of their behaviour. But, for other viewers in the group the fact that these tourists know they are being filmed for a reality programme is a good indication of the falseness of their behaviour. One viewer refers to the commonsense belief that in order to create entertaining television you need people to be entertaining – 'if it was real life I'd be watching someone sitting down watching telly all day'. The effect of the final statement is to end discussion – case closed. [...]

The following discussion is based on a story in *Ibiza Uncovered* about two married men on holiday with their wives and children. The two men are 'Jack the lads', who are out on the town, looking for some action of the female persuasion. We follow them as they drink in bars, flirt with single girls, some of whom flash their breasts, or bottoms at the men (and the cameras), and stagger home at the end of the night, somewhat the worse for wear. From the point of view of the programme itself, the authenticity of the talk and behaviour of these two guys is presented very much as true to their experience – this is what we are normally like on holiday in Ibiza. From the point of view of the audience, the programme's truth claims are treated with suspicion, but not rejected outright. These male viewers (aged 18–44) draw on their own experience to assess the authenticity of the behaviour of the two men on holiday:

Max You go to Southend, it's like filming Southend on a Friday or Saturday night, you see exactly the same thing.

Shaun I think that's rubbish what they've put on there, if the camera's there, everyone is going to act up

Max Yeah, that's right, especially on holiday ...

Shaun They were in the bar, had a drink, turned around and that was it, straight away. It doesn't work, not so quick as that, but because the cameras are there, the girl sees the camera, thinks 'Oh I want to be on TV' ...

Max And the thing is, it starts them off sober and we're going out clubbing, you see them as they get ... as they're getting a little bit tipsy but they're getting a little bit, they're getting tipsy a little too quick for my liking ... and then it shows them being childish ...

Brian I think that they'd be worse if the cameras weren't there!

Max   In fact, I think it could have got naughtier ... they were being a little bit the boys ... people go out there and doing what they were doing to those girls, they wouldn't still be on that dance floor, I tell you that now. Not a chance, not a chance ...

Terry   I've been to Spain and all that, with the boys and everything, and I've never seen anything like that ...

Max   Let's face it, if you had two other guys who weren't two guys who were coming across Jack the lad. I mean, all of us guys have been Jack the lad at some stage, most probably some of us still are, but, if they picked another two guys that were more, er, nervy, then how would it have gone. The entertainment might not have been there.

Brian   But they might have been actors, mightn't they?

Max   But, you won't get ... I don't think they were actors cos any guy that they says 'Right, there's a camera, we're making this, do you mind us filming you?' and they would have looked at these guys and said 'Well, like, they're a bit Jack the lad, they're game and we're in there.' Boom, that's what they got.

Barry   You've got to find someone whose wife, who'd let them go and film them anyway. I mean my wife wouldn't let me do that. I mean I'd love to go and do it. I mean it'd be a good crack ... [laughs]

Terry   She'd know exactly what you were going to get up to!

There are several overlapping points being made by these male viewers about the authenticity of this scene from *Ibiza Uncovered*. Most of the viewers referred to their own experience of being out for a night on the town, being 'a bit Jack the lad', to make sense of the scene. For Shaun, the two men attracted an unnatural (i.e. instantaneous) interest from girls precisely because there were cameras present. This meant the situation was unnatural, and the men weren't themselves – 'they were in a different skin'. For Max, the scenario seemed false because the men didn't act the way he imagined they would act – they were drunk too quickly, they didn't flirt enough, 'it could have got naughtier'. Thus, the scene wasn't true to this viewer's experience of similar situations (Southend on a Friday night), and the men weren't true to themselves, in the sense of being red-blooded males. There was certainly agreement the men performed well, and provided entertainment – one viewer even suggested the men were actors. But, the fact that the men gave such good performances drew attention to how the programme was constructed. The final reality check comes from one viewer who judges the scene untrue in relation to his own experience of being married – were those men really given permission by their wives to behave badly?

Reading source
Hill, 2004, pp.74–77 ▪ ▪ ▪

As Hill's discussion brings out, there are conflicting currents in what her interviewees say. On the one hand, they may draw on many aspects of their own experience to judge whether details of on-screen behaviour are authentic or not (how quickly people appeared to get drunk, and so on); they do so apparently on the basis that the truth of what is presented in the programme is worth debating, rather than its falsity and constructedness being a foregone conclusion. On the other hand, cutting across this is some interviewees' sense that people necessarily act up in the presence of a camera. Take Shaun's comment in Hill's second extract: 'because the cameras are there, the girl sees the camera, thinks "OK, I want to be on TV" ...'. This sense of the *power* of the camera may be connected to another interviewee's ironic sense that the events shown in 'reality' television in fact bear only a limited relation to his life as an audience member: (Paul in Hill's first extract) 'if it was real life I'd be watching someone sitting down watching telly all day'.

What we see here are the complex, at times contradictory, positions that audiences take up in discussing 'reality', and the awareness, implied in what audiences say, of the power of the television camera (compare my discussion of media institutions' 'symbolic power' in Section 3). Audiences of reality TV are well aware of what the US media critic Neal Gabler calls 'the sanctification of the television camera' (Gabler, 2000, p.187). The idea that media, particularly television, confer social status, and that this might be one of the most important dimensions of media's power, is an old one, first noted in 1948 at the beginning of media research by Paul Lazarsfeld and Robert Merton (republished as Lazarsfeld and Merton, 1969).

Lazarsfeld and Merton were writing at a time when television was in its infancy and appearances of non-media people in any medium were exceptional. This is clearly no longer the case. One interesting question about the contemporary audience, if we consider it in the 'extended' fashion suggested at the end of Section 3, is how media performance (its possibility and attractions) is reflected upon by audiences. What are the consequences of the frequent representations of 'ordinary people' in media for our everyday understanding of what is important, authentic, 'real' in everyday life?

These are the sorts of questions opened up by a consideration of the reality TV audience. We will return in Section 4.4 to these broader questions, but first we should look a little more closely at how our sense of what audiences *do* has been extended by audience reactions to reality TV in particular.

4.3 *Big Brother* – the final night!

Audiences of reality TV, or at least many of them, do more than just *watch* a programme, as Kim Schrøder and his colleagues argue (Schrøder et al., 2003, pp.3–5) (see Figures 5.4 and 5.5). They may read articles about the participants in celebrity magazines, visit the programme website, email contestants, join online chat groups about the programme, or receive SMS messages on their mobile phones about what is happening 'right now' in the *Big Brother* house. They may also, of course, vote by phone or text message in the weekly decision about who stays in the house – all this in addition to sitting down to watch the programme and subsequently talking about it to friends or people at work, the two activities on which earlier audience research concentrated.

Figure 5.4 *The fans of Tom, a participant on* Big Brother, *wait outside the Big Brother household and make their feelings known*

It is clear, then, that 'the modern audience experience ... is becoming increasingly multi-dimensional and multiply interactive' (Schrøder et al., 2003, p.4). More poetically, Schrøder and colleagues see the audience member changing from 'couch potato' to 'semiotic juggler'. Leaving aside this rather romantic proposal (is this new interpretative flexibility of the reality TV audience as extensive as Schrøder suggests? Even if it is, is it new?), it is clear

Figure 5.5 *Craig, the winner of the first UK series of* Big Brother, *being escorted by the presenter of the programme, Davina McCall*

that most of these extended dimensions of audience engagement only emerged through the availability of new media *technologies*, particularly the convergence of traditional electronic media (television, video) with computer-mediated communications. A major television product such as *Big Brother* may transcend the divides between specific media to create a total, all-consuming 'event' which merits continuous monitoring.

Or so it seems. We should beware of exaggerating the changes here: as Hill points out, actual accessing of websites linked to reality-TV programmes is a minority pursuit (15 per cent in her survey of audiences in 2000, the year of *Big Brother*'s introduction to the UK: Hill, 2002, p.332). Similarly, we should acknowledge how the vision of total connectedness (the idea repeated in Schrøder et al. [2003, p.4] of 'the network society of the future characterized increasingly by communicatively hyper-complex phenomena like *Big Brother*') is precisely part of the hype that various media technology producers and suppliers want to create. As one newspaper commented in 2001 just before the second series of UK *Big Brother* started: 'ultimately the [enhanced] SMS services may all boil down to the quality of the content and characters, not forgetting the giddy excitement that can be generated from a message telling Big Brother obsessives of two housemates being in bed together – "live on the internet now"' (*The Guardian*, *Online* section, 24 May 2001, p.5).

Leaving aside the hype, however, there remains, as Schrøder et al. note, a strong argument for a multi-focused approach to studying a phenomenon as complex as the *Big Brother* audience.

Once we have a clearer picture of the distinctiveness of how audiences engage in a multimedia output such as *Big Brother* (and, as we have seen, what is important is the evidence here, which may be much less dramatic than the marketing hype), we still need to ask how, within the tradition of audience research, to make sense of this phenomenon. Much of the interest around *Big Brother* among academic writers and general cultural commentators is based on a claim that the *Big Brother* audience (and audiences for similar participatory 'reality' shows) signifies not just a new form of interactive media entertainment, but a significant new form of social participation.

Activity 5.2

Take a reality TV programme you or (if you do not watch such programmes) a friend watches regularly. Make a list of all the things you do (or that friend does) in connection with that programme over and above watching it.

- How important are these additional activities to your (or your friend's) enjoyment of the programme?
- Does it make sense to say these activities involve you (or your friend) in a 'community' with other viewers of the programme? ∎ ∎ ∎

A number of writers have argued that there is an important social dimension to this behaviour which constitutes a new type of event-based sociality, something particularly significant in societies that, in other ways, feel increasingly fragmented. One such writer is the French sociologist Michel Maffesoli who introduced the notion of contemporary societies as 'neo-tribal' (Maffesoli, 1996), based less around old-style stable group markers such as class and ethnicity, and much more around micro-distinctions between those who share specific tastes and passions, particularly tastes orchestrated through media. Without getting into wider debates about the overall nature of contemporary social order, which would take us too far afield, there is certainly something intriguing in Maffesoli's claim (made before reality TV's explosion, but with early forms of participative television in mind) that such media-focused events produce '"instant condensations" [which] can operate periodically, which are fragile, but in the same moment elicit strong emotional investment' (Maffesoli, 1993, pp.xv–xvi). Maffesoli argues boldly that there is a transformation of the social bond going on, which links individuals not through old forms of group loyalty, but through temporary, localised moments of commonality that Maffesoli calls 'tribal' – in our case, the discovery that your friends share a similar passion for *Big Brother* or, more specifically, a liking for the same character! The result of this 'magical participation' according to Maffesoli is to constitute a 'new communal identity [that returns us] to a type of community ideal that is that of ancient societies' (interview with Maffesoli, quoted in Mehl, 1996, p.147).

These are heady claims indeed, but they illustrate how debates around the extended audience intersect with much larger debates about the changing forms of order and community in increasingly complex and mediated social worlds. We are not so far here from claims made about forms of community on the internet (Rheingold, 1994) and their heralding a new form of social organisation. If doubts have grown about those early claims for internet-based community, we should perhaps be equally cautious about claims for the temporary social connections formed around reality TV.

Rather than pursue this line of speculation, I want to end this section by considering some less positive readings of the 'extended' reality TV audience, and its implications for questions of media power.

4.4 Reality TV and the 'regulation' of social behaviour

What alternative readings of the reality TV audience are possible? Firstly, we should notice how positive accounts of the audience 'community' around reality TV shows fit all too neatly into the language of marketers who see the reality TV formats (with their accompanying hype and sense of short-term compulsory viewing) as delivering a new type of audience for advertisers. Consider this quotation from the director of interactive media at Endemol, *Big Brother*'s producer, which had just acquired the online marketing agency Victoria Real:

> The next stage is brands wanting a relationship with a programme all year, not just when it's on air, and that can be done through the web and interactive media ... [the advantage of a reality-based show here was that] you had these incredibly committed small communities that obsessed over every last detail of the show. That's a powerful thing for a sponsor to tap into.
>
> Peter Cowley, quoted in *The Guardian*, *Online* section, 16 June 2003, p.47

The plan was for the corporate sponsor, such as a telecommunications corporation, to become involved in every aspect of the reality programme's promotion, including text updates to people's phones. Branding ideas, on this model, are 'central to the [programme] format idea from the start' according to Cowley, which suggests that much of the spontaneous 'participation' around reality TV may be coordinated within a fully branded and commercially pre-planned 'interactive' environment. If the audience is dispersed, so too, perhaps, will be the advertiser and the corporate sponsor.

Activity 5.3

Look at the prediction of a reality TV audience 'community' by media executive Peter Cowley, just quoted. Suppose you were asked to test the accuracy of his claim for the audience of a specific reality TV show: make a list of the things you would want to observe and where you would plan making those observations.

The kinds of things you might want to observe are: people watching the programme together, people talking about the programme, voting and telling each other how they voted, comparing interpretations, and acting out scenes from the show. Observation of these different kinds of audience participation offers important insights into the multi-dimensional nature of viewing 'Reality TV' and branded contexts of interactivity. ▩ ▩ ▩

Branded contexts of interactivity are just one of many sites where reality TV audiences in the extended sense raise questions about power. How, for example, are we to interpret the rise of reality TV programmes based on surveillance against the background of societies (such as the UK) which have seen an extremely rapid growth of surveillance in managing public behaviour (Lyon, 2001; Palmer, 2002)? What is the relationship between our watching surveillance footage as 'reality'-based entertainment and the increasing social acceptance of surveillance as an instrument of order? Is there a relationship, more generally, between the norms of behaviour implied by reality TV (if generalisations are possible) and changes in social norms generally (cf. Couldry, 2004)? Can we see reality TV as a form not just of entertainment, but also of the education of subjects?

There are interesting links here back to the methodological questions discussed in Chapter 1 in relation to the early form of audience research known as cultivation research. Cultivation research, if you remember, ran into difficulties because it wanted to prove scientifically the causal chain between heavy television viewing and various undesirable social traits. In thinking about the wider consequences of 'reality TV' for everyday life, we would not want to repeat cultivation research's problems in specific and detailed 'effects' from television texts to audience behaviour. A more useful approach would be to consider in a more open fashion the possible interrelations between the language, plots and implicit behaviour norms of reality TV and the norms of everyday life, and the links which viewers *themselves* make between the two, when talking about themselves. What weight do people give not just to the 'reality' of reality TV shows, but also to their relevance as guidance for their own and others' behaviour? This is not to claim that television programmes have 'power over' audiences in any simple sense, but to consider how far the values and thought patterns mobilised in reality TV programmes are accorded by audience members as sources for regulating conduct (see discussions of self-regulation of conduct in chapters 2 and 4).

In the final section, I want to follow this expanding agenda of audience research into one further question: space. What are the implications of the growing fluidity in the relationship between the audience's spatial location and media industries' spatial location? This returns us, against the background of our detailed examination of the reality TV audience, to the question asked in Section 2: what *and where* is the contemporary audience?

5 The mobile audience

An older model of the audience focused, implicitly, on the relationship between two types of place: a centralised site of production (whose detailed study could be delegated to work on media production) and the myriad, mainly private, sites where media is consumed (where audience research was conducted). Our understanding of this spatial relationship, however, is undergoing a transformation, firstly because of our increasing awareness of the journeys audiences make to sites of production and, secondly, because of the mobility of media production resources themselves. I will look at each of these spatial transformations in turn; both develop our understanding of what the 'extended audience' involves and both (especially the latter) return us to the power relations between audiences and media industries considered in Section 3.

5.1 On the set

We started this chapter with audiences travelling to a site of film production to take part as extras, as a reward for buying shares! This is a specific example of a wider trend towards people visiting media locations, particularly the sites of television or cinema production.

Here, an extended audience study intersects with the sociology of tourism, which has addressed the growth since the 1970s of new sorts of tourism beyond the traditional forms of museums, ancient buildings, central sites of political power and national history, and sites of pure leisure interest such as beaches and mountains. Tourism now may take us to sites which from many perspectives are quite banal, but offer an otherwise unobtainable view of an aspect of other people's everyday life. Unlike the traditional historical or purely leisure-focused tourist site, these destinations for late modern tourism offer, as the pioneering sociologist of tourism Dean MacCannell (1976, p.55) put it, staged but seemingly authentic images of 'society and its works'. We go to such places to see how a particular type of work is done, or in the heritage version, was done in the past – by 'ordinary people', not elites. Visits to sites of media production are a further example of this type of tourism.

This, however, only captures part of what is interesting about audiences' journeys to media locations. Another important point is that, like all tourism, media locations offer a promise of seeing the 'extraordinary' in contrast to the 'ordinary' everyday life from which we are taking a break: this, according to another sociologist of tourism, John Urry (1990, pp.11–12), is a crucial feature of how any site gets constructed as a site of tourism. What is 'extraordinary' about media locations derives from an aspect of the everyday experience of audiences so obvious that it is easy to overlook: audiences are generally distant, as they sit in their living room, from the places where the media they watch are normally produced. Visiting a media location is 'extraordinary' therefore by opposition to the 'ordinary' distance audiences have from principal sites of media production. This spatial contrast is only another aspect of the difference in symbolic power between audiences and media discussed in Section 3.

There are many types of media location which audiences visit (Couldry, 2000, Part 2). There are the internationally famous sites such as Disney–MGM Studios and Universal Studios in the USA which are on a huge scale: the former cost Disney an initial investment of $500 million (Wasko, 1994, p.56). There are the important national media sites such as Granada Television's Granada Studio Tours, home of the external set of *Coronation Street*, opened in 1988 but closed in 2003 as part of Granada's shifting of its resources away from the North of England (see Figure 5.6); many smaller commercial sites promoting other programmes also fall into this category. Then there are more informal not-yet-commercialised locations where people can visit for free the locations where a particular television programme or film was shot: for example, the sections of Vancouver where *X-files* episodes were shot have attracted large numbers of visits by fans of the series (discussed in Hills, 2002, Chapter 5).

All of these sites rely on the attraction to audiences of visiting for themselves the place they have already seen on television or in the cinema. Some writers have found this puzzling (Rojek, 1993, p.70): why spend what is often a considerable amount of time and/or money visiting a place that you have already seen, maybe hundreds of times? Umberto Eco, in his book *Travels in Hyperreality*, seizes on this type of tourism, and its frequent combination of extreme artificiality and constructedness with great claims to authenticity, as an example of a 'postmodern' truth that we live in a world in which the 'completely real' is identified with the 'completely fake' (Eco, 1986, p.7, quoted in Rojek, 1993, p.160).

This raises large issues about the contemporary organisation of space and place that go far beyond audience studies, but for our purposes we can ask whether such a judgement ignores the possibility that sites of media production – the sites where popular programmes are actually made – *do* have a significant 'reality' of their own. Indeed, in Susan Davis's view, it is precisely this sense of those locations' privileged relation to the media production process that enables media corporations to exploit them as 'pilgrimage sites' for tourists (Davis, 1996, p.411).

Figure 5.6 *The set of* Coronation Street. *Fans wander around the set during a Granada Studios Tour (June, 1996)*
Source: Couldry, 2000, p.71

Reading 5.3 Activity

You should now read James Langton's 'Meet the Waltons' (Reading 5.3) (from a feature article on visitors to the Los Angeles set where the US television show, *The Waltons* (USA, CBS, 1972 to 1981), was filmed), and answer the following questions:

- What are the main reasons identified in this report for why people visit this site?
- Have you ever visited a tourist site (not necessarily a media site) and experienced something similar to the experiences described here?
- What does the article suggest about the attitude of its author to the site's visitors?

Reading 5.3

James Langton, 'Meet the Waltons'

An American pastoral loved by Jimmy Carter (former US President), *The Waltons* was the most wholesome television show ever, and still lives in the hearts of its fans. As the family releases a Christmas album, James Langton joins the faithful at the home of John-Boy and Jim-Bob.

[...]

Certainly, the fans here in LA are deeply devout – so devout that they have flown in from all over the States, though most of them are from the Midwest and the old South. This particular group is here for three days of all things Walton, including a gala dinner with as many of the stars as can be rounded up. First stop is the lot where the series was filmed. Their guide is Earl Hamner: the series is based on *The Homecoming*, a bestselling novel Hamner wrote in the early Sixties which in turn was based on his memories of growing up in the small town of Schuyler, Virginia. Aged 76 now, Hamner is a tall, silver-haired patriarch who arrives at the lot in a forest-green Range Rover and is greeted like a favourite uncle with a pocketful of sweets. The female fans, in particular, like to be photographed cocooned in his embrace, their faces becoming extraordinarily calm and happy, like those of small children who realise that they are safe and that nothing in the world can touch them. 'If you've got a question', says Earl, 'then please do talk loudly because I've got a new hearing aid and I can't hear a thing'. They know most of the answers anyway. They know which is the screen door through which the kids would come in for meals. They know that the Waltons' house has been caught moonlighting in *Bonanza* and *F-Troop*. Above all, they know that John-Boy's bedroom window is the one on the first floor at the left, and that Earl modelled the character on himself, and that with very little persuasion he will climb the rickety ladder in the hollow interior of the house and wave for pictures. [...]

Earl has by now clambered down from his perch and is gathering everyone up. On the way back to the car park, the ragged crocodile passes a brick Colonial house which everybody recognises as the home of Miss Emily and Miss Mamie, the two elderly and reclusive Baldwin sisters who jollied up the series – and their lives – by brewing moonshine.

The fans push through the front door and discover another dank shell. Earl shoos everyone out, explaining that they're not covered by the Warner Brothers' insurance policy. 'They call these things "flats"', he explains. 'They're nothing but a façade. Which tells you everything you need to know about Hollywood.'

[...]

The gala dinner – the high point of the weekend – takes place on Saturday evening. The fan club has hired a somewhat overheated reception room at their hotel, the Beverly Garland Inn. There is a long table at which souvenir photographs are being sold, and at least a dozen smaller ones set for dinner. A bar in the corner is selling house wine and ready-mixed margaritas.

Earl is sitting with his wife Jane on what is, effectively, the top table. He is, after all, *The Waltons* – or rather *The Waltons* are him. He invented them; he cast them; he produced them; and in due course he saw them banished from prime-time. In his scripts, the Waltons survived the Depression and the Second World War; but by the time the fictional family emerged into the Fifties, in the real world it was the early Eighties, and the TV landscape had undergone seismic changes: The traditional family hour was dead, and the networks were losing their grip to a multitude of new channels and to cable. The kids were watching MTV and Dad had the sports channel. Mum might have wanted to watch *The Waltons*, but she didn't carry the advertising or the demographics. After nine seasons the show was finally cancelled.

And there it might have ended. There were a couple of TV specials, but the Waltons' story seemed to be over. The cast broke up. Some of the older actors retired. Earl Hamner wrote *Falcons' Crest*, a steamy soap about a wealthy and ruthless family who owned a vineyard in the Napa Valley.

But *The Waltons* refused to go away. Shown on the Family Channel in the early Eighties, the repeats became the number one show. Many of the cast members stayed in touch. And when, in 1992, a Waltons museum was opened at the old schoolhouse in Schuyler, under the shadow of the real mountain, the organisers found themselves swamped by 5,000 fans on the opening day.

The fan club was formed shortly afterwards. Carolyn Grimmel, until then just an ordinary mother of two from North Carolina who happened to have three walls of her study covered in Waltons' memorabilia, went to the opening of the museum and found thousands like herself. 'It was phenomenal', she remembers. 'And so moving to see all those people. We just sat in my room and talked all night.'

Reading source

Langton, 1999, pp.25–7 ■ ■ ■

As you will have noticed, one of the most striking themes from the last reading is the role of *The Waltons* site as a focus around which audiences could gather to exchange memories of the programme. The final paragraph of the extract is particularly interesting for two reasons. Firstly, the fan who speaks of how moving it was suddenly to meet people who shared something quite personal with her (fandom for this programme) suggests something very much like the moments of 'neo-tribal' sociality that Maffesoli (discussed in Section 4) detects in today's fragmented societies; this is a dimension of audience experience (usually latent as we sit in the privacy of our own living room or bedroom) that would repay further investigation. Secondly, notice the tone adopted by the writer, particularly the description of this fan as 'just an ordinary mother of two' before she came to the site. Why emphasise 'ordinariness' here? Is there implicitly a contrast with the extraordinariness of the media celebrities she meets there or of the place itself? Or is this a further example of how, even in an age when the audience is 'diffused' in one respect, an implicit social division between audience and media remains?

5.2 A webcam in every bedroom?

The distance between audiences and media industry is still, for most purposes, a real one. It can be crossed, symbolically, as when we visit a media location, and it can also be celebrated, as when crowds at the end of each series of the UK *Big Brother* cheer the 'ordinary' inmates and ex-inmates who are preparing to leave the media world of the *Big Brother* house and return to the everyday world. In both cases, the underlying distance is unaffected.

In one way, however, new media technologies – specifically the digital camcorder and the possibility of transmitting camcorder footage, like any digital data, via the internet – may be undermining the distance between audience and media industries. Any audience member with the right equipment can now, in principle, broadcast images to an unpredictably large Web audience, including 'reality' footage of their own lives. Is the power relation between media consumers and producers here being reversed or bypassed?

Experiments with webcam reality footage have attracted considerable attention since the late 1990s: for example, Jennifer Ringley's site www.jennicam.org, widely regarded as having pioneered the 'webcam in the bedroom' approach. This was eventually closed down by the company that handled subscriptions to the site, because of their reservations about the 'explicitness' of some of the material (see *The Guardian*, 3 January 2004, p.13). There are also umbrella sites where the visitor can select from a wide range of individual camcorder sites (such as www.camcentral.com). What questions do such sites raise for our understanding of the contemporary audience, and particularly of how audiences' relationship to the media industries may be transformed by technological change? How are we to make sense of the proliferation of *self*-surveillance as a voluntary activity?

Reading 5.4 Activity

You should now read Mark Andrejevic's 'The digital enclosure of DotComGuy' (Reading 5.4) and consider the following questions:

- What power issues does Andrejevic identify in the webcam 'subculture'?
- Do you agree with his assessment?
- Are there any positive readings of what DotComGuy does as a media producer, which Andrejevic does not consider?

Reading 5.4

Mark Andrejevic, 'The digital enclosure of DotComGuy'

Since Jennicam first went online from Dickinson College in 1996, hundreds of imitators have followed suit, and many of them have attempted to tap into the commercial potential of home webcasting. One of the most recent imitators, a 26-year-old former computer systems manager who changed his name to DotComGuy when he decided to live his life online for a year, served as a round-the-clock advertisement for the ostensible benefits of the de-differentiation of work, leisure and domestic space within the digital enclosure. DotComGuy's stated goal was to prove to the world that he could order everything he needed to survive over the Internet – without leaving home for all of the year 2000. Furthermore, he attempted to earn a living while shopping, budgeting himself a $98,000 salary based on the revenues he hoped to earn from online sponsorships and advertising. The project got off to a strong start: during the early months, DotComGuy's website boasted an average of one million hits a day (Eldredge, 2000), and he built up an impressive list of online sponsors. However, his timing was bad. The dot.com crash was in full swing by the time he had spent half a year in the DotComPound, and he left the house at the end of the year with nothing to show for his efforts but a few of the products that had been donated by sponsors. Despite its failure as an entrepreneurial endeavour, the DotComGuy website made explicit the role that surveillance played in transforming domestic and leisure-oriented spaces into spaces of production. One newspaper account put it succinctly, describing DotComGuy (a.k.a. Mitch Maddox of Dallas, Texas) as a 'guy who sold his own life – whose journals are posted on-line, whose everyday speech is riddled with endorsements, whose movements even in sleep are scrutinized by millions of viewers' (Copeland 2000:C1).

DotComGuy, in short, overcame the spatial divisions of modernity described by Giddens (1981). When he was in the DotCompound (which included a backyard for DotComDog), he was, in some sense, always working. Even when he was sleeping, a viewer who logged onto the site could find an image of him in bed surrounded by the flashing banner ads that helped pay his salary. In addition to turning his life into a series of product endorsements (from online grocery and maid services to software products and even an online athletic trainer), DotComGuy served as a branded advertisement for the promise of the online economy. This promotional function was not a by-product of the project, but its explicit goal, as stated on DotComGuy's website:

> It started with an observation: ... E-commerce can provide anything you could ask for, and you'd never have to leave home ... Most people still think the Internet is an infant. This then, is a unique opportunity to help bring that baby up and help others learn to trust it ... This project can help take some of the drudgery out of day-to-day purchases, and even help turn people on to a world they might not otherwise embrace.
>
> DotComGuy.com, 2000

In short, DotComGuy's life became a round-the-clock advertisement for a lifestyle that corresponded to a new way of consuming. It was by no means a fluke that this advertisement took the form of perpetual surveillance for such is the nature of the lifestyle being advertised. Online, we may well all become DotComPeople, under perpetual surveillance, ostensibly for our own convenience and profit. DotComGuy's advertising campaign, then, makes a pitch not just for the convenience of online shopping, but for the advantages of being watched. By agreeing to live his life on camera, DotComGuy enacted the appropriate attitude of the wired consumer: a thoroughly contemporary, almost 'hip', lack of squeamishness toward surveillance.

This is the attitude of the youth celebrities on MTV's *Real World* and of would-be contestants on reality game shows like *Survivor* and *Big Brother*. It is also the characteristic attitude of the webcam celebrity. Jennifer Ringley, for example, equates the retreat into privacy concerns as a form of self-delusion. 'I honestly think the concept of privacy is a mental fabrication. It's a convenient way to imagine we're hiding the things we like least about ourselves, and therefore negates us from responsibility for them. ... Realistically ... we should be able to defend our actions to ourselves, to know why we do what we do and to come to peace with it' (Ringley, 2000). Perpetual surveillance, in other words, is nothing to be afraid of – so long as we are honest with ourselves. Comfort with self-disclosure signifies a healthy openness and self-awareness. It is no longer surveillance that is stigmatized, but fear of it. This attitude nearly aligns itself with the marketing promise of e-commerce – that willing submission to perpetual self-disclosure should be viewed neither as an intrusion nor as an inconvenience to be tolerated, but as an advantage to consumers. One of the reasons that the mass market felt like a homogenizing force was that our individual natures were shielded in privacy that failed to let marketers discern the idiosyncrasies of our desires. Thus, if we are to counter this tendency, we must open ourselves up to the process of self-commodification as self-expression.

References

Copeland, L. (2000) 'The cyber-house rules: Dallas's DotComGuy makes a domain name for himself', *Washington Post*, 8 July, C01.

Eldredge, R.L. (2000) 'Peach buzz: June looking good in profile', *Atlanta Constitution*, 5 July, 2C.

Giddens, A. (1981) *A Contemporary Critique of Historical Materialism*, Berkeley, CA, University of California Press.

Ringley, J. (2000) 'Book chapter request', email to M. Andrejevic, 14 September.

Reading source

Andrejevic, 2004, pp.199–201 ■ ■ ■

Andrejevic uncovers some disturbing paradoxes in the apparently 'free' spaces of webcam production. Webcam site producers exhibit an apparent 'openness' to living in public without secrets: *The Guardian* quotes Jennifer Ringley as saying 'I keep Jennicam alive not because I want or need to be watched, but because I simply don't mind being watched'. But at least in the case of DotComGuy (it is less clear with Jennicam), this surface openness is less an openness of self and more an openness to the *commodification* of self, a willingness to offer a view of one's private life in return for financial reward.

Such practices take us a full 180 degrees from the traditional focus of audience research (someone sitting in the guaranteed privacy of their own home watching the publicly circulated productions of a centralised media industry). With webcam sites, the audience member has become the producer, opening up his or her life to an unseen audience.

Is the result of 'audience-cum-producer' a democratisation of media production that genuinely erodes the power differentials between audiences and media performers? Or will those differentials go on being reproduced in Web auto-production, even if in new forms? In support of the second possibility, listen to the language of one Jennicam fan commenting on the site's closure (which we should remember was forced upon Jennifer Ringley by the site manager): 'I am glad she could get much more than her share of 15 minutes of fame [through her website] ... Furthermore, she has a good chance to resume normal (albeit boring) life' (quoted in *The Guardian*, 3 January 2004, p.13). The implicit division between the glamour of media attention (and the media world) and the 'boring' nature of life beyond the camera (the everyday life, that is, of *the audience*) is here reproduced as clearly as ever (cf. Couldry, 2000, pp.44–50).

6   Conclusion

It is up to you, the reader, to decide where you stand on such questions of power. But this chapter has at least, I hope, convinced you of the scope for extending (and the need to extend) the focus of audience research beyond the original act of watching, listening or reading that traditional audience research considered.

To conclude, it may be useful to recall the three challenges to audience research with which I started this chapter: technological, social/ spatial and experiential. I argued that the very nature of the audience is being transformed not only through changes in the technological interfaces that media involve, but also through changes in the social and spatial forms that 'audience-hood' is taking, with the result that being a member of a media audience is becoming a different experience from what it was in the past. The challenge to audience research is to keep up with those changes without overestimating the speed and breadth of change.

We have seen that any understanding of the contemporary audience must address how being an audience member involves doing more things in more places and in relation to more interconnected media than previously. It is this shift that is captured, variously, by terms such as the 'diffused audience', 'media culture', and the 'extended audience'. We have seen examples of this from reality TV, particularly the game-based reality show *Big Brother*, from visits of viewers to the set of an enduring form of popular television, the soap opera, and from the quite new phenomenon of the self-produced webcam site.

At the same time, I have argued that older questions of power – not only the power relations between media institutions and audiences, but also the consequences for wider power relations of media culture – have not disappeared. Indeed, they continue to emerge in new forms. It would be surprising if, in media-saturated cultures, media had become sufficiently detached from questions of power for audience research to put such questions to one side.

Not that the questions raised by audience research are susceptible to ready-made answers. Indeed, if the 'ordinary life' of audiences continues to generate revenues for media corporations as it did in the late 1990s and early 2000s, even the boundary between the study of audiences and the study of media production cannot be assumed. For, as we have seen, the worlds of the audience and media production are not sealed off hermetically from each other (see **Toynbee, 2006**), but intersect in what particular audience members do. Each of those 'worlds', after all, is just one aspect of the larger picture of media's role in the social world – a good note, perhaps, on which to end.

Further reading

Abercrombie, N. and Longhurst, B. (1998) *Audiences: Towards a Theory of Performance and Imagination*, London, Sage. A theoretical account of the shifts in contemporary audiences and research.

Alasuutaari, P. (1999) 'Introduction' in Alasuutaari, P. (ed.) *Rethinking the Media Audience*, London, Sage. Key researchers offer thoughts on the future of audience research.

Couldry, N. (2000) *The Place of Media Power: Pilgrims and Witnesses of the Media Age*, London, Routledge. This offers a fresh approach to audience research and questions of power.

Davis, S. (1996) 'The theme park: global industry and cultural form', *Media Culture & Society*, vol.18, no.3, pp.399–422. This explores the nature of audience experiences of global cultural forms.

Schrøder, K., Drotner, K., Klin S. and Murray, C. (2003) *Researching Audiences*, London, Arnold. This gives a very comprehensive overview of quantitative and qualitative approaches to audience research with useful case studies.

Thompson, J. (1995) *The Media and Modernity*, Cambridge, Polity. A stimulating, theoretical account of the changing role of the media in modern societies.

References

Abercrombie, N. and Longhurst, B. (1998) *Audiences: Towards a Theory of Performance and Imagination*, London, Sage.

Alasuutaari, P. (1999) 'Introduction' in Alasuutaari, P. (ed.) *Rethinking the Media Audience*, London, Sage.

Andrejevic, M. (2004) 'The webcam subculture and the digital enclosure' in Couldry, N. and McCarthy, A. (eds) *MediaSpace: Place, Scale and Culture in a Media Age*, London, Routledge.

Corner, J. (2002) 'Performing the real: documentary diversions', *Television & New Media*, vol.3, no.3, pp.255–71.

Couldry, N. (2000) *The Place of Media Power: Pilgrims and Witnesses of the Media Age*, London, Routledge.

Couldry, N. (2004) 'Teaching us to fake it: the ritualized norms of television's "reality" games' in Murray, S. and Ouellette, L. (eds) *Reality TV: Remaking Television Culture*, New York, New York University Press, pp.57–74.

Davis, S. (1996) 'The theme park: global industry and cultural form', *Media Culture & Society*, vol.18, no.3, pp.399–422.

Dovey, J. (2000) *Freakshow*, London, Pluto.

Eco, U. (1986) *Travels in Hyperreality*, London, Secker and Warburg.

Foucault, M. (1980) *Discipline and Punish*, Harmondsworth, Penguin.

Gabler, N. (2000) *Life: The Movie*, New York, Vintage.

Gitlin, T. (2001) *Media Unlimited*, New York, Metropolitan Books.

Hermes, J. (1999) 'Media figures in identity construction' in Alasuutaari, P. (ed.) *Rethinking the Media Audience*, London, Sage.

Hill, A. (2002) '*Big Brother*: the real audience', *Television & New Media*, vol.3, no.3, pp.323–40.

Hills, M. (2002) *Fan Cultures*, London, Routledge.

Kilborn, R. (1994) '"How real can you get?" Recent developments in "reality" television', *European Journal of Communication*, vol.9, no.4, pp.421–40.

Langton, J. (1999) 'Meet the Waltons', *Sunday Telegraph* Magazine, 21 November, pp.25–7.

Lazarsfeld, P. and Merton, R. (1969) 'Mass communication, popular taste and organised social action' in Schramm, W. (ed.) *Mass Communications* (2nd edn) Urbana, IL, University of Illinois Press.

Lyon, D. (2001) *Surveillance Society*, Buckingham, Open University Press.

MacCannell, D. (1976) *The Tourist*, London, Macmillan.

Maffesoli, M. (1993) *The Shadow of Dionysus*, New York, State University of New York Press.

Maffesoli, M. (1996) *The Time of the Tribes*, London, Sage.

Mehl, D. (1996) *La Télévision de l'intimité*, Paris, Le Seuil.

Palmer, G. (2002) '*Big Brother*: an experiment in governance', *Television & New Media*, vol.3, no.3, pp.295–310.

Rheingold, H. (1994) *Virtual Community*, London, Secker and Warburg.

Rojek, C. (1993) *Ways of Escape*, London, Routledge.

Schrøder, K., Drotner, K., Kline, S. and Murray, C. (2003) *Researching Audiences*, London, Arnold.

Thompson, J. (1995) *The Media and Modernity*, Cambridge, Polity.

Toynbee, J. (2006) 'The media's view of the audience' in Hesmondhalgh, D. (ed.) *Media Production*, Maidenhead, Open University Press/The Open University (Book 3 in this series).

Urry, J. (1990) *The Tourist Gaze*, London, Sage.

Wasko, J. (1994) *Hollywood and the Information Age*, Cambridge, Polity.

Williams, R. (1975) *Drama in a Dramatised Society*, Cambridge, Cambridge University Press.

Beyond the living room: re-thinking media audiences

Marie Gillespie

In this book we have explored the value of audience research. We have examined different theoretical and empirical approaches to television and film audiences: from media effects studies and reception research to ethnographic approaches to television and everyday life. We have looked at how the media shape our bodily, sensory and social experiences as well as how audiences are constituted as citizens and publics, consumers and markets. We have also considered the different ways of thinking about and researching audiences that have emerged in response to changing media technologies, and institutional and social circumstances. I hope you have come to appreciate why the study of audiences is valuable and necessary, and are now in a better position to evaluate what makes for good quality empirical audience research and robust audience theory.

As television and cinema screens morph into computer and mobile phone interfaces, both they and their audiences are increasingly global and mobile, privatised and individualised. Audiences don't just sit and watch and/or listen anymore; they do a wide variety of other things with their screens – from shopping and dating to voting and learning. The boundaries between entertainment, information and education grow blurred. Whereas television audiences were once conceived of and researched in laboratories or in their living rooms, a new generation of audience research is now required to capture new forms of interactivity and connectivity.

In this concluding section we return to the main themes of this book a) media power and audience empowerment, b) the role of the media in shaping audiences' knowledge, values and beliefs, and c) social and technological change and continuity and its impact on audiences.

Power

What can we conclude about the power of the media from the various studies presented in this book? We have seen how 'media effects' research tends to be based on a model of the communication process that posits a direct, uni-linear, casual relationship between senders and receivers of messages. At the very beginning of this book, in the Introduction, we mentioned that audience research has tended to fall into one of two broad approaches: audience as passive and the audience as active. Throughout this book, however, we have challenged the view that media power lies mainly or even exclusively in the hands of media producers and institutions, and that audiences are predictable or powerless. We have argued that, in order to fully understand the power of the media, we need to study media audiences in relation to media institutions and media texts. We have also demonstrated that it is important to situate these essential elements in studies of media (audiences, texts and institutions) within a dynamic model of communication – a model that is capable of dealing with both *actors* (producers and audiences) and *processes* of communication.

The power of the media operates in different ways. As you progressed through the book you might have noticed that we discussed 'power' in different ways. Firstly, our ideas about audiences are shaped by competing discourses which define them in different ways: as vulnerable or creative, powerful or powerless. We examined the *power of discourse* to shape the available ways of thinking about studying and even behaving as audiences. In Chapter 1, we examined how 'critical' discourses conceive of audiences as the subjects of, and subjected to, powerful economic and political interests. In contrast, 'liberal–pluralist' discourses tend to see audiences as more active, selective and creative. These discourses about audiences are not entirely uniform, consistent or coherent; they bear their own internal contradictions and inconsistencies. Nevertheless they provide us with useful points of orientation that help us to situate different arguments and types of evidence about the relative power of audiences and media in society.

Secondly, we have considered how different forms of *economic* and *political power* exert pressure on media organisations from outside. Given the commercial and profit-seeking imperatives of the media industry, media institutions and producers cannot avoid responding to the vested interests of powerful groups. Power elites, including state and government actors, work on and through media organisations and audiences, but typically in ways that are indirect, long-term and diffuse. The long-term ideological effects of media on audiences brought about by these processes are very difficult to research empirically. There are no readily available methods that would make this task easier. However, the case studies presented on television audiences in Israel, India and in Egypt provided us with good examples of how these long-term, diffuse processes of power work, often in unexpected and unintended ways with unanticipated outcomes.

Thirdly, media institutions (including multinational corporations) and producers exert *institutional* and *symbolic power*. They shape the media forms and content that are available to us and how media products are distributed. They mould the nature of media texts, provide templates that frame perceptions of the social world, and encourage and promote certain kinds of responses in audiences. The genres, narratives and ideological discourses of television and film texts are produced and reproduced in accordance with producers' knowledge and beliefs about what audiences will enjoy and what they may want to consume again and again, and what will therefore make profits or get high ratings. The programmes that appear in our television schedules, or the films available to us at our local cinemas, are the result of choices and decisions by powerful actors. They constitute an ever expanding array of choice. But our choices are delimited by the standardisation and reproduction of popular genres and by the pursuit of profit in commercial media (**Hesmondhalgh, 2006**).

Although institutions exercise symbolic power through the organisation and distribution of symbolic goods in society, the symbolic meanings of texts are not obvious or 'given' but a matter of interpretation – individual and collaborative. Texts are polysemic. The same text is open to multiple, competing and often opposing interpretations, as audience reception analysis has usefully demonstrated. There is no direct or inevitable relationship between the producers and receivers of media messages. The kinds of meanings intended by producers are mediated by the often unpredictable ways in which active audiences negotiate meanings.

A fourth form of power that this book has highlighted is the *interpretative power* of audiences. Interpretations are subject to a variety of contingent and contextual factors; meanings cannot simply be assumed but have to be researched empirically. It is also important to consider the contextual and contingent factors that intervene in processes of meaning making. Gender, class, ethnicity and age, among other factors, shape not only what we consume but how, and with whom, and can disrupt power relations. And the contexts of media use can be as, if not more, important than media producers or texts themselves in determining meanings. Audiences have the power to challenge and resist dominant meanings 'encoded' in texts and to use media for a variety of empowering purposes. But does this reduce the media's power over us?

'Critical' approaches tend to see the media as exerting power *over* us. The 'media imperialism' model of international communications and research in the 'media effects' tradition are two examples of this approach. This book has challenged them in their simpler forms. Liberal–pluralist approaches tend to see power as more evenly distributed among a range of actors and often emphasise the ways in which audiences may be empowered by the media.

Chapters 3 and 4, via case studies, examined Gramscian conceptions of power as hegemony. In this approach, media and popular culture are understood as 'sites of struggle' over meaning and power. Audiences may use the media in empowering ways to contest, resist and negotiate dominant meanings, beliefs or values around, for example, consumerism, femininity, national identity or religious nationalism. But, depending on their circumstances and the contexts in which they consume and discuss media, they may absorb and accept dominant media representations of social realities that serve to reinforce inequalities. The main point here is that we cannot presume in advance what the effect of any particular example or diet of media will be and that empirical enquiry is therefore crucial to avoid assuming that we know how audiences think and behave. This approach is valuable in that it validates the ways in which audiences can actively negotiate texts and the ways in which their readings may be contradictory, both compliant with and resistant to the workings of power and inequality. However, as the case studies indicate, the dynamic between compliance and resistance is not always an adequate way of understanding how people engage with media texts, not least because dominant meanings are in any case sometimes hard to identify or pin down, especially in richly polysemic texts.

A Foucauldian approach to power, in contrast, suggests that we should not simply study power by examining particular people or institutions and how they secure, and possess power, contest or collude with power. Rather we should look at how relations across a wide social field, including the relations between media audiences and media forms such as melodrama or news, contribute to sustaining certain kinds of power relations that may be racialised, gendered, nationalised and/or classed. This book has highlighted the possible different ways in which media power works *through* us – through our bodies as well as our minds to shape perception, subjectivities and the nature of social and political life.

This more diffused conception of power seems appropriate to the more diffused conception of audiences that we considered in the final chapter of the book. However, as Nick Couldry argued, a diffused approach to power should not be confused with either a dilution or weakening of the power of media producers and institutions, even if new technologies are, arguably, shifting the balance of power in favour of audiences and users. As Tony Bennett argued in Chapter 2, the power of the media works profoundly on our senses, producing us as disciplined, attentive, individualised citizens. A diffused conception of power eschews crude theories of media domination or manipulation. Rather, as the case study on melodrama in Egypt in Chapter 4 suggested, 'techniques of self' are deployed in ways that secure our involvement in the forms of self-regulation and self-management that are core strategies of 'liberal governance'.

To sum up then, we have examined different theoretical perspectives on the workings of media power: power working *over* us from above; power working through us and our social relations in a more diffuse way; and finally media as enabling forms of empowerment as well disempowerment under particular circumstances that require empirical investigation.

We should not ignore the fact that empirical research with audiences also involves power relations. We have seen how different qualitative methodologies, reception research and audience ethnography in particular, tend to emphasise the active, selective and creative ways in which audiences appropriate and are empowered by media, without necessarily over-celebrating the emancipatory potential of media. But empirical research always sets up its own power and knowledge relations. Research methodologies may be more or less intrusive or exploitative, coercive or covert, depending on how they are used in specific contexts. Researchers and those who fund academic research exert power to shape the kinds of knowledge that get produced and circulated about audiences – what we know and how we come to know it. Such epistemological questions, as we have seen, need to be carefully balanced with ethical questions about how research is conducted, its ethos and politics and how the audiences under study are treated and represented.

Knowledge, values and beliefs

What stories do the different chapters of this book tell us about knowledge, values and beliefs? Clearly, questions of media power are inextricably linked to the ways in which media shape what we, as audiences and social subjects, come to know, value and believe. News media play a vital role in informing citizens, but information is not knowledge. Information has to be processed through analytical frameworks to become useful. Invariably, media information is interpreted through culturally specific frameworks (as we saw in the case study of Israeli news audiences), and transformed into knowledge that can be used for a variety of purposes: to make an argument; to assess a situation; to form the basis of social action. From issues of censorship to allegations of 'dumbing down', there are endless controversies about media as information, knowledge and power.

State public television channels around the world aim to educate and inform as well as entertain their 'national' audiences. We have seen how in India and Egypt state television projects seek to produce the informed citizens needed by functioning democracies. Similarly, early cinema encouraged the kind of focused attentiveness that was required for mass citizenship. Citizens may be informed and empowered at the same time as they are managed and regulated. Our knowledge of markets and consumer goods via the media helps us exercise choice. At the same time the cultures of media consumption that we inhabit reproduce us as 'consumers'. There seems to be no easy way out of the paradoxes of living with media: between media power and audience empowerment, choice and control, activity and passivity, creativity and constraint. Perhaps the ambiguity that lies at the heart of audience studies is something we need to hold on to rather than attempt to explain away. We have argued that we need to study this ambiguity in concrete social settings, linking the local and global, national and transnational dimensions of media and audiences today.

In empirical studies presented in this book, audiences talk about 'reality TV' and US and Indian soap operas in ways that suggest that global television forms are appropriated and transformed into locally useful knowledge that is used as a resource to make meaningful local worlds and identities. Viewers bring prior knowledge to their experiences of media, so we cannot presume effects. Staple media narratives, especially continuing serials like melodrama (and news), depend on the knowledge of the serial that audiences bring to each episode. This knowledge is used as an interpretative resource. The mobilisation of media knowledge, and the cognitive activities that go into making sense of television narratives, account in large part for the pleasures and emotions that are generated by these media experiences. Whether this knowledge or experience is valued, and by whom, is another question.

Values are notoriously difficult to study but what this book shows is that we cannot assume that US or 'Western' values (Christianity, capitalism, individualism) are transmitted directly across the world as a result of the globalisation of media. Empirical studies suggest that there are profound tensions between different sets of values: modernity and tradition, fundamentalism and cosmopolitanism, neo-conservatism and liberal–pluralism, religious and secular, democratic and authoritarian values. The audience studies examined here indicate that these seemingly conflicting value systems can and do co-exist in individuals, families, localities, and in national and transnational 'communities'. The media play a vital role in provoking audiences to think through the dilemmas posed by the competing value systems that shape our lives.

Media may reinforce existing systems of religious belief as we saw in the case studies of the Indian epics but they also transform religious beliefs and practices in the process. Theorisations of media and of modernity have long assumed the decline of religion and the growth of secular thinking. Clearly this is not happening. Fundamentalist religious beliefs of various forms, Christian, Islamic, Hindu and other, all receive sustenance from the persuasive powers of modern media techniques.

Media as cultural technologies shape and regulate our senses and what it becomes possible to see, to believe and to know. It is often said that 'seeing is believing'. Israeli interpreters of news about the Israeli–Palestinian conflict operate according to their beliefs about whether news programmes can be trusted to tell the truth, and according to whether they are 'hawks' or 'doves'. Viewers also interpret what they see through realist or 'reflectionist' (news is transparent and real) as well as constructivist (news is manufactured according to convention) lenses, often commuting between these, and this affects the resulting knowledge that they produce.

Change and continuity

Finally, what stories does this book tell about change and continuity? Technological change poses a challenge to conventional ways of researching audiences and this book has attempted to rise to that challenge. Digital and satellite technologies are bringing about an increasing diversification and fragmentation of audiences. This may, as our case study of audiences for the Indian epics revealed, increase political participation among viewer-publics at the same time as narrowing public debate and closing down political discourses, in this case debate and discourse over what it means to be an Indian. One of the most important directions for future media audience research is to examine the twin tendencies towards homogeneity and fragmentation. Quite how communities and identities will be forged in this new media environment is uncertain and difficult to predict. What is clear is that new kinds of alliances are being forged that transcend national and cultural boundaries. These pose new challenges to audience researchers.

Another challenge to conventional audience studies is posed by the new modes of mobility and interactivity. Audiences-cum-users develop increasingly individualised pathways that transform media experiences and sociality, as well as temporal and spatial relationships. The use of webcams and blogging and digital recording technologies is shifting the balance of power between media producers and consumers. This is another very fruitful avenue for audience research to take.

One clear message across the chapters is that media studies can only benefit from developing historical and cross-cultural perspectives on media audiences. Media studies have tended to emphasise change at the expense of continuities. Sonia Livingstone has shown the advantage of taking an historical approach to debates about the activity or passivity of audiences. We have seen the continuities and changes between film and television audiences and Greco–Roman theatre audiences, folk theatre and village performances of the Indian epics and early film audiences. The continuities suggest the undying appeal and enduring significance of narrative forms and the deep engagement and sheer vitality of audience practices. We have considered how technologies crystallise habitual modes of perception, forms of involvement and detachment, focused attention and distraction. The effects of technologies may work not so much at the level of opinions, beliefs and knowledge as at the level of our senses and practices of looking and seeing. An historical and cross-cultural perspective on audiences helps us to put our arguments and assertions about the transformative effects of the media into perspective, and to challenge overblown accounts of epochal change that are so current in media and academic discussion.

This book has also shown that technologies do not have predestined uses or effects. Media technologies and their uses come into being at particular socio-historical conjunctures. They shape and are shaped by cultural and social dynamics but developments could always have been different. Maybe one of the most useful suggestions to readers is – 'mind the gap'. It is in the gaps between the production and interpretation of meaning, between intended and actual uses, that many of the unintended consequences of media technologies and communication occur. Historical and comparative research on audiences suggests that the unexpected and unanticipated responses of audiences to media are a powerful testimony to human resourcefulness and creativity. The engagements of audiences with media, even in the least auspicious of circumstances, be it political conflict or war or environmental disaster, bear witness to the ongoing human creative endeavour to make sense of self and others.

Reference

Hesmondhalgh, D. (2006) (ed.) *Media Production*, Maidenhead, Open University Press/The Open University (Book 3 in this series).

Acknowledgements

Grateful acknowledgement is made to the following sources for permission to reproduce material within this book.

Chapter 1

Figures

Figure 1.1: Copyright © Photolibrary.com; Figure 1.2: Copyright © Solo Syndication; Figure 1.3: Hulton Archive / Getty Images; Figure 1.4: Copyright © Mark Richards / Solo Syndication; Figure 1.5: Copyright © Albert Bandura; Figure 1.6(a): McQuait, D. and Windahl, S. (1993) Communciations Model, Pearson Education Ltd; Figure 1.6 (b): Hall, S. (ed) (1980) Culture, Media, Language: Working Papers in Cultural Studies, 1972–1979, Routledge; Figure 1.7: Livingstone, S.M. (1990) Interpreting a Television Narrative: How Different Viewers see a Story, Journal of Communication, Vol. 40, No. 1, Winter 1990, page 73, Oxford University Press, Inc.; Figure 1.8: Livingstone, S.M. (2002) Young People and New Media, Sage Publications Ltd. Reproduced by permission of Sage Publications, Thousand Oaks, London and New Delhi.

Readings

Reading 1.1: Butsch, R. (2000) The Making of American Audiences, © Richard Butsch 2000, published by Cambridge University Press, reproduced with permission; Reading 1.2: Seiter, E. (1999) Television and New Media Audiences, Oxford University Press; Reading 1.3: Allen, R. C. (1994) To be Continued .... Soap Operas around the World, Routledge. Taylor and Francis Books Limited, www.tandf.co.uk & www.eBookstore.tandf.co.uk.

Chapter 2

Figures

Figure 2.1: Copyright © Australian Broadcasting Corporation, ABC Content Sales; Figure 2.2: By permission of The British Library; Figure 2.4: Nelson Evans; Figure 2.7: Copyright © Kunsthalle Wien; Figure 2.14: Science Museum/ Science & Society Picture Library.

Readings

Reading 2.1: Gunning, T. (1989) An Aesthetic of Astonishment: Early Film and the (In)credulous Spectator, Art & Text 34. Copyright © Tom Gunning; Reading 2.2: Dyer, R. (1997) White, Routledge; Reading 2.3: Singer, B. (1995) Modernity, Hyperstimulus, and the rise of popular sensationalism, in (eds) Charney, L. and Schwartz, V.R., Cinema and the Invention of Modern Life, University of California Press. Copyright © 1995 The Regents of the University of California.

Chapter 3

Figures

Figure 3.1: BBC; Figure 3.3: Getty Images; Figure 3.6: Copyright © News International Syndication; Figure 3.7: Cohn-Sherbok, D. and El-Alami, D. (2002) The Palestine-Israeli Conflict: The Beginner's Guide, Oneworld Publications; Figure 3.8: Copyright © Menahem Kahana/ AFP/Getty Images; Figure 3.9: Copyright © Abid Katib/Getty Images.

Reading

Reading 3.1: Liebes, T. (1997) Reporting the Arab-Israeli Conflict, Routledge.

Chapter 4

Figures

Figure 4.1: Copyright © Lorimar/The Kobal Collection; Figure 4.2: Jeremy Paul; Figure 4.3: Copyright © Reuters/Vasily Fedosenko; Figures 4.4 and 4.5: Copyright © Heather Clarke; Figure 4.6: Copyright © CBS Entertainment Production / Ronald Grant Archives; Figure 4.7: Archivos de la Filmoteca; Figure 4.8: Motherland, November 1997; Figure 4.9: B.R. Films.

Readings

Reading 4.3: Abu-Lughod, L. (2002) Egyptian Melodrama, in (eds) Ginsburg, F. D., Abu-Lughod, L. and Larkin, B., Media Worlds: Anthropology on New Terrain, University of California Press. Copyright © 2002 The Regents of the University of California.

Chapter 5

Figures

Figure 5.1: Wilde Films PLC; Figure 5.2: Copyright © BBC; Figure 5.3: Copyright © ITV Granada; Figure 5.5: Copyright © Reuters/Ferran Paredes; Figure 5.6: Copyright © Nick Couldry.

Readings

Reading 5.1: Abercrombie, N. and Longhurst, B. (1998) Audiences: A Sociological Theory of Performance and Imagination, Sage Publications. Reproduced by permission of Sage Publications, Thousand Oaks, London and New Delhi. Copyright © Nicholas Abercrombie and Brian Longhurst, 1998; Reading 5.2: Hill, A. (2004) Reality TV: Audiences and Popular Factual Television, Routledge; Reading 5.3: Langton, J. (1999) Meet the Waltons, Sunday Telegraph Magazine, 21 November 1999 © Telegraph Group Limited 1999; Reading 5.4: Andrejevic, M. (2004) The Webcam Subculture and the Digital Enclosure: The Digitial Enclosure of DotComGuy, in (eds) Couldry, N. and McCarthy, A., Media Space: Place, Scale and Culture in a Media Age, Routledge.

Colour Section

Plate 1: © Copyright The Trustees of The British Museum; Plate 2: Bridgeman Art Library; Plate 3: Copyright © INDIA TODAY.

Cover image

Zefa Visual Media Ltd.

Every effort has been made to contact copyright holders. If any have been inadvertently overlooked the publishers will be pleased to make the necessary arrangements at the first opportunity.

Index

Abercrombie, Nicolas
and Longhurst, Brian 45–6, 186, 187, 189
'Diffused audiences' 190–4, 195–6

Abu-Lughod, Lila 170–7, 180
'Egyptian melodrama - technology of the modern subject?' 171–7

access to media, and audience research 187

active audiences 17–18, 20–1, 224, 229
culture and media influence 99
and ethnography 152
and interactivity 47
and international communication 147
and reception theory 43

'active' model of the audience as public 99

Adamson, Robert 72

aesthetic of astonishment
and film spectators 61–4, 86
and sensationalism 86–7

Afghanistan, radio drama in 145–7

age
and audience reception 41, 42
and the interpretative power of audiences 225

Alasuutaari, Pertti 185, 189, 193, 196

Allen, Robert C., 'To be continued... soap operas around the world' 35–9

Amira (Egyptian domestic servant), and modern subjectivity 171–7, 180

Anderson, Benedict 140, 162

Andrejevic, Mark, 'The digital enclosure of DotComGuy' 216–18

anthropology, and ethnographic fieldwork 153–4

The Archers 145–7

Arnheim, Rudolph 74

attribution theory, and televised conflict 126–7, 128–9

audience ethnography *see* ethnographic research

audience reception research *see* reception studies

audience talk, about reality TV 199–205

authenticity
and reality TV 200, 201, 203–4
'cultural authenticity' 143, 144, 153–4, 162, 179, 200–204, 210–11

bacchanal, and television soap opera in Trinidad 156, 157, 158–9

Bandura, Albert 24–5

BBC, and radio drama in Afghanistan 145–7

behaviour
different conventions of audience behaviour 19–20
and media effects research 22, 23–6

beliefs 228–9
and media audiences 2, 3–4
and media effects research 23, 25
and modern subjectivities 175
and moral panics 12–14
and power 225
and television 138–9, 180

Benhabib, S. 106

Benjamin, Walter 63, 81, 82, 89, 90, 91

the Bible, and media sensorium 57